LESSONS IN LANDSCAPES

PAINTING TREES

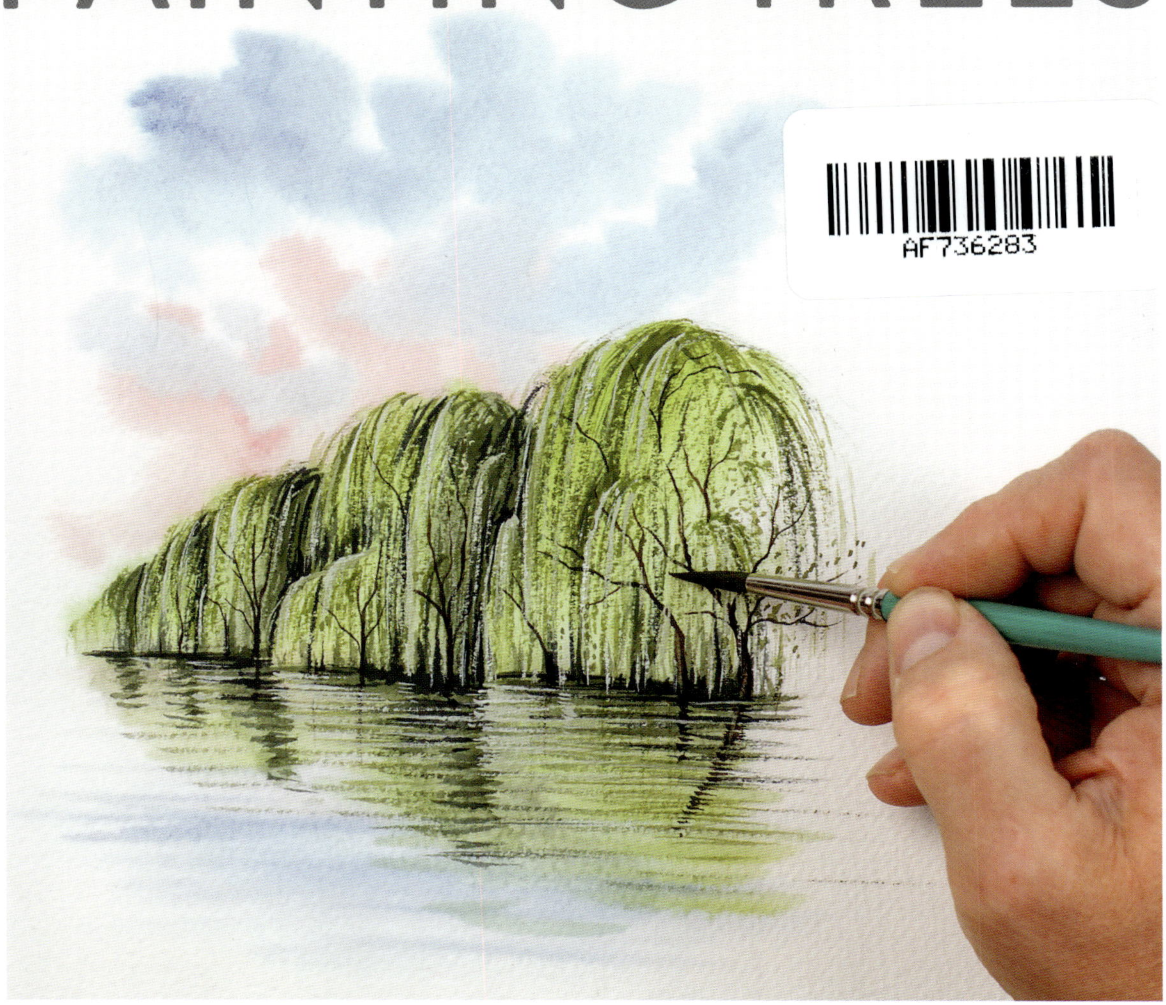

IN WATERCOLOUR

DEDICATION
This book is dedicated to Daisy, a wonderful pet for over 20 years.

First published in 2027
Search Press Limited
Wellwood, North Farm Road,
Tunbridge Wells, Kent TN2 3DR

1 2 3 4 5 6 7 8 9 10

ISBN: 978-1-80092-273-0
ebook ISBN: 978-1-80093-272-2

ABOUT THE AUTHOR
To learn more about Matthew, and for more watercolour inspiration, visit watercolour.tv

BOOKMARKED HUB
For further ideas and inspiration, and to join our free online community, visit www.bookmarkedhub.com

PUBLISHERS' NOTES
Metric measurements are used in this book; the imperial conversions are rounded to the nearest ¼in. Always use either metric or imperial measurements, not a combination of both.

The Publishers and author can accept no responsibility for any consequences arising from the information, advice or instructions given in this publication.

All our books are proudly human-made: by creative people, for creative people.

For errata, please visit the Search Press website (www.searchpress.com) or the Bookmarked Hub website (www.bookmarkedhub.com).

GPSR information can be found at www.searchpress.com

Printed in China, RRD072026

FSC www.fsc.org MIX Paper | Supporting responsible forestry FSC® C144853

LESSONS IN LANDSCAPES

PAINTING TREES IN WATERCOLOUR

MATTHEW PALMER

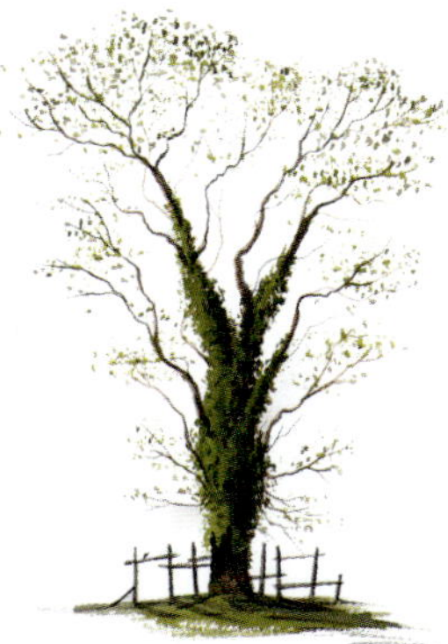

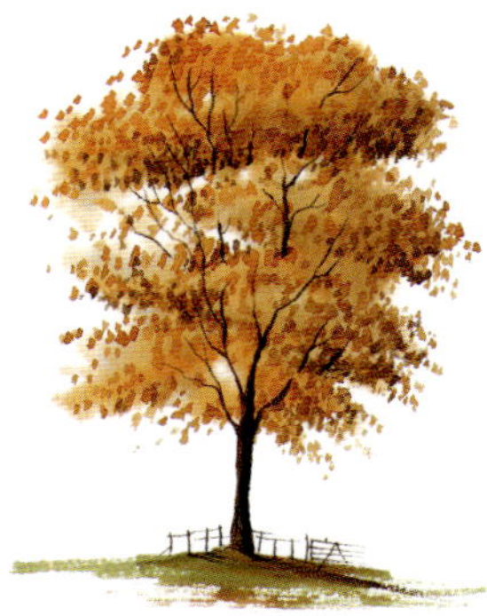

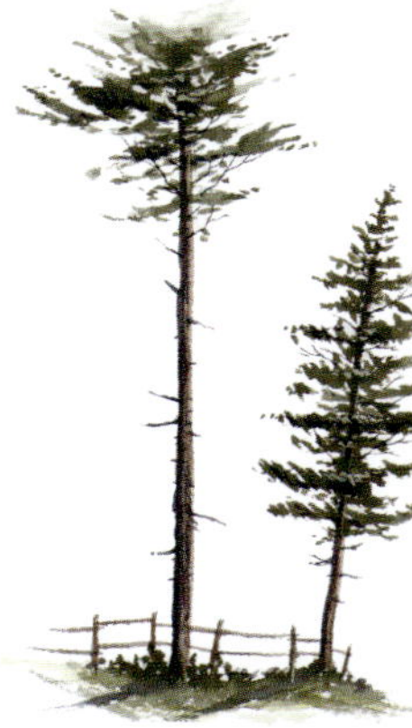

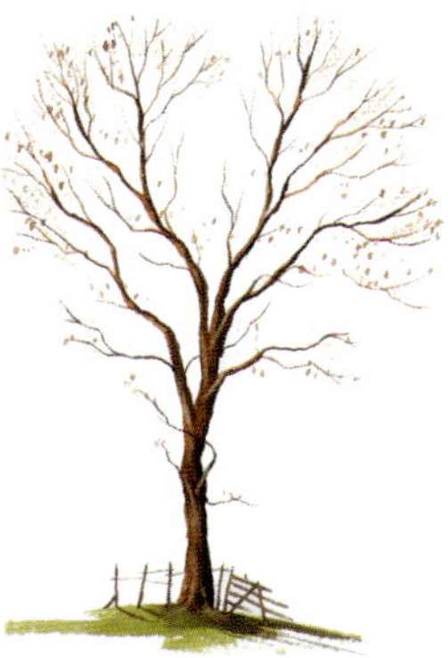

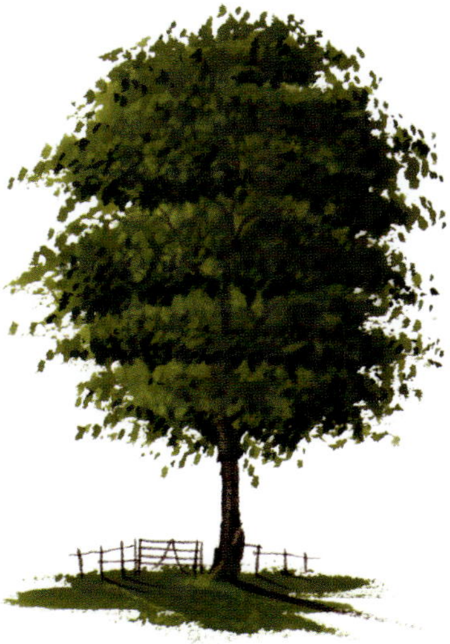

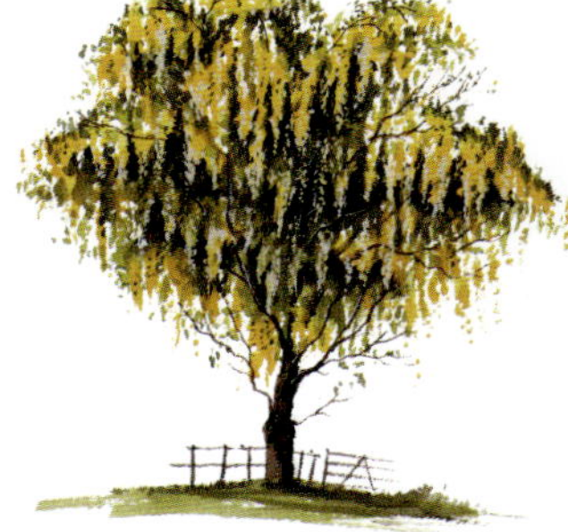

SEARCH PRESS

CONTENTS

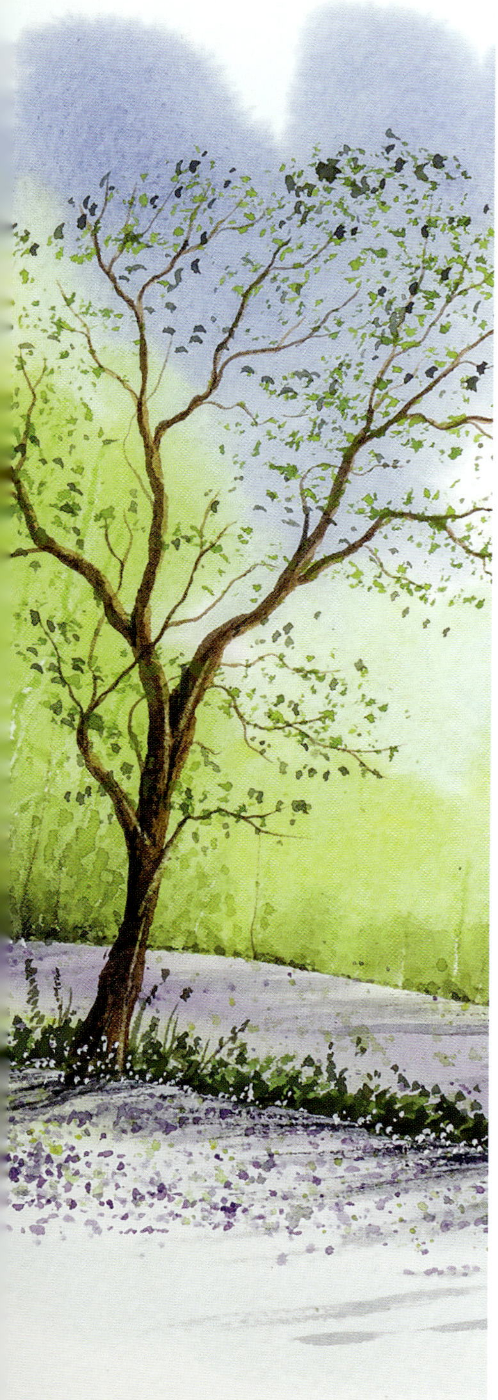

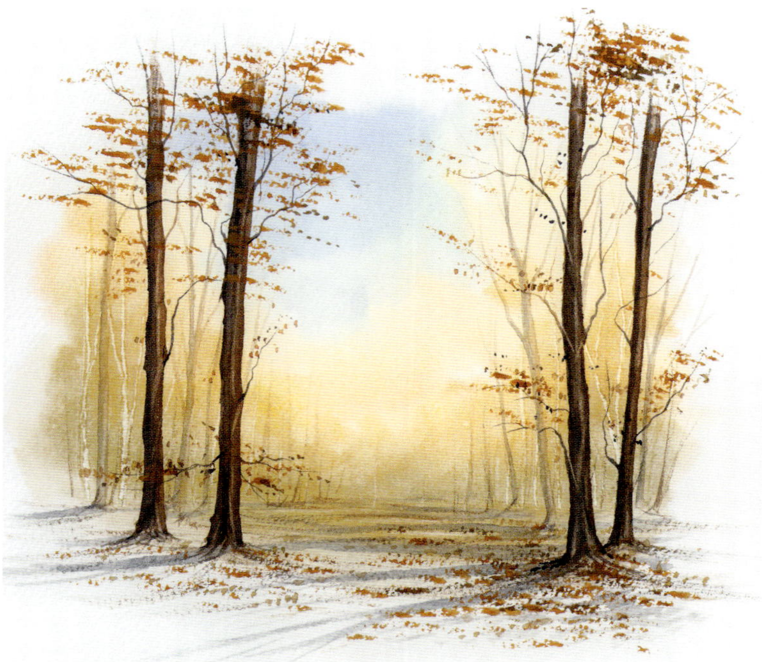

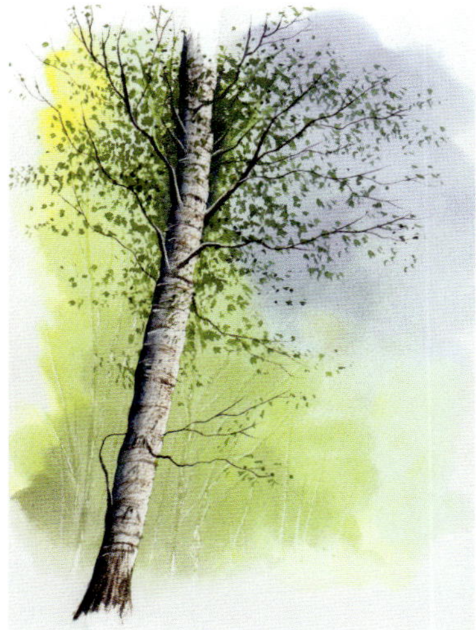

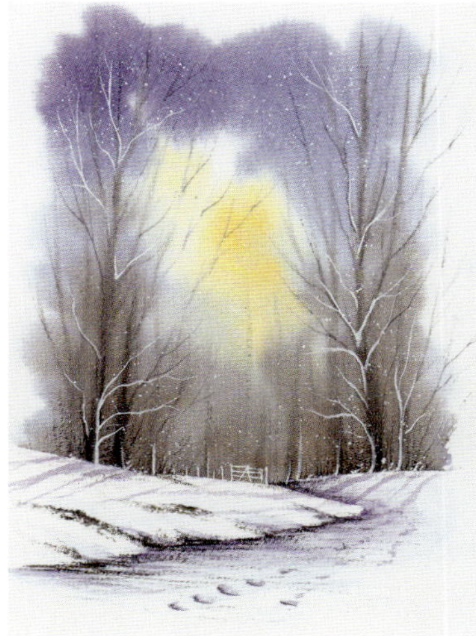

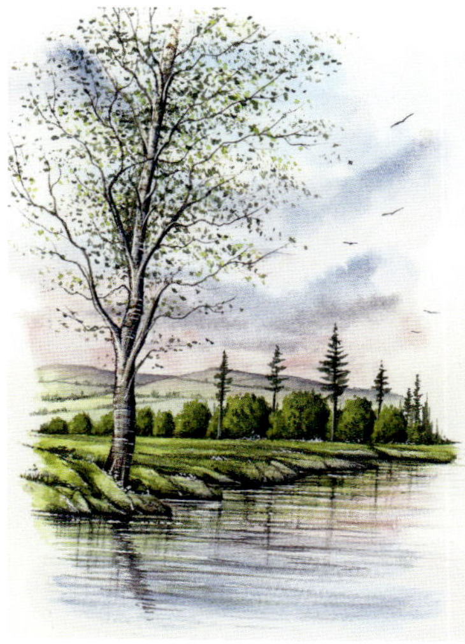

INTRODUCTION

I'm often asked what my favourite subject is to paint. It's a question I find hard to answer, but landscapes is certainly towards the top. I love painting scenes throughout the year, and you may be surprised to learn that by using just a few colours, you can produce some truly beautiful landscapes.

When I started on my watercolour journey over 30 years ago, I knew that trees played an important part in a landscape. However, I also knew they could be a challenge to paint, especially in summer and autumn when there are lots of features to be mindful of – from the colours of the leaves to the textures of the trunks.

So, I set out with my sketchbook to study trees, making notes, sketches and colour samples. I spent many months working on this. At the time this felt like a lot of work but now, in hindsight, that groundwork and research really paid off. Soon I developed my own way for painting trees from all seasons, and these techniques have followed me through many a workshop and lesson, and feature in this book.

The tips, tricks and methods you'll see in this book are the result of my 30-plus years of work, which I hope will transform your own artworks, and excite you enough to get out your paints and brushes and have a go yourself.

Matthew Palmer

www.watercolour.tv | @mattyartist | @MatthewPalmerArtist
@matthewpalmerartist

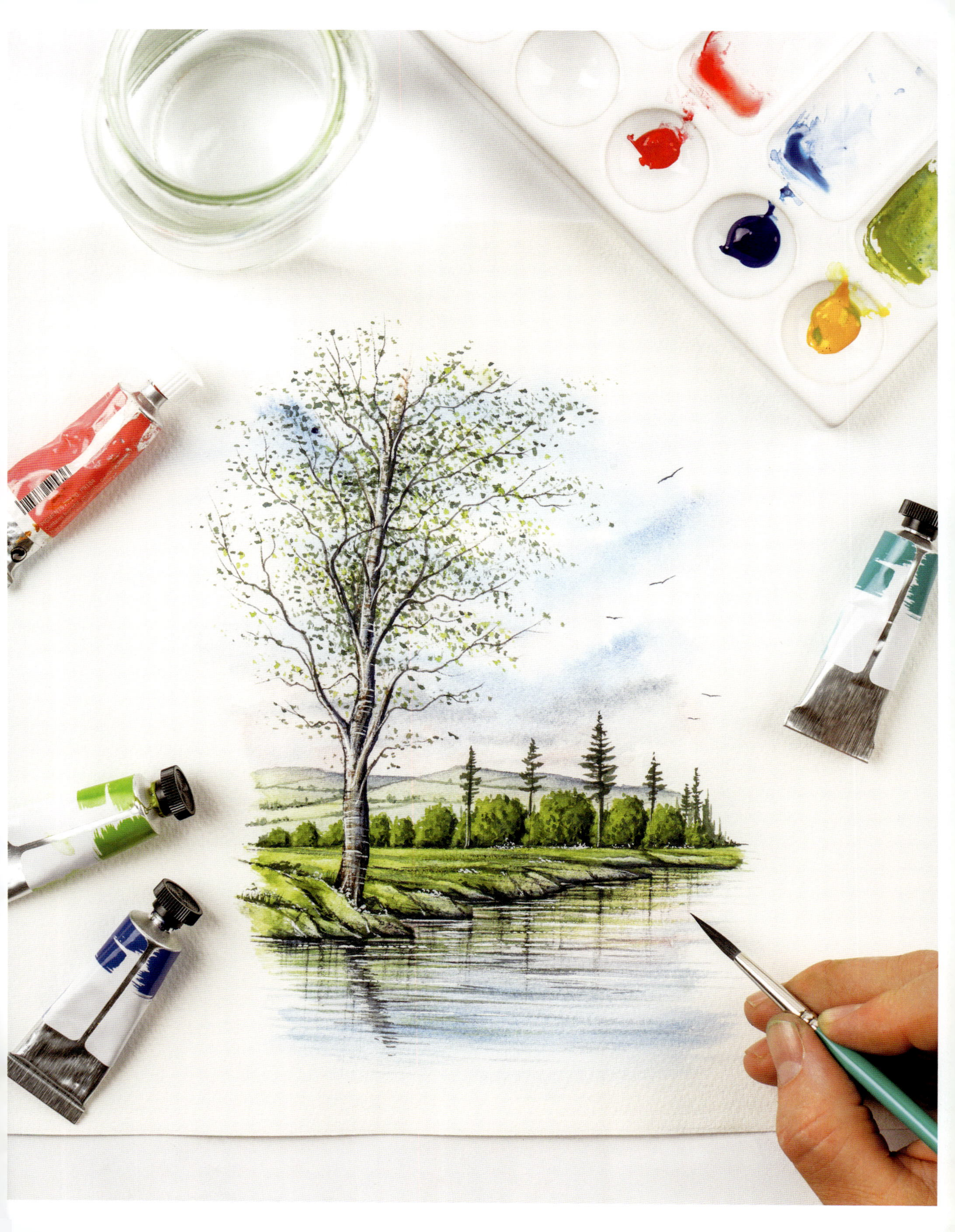

TOOLS AND MATERIALS

Paint

There are two standards of watercolour paint – 'artist quality' and 'student quality'. The main difference, apart from the price, is the pigments used in the paint: artist-quality watercolours are made from the finest of pigments with a gum arabic binder. To start with, however, a **good student-quality paint** is perfectly fine to use.

Watercolour paint comes **in tubes or pans**. A pan is hard dry paint normally in a rectangular block, and you add water to it to lift the colour. I prefer to use tubes as a little bit goes a long way, and the colours are more concentrated and vibrant than those from pans.

Since I've been teaching, I've encouraged my students who are starting out to **buy and use primary colours** – red, yellow, blue – since these can be mixed to create lots of different colours. There are so many variations on primary colours you can buy, from bright yellows to dark yellows, so you can achieve the right shade for your painting. We'll be using lots of greens in this book, but I'd still encourage you to mix these yourself – more often than not, ready-mixed, off-the-shelf greens just don't look natural.

If you decide you'd like to buy ready-made greens, I have my own range of watercolours called Matthew Palmer's Natural Collection. These are artist-quality colours designed to replicate shades in nature.

A bit on white paint: many years ago, white paint in watercolour painting was considered to be a bit of a no-no! But nowadays, it's in most people's palettes. I use white paint quite a lot, and I love the highlights you can create with it. Regular white watercolour paint can disappear once it's dry, so you'll need a good opaque white. Diluted white gouache paint (such as Titanium White) is also a good alternative; in my own range of paints, you can find a Natural Opaque White, too.

Paper

As with paints, there are different qualities of watercolour paper. Through my many years of experience, I've found watercolour paper is the most important thing to get right so go for quality over quantity, and **get the best you can afford**.

The right paper can make your painting journey so much more enjoyable and straightforward. Paper made entirely from wood pulp is cheap, but struggles with the wetness of watercolour paint and doesn't absorb water evenly, creating more disappointing results. It is for this reason that I always use a **100% cotton watercolour paper**, as it's more durable and absorbs water more effectively. The nature of watercolour means your paper needs to cope with large amounts of water applied to it. Ordinary paper can warp or tear when water is applied and your paints can spread uncontrollably or get absorbed so quickly that you can't create attractive washes. Using a good-quality cotton watercolour paper will prevent this happening.

There are different paper textures too. I like to use **paper with a NOT (also known as cold-pressed) surface**; this means that it has a medium level of texture, so is neither too rough nor too smooth. You can also buy smooth (also known as hot-pressed) paper and rough paper, each ideal for certain kinds of paintings, but for me NOT grain is the perfect middle ground, and the best to start out with as a beginner.

What weight paper you choose makes a difference as well – too thin a paper will 'buckle' (go wavy) when you've added lots of water to its surface. A **300gsm (140lb) paper is a good average**, and I would try not to go below this. You might be tempted to choose a thicker paper for painting on, but this has its own set of difficulties – very thick paper demands a lot of water and paint, and you may find you're forever running out of paint and spending more time painting an area too.

For the lessons in this book, I used 23 x 30.5cm (9 x 12in) sheets of 300gsm (140lb), which I taped to a board to secure and prevent buckling.

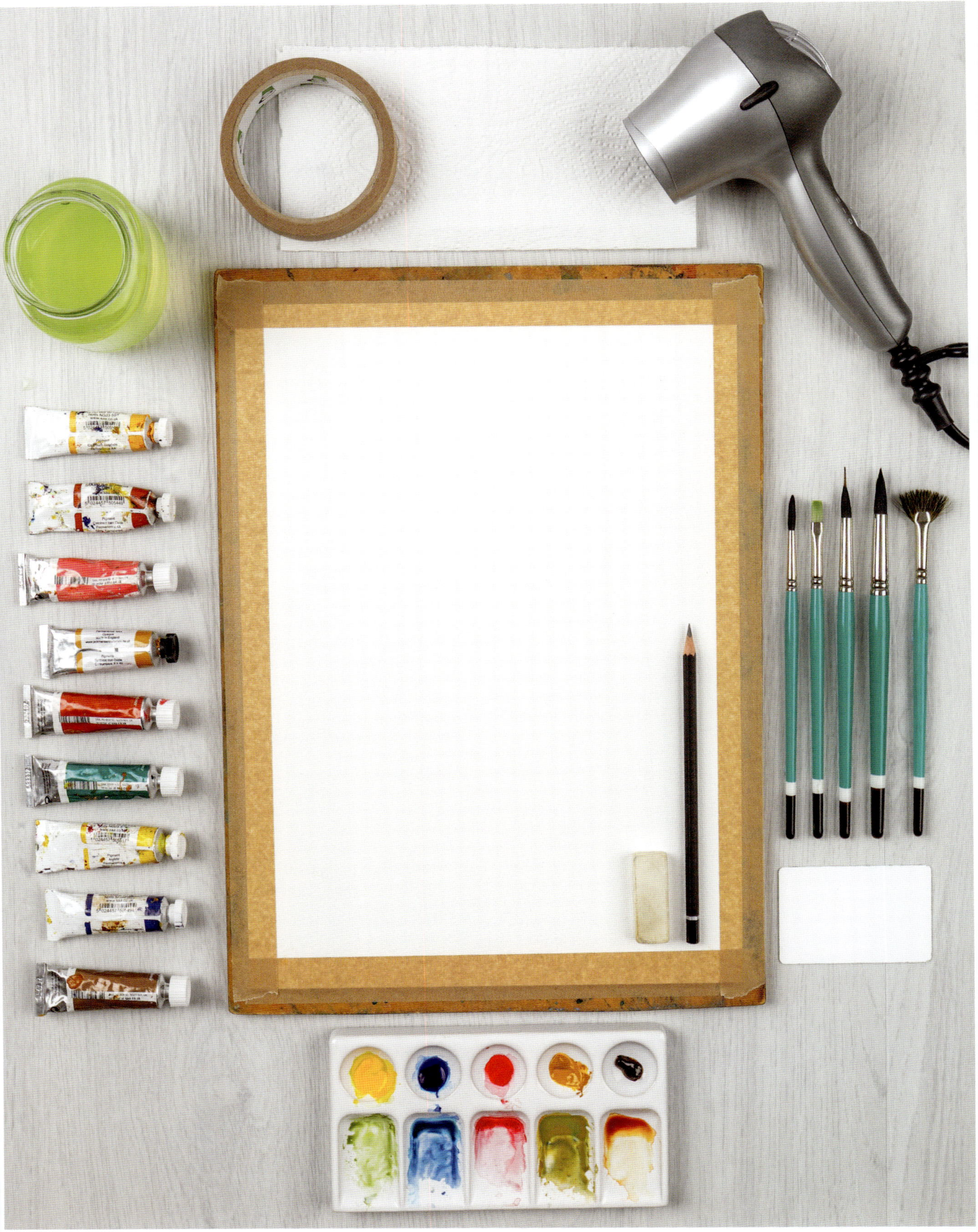

Brushes

There are so many types, sizes and qualities of brush, and it's very easy to buy every single one you encounter – but this isn't necessary! Five brushes are all you need when you're starting out: large, medium and small Round brushes, a fine brush and a Flat brush.

For most work, you'll need a Round brush. I like to use a **size 10 or 12 Round** for painting large areas (like the washes for a sky), and a **size 6 Round** as my 'worker' brush – i.e. the one I use for most of my painting.

For more detailed work, you'll need a fine brush like a **Rigger**. A Rigger has very few bristles and a pointy tip, perfect for painting tiny elements. It's important you angle the brush when you use it so that you only paint with the tip of the brush, not only to achieve finer brush strokes but to avoid damaging the brush too. I recommend a size 2 Rigger if you're an absolute beginner. Riggers run out of paint very quickly because of their few bristles. My version of a Rigger brush is called a '**Branch & Detail Brush**' (or '**Detail**' for short); this is similar to a Rigger but the bristles form a large, bulbous belly before tapering to a fine tip; picking up the paint with the 'belly' allows you to keep feeding the tip with paint.

A **Flat brush**, also known as a chisel brush, has a wide brush head with a flat tip. I tend to use a small one (6mm / ¼in) for 'lifting out' – i.e. removing paint. Lifting out paints allow you to create subtle highlights, but it's also useful for removing accidental paint marks (we all make mistakes, right?). A large Flat brush, which I don't use personally, would make a nice investment brush if you plan to paint large washes for backgrounds and skies in future paintings.

SPECIALIST TREE BRUSHES

When painting trees in particular, you may find certain brushes will make creating some textures much easier, but these are by no means essential.

A **Fan brush** is very useful for stippling and making feathering strokes too, ideal not only for leaves but also grasses and bushes. Personally, I have founded the wider and thicker the fan tip the better, as I find this prevents 'spiky', unrealistic shapes with the paint. I have my own version of a fan brush called 'FANtastic Brush', which is made from natural hair, is thick and wide, and the hairs are different lengths too for realism. In this book, I've used just one size Fan brush – a medium.

Stipple or Stencil brushes can be used for creating dense leafy textures too. I haven't used one in this book, but you may find it makes filling in tree foliage much quicker. My version of stipple brush, 'Tree and Texture Brush' has a slightly slimmer, taller brush head for more controlled stippling.

Synthetic or natural?

Brush hairs can be synthetic or natural, or a mix of both. Synthetic brushes are the cheapest you can buy; while they don't hold a great deal of water they have good shaped points and are relatively durable. Pure natural-hair brushes, often made from sable, hold water well but are very expensive, not very durable and have ethical concerns too. If I'm honest, they are not worth buying. Using a sable-synthetic blend as your brush gives you the best of both worlds – they feature a low percentage of natural hair and a high percentage of synthetic hair, which means they hold water nicely, are durable and the tips stay nice and pointy.

Other equipment

To support your painting and allow you to angle it in a way that suits you, I recommend a **board** to rest your work on while you paint. These can be purchased, but an old bit of wood leftover from a DIY project, or sold cheaply at a hardware store, is good enough.

Masking / painter's tape is used to attach your paper to your working surface or board, to stop it moving around. You can also use masking / painter's tape to cover up certain areas of your artwork to create white spaces, or to mark and preserve areas above or below a specific area that you will work on later (see Lesson #7, for example).

A **water pot** for cleaning your brushes can be anything, from an old jam jar to a purpose-built ceramic pot. When travelling, I use a fold-out silicone pot. One water pot is good enough when you're starting out, but you may find two pots are useful – one for clean water only, and one to use for mixing.

When selecting a **mixing palette**, ideally you want one that has both small and large areas – the small wells are for squeezing your pure colours into, and the large wells are for mixing. (If you prefer to use pan colours, these often come as sets in tins which have wells in the tin lid.)

Kitchen paper is an artist's best friend! It's essential for dabbing excess paint and water from your brush, but also for lifting out wet paint on the paper.

For any sketching, you'll need a **pencil and soft eraser** to hand. Use a 2B pencil for drawing, as its lead is not too hard and won't damage the surface of the paper; it's also easy to erase.

To gently scratch out marks in the paint, you'll need a small piece of **hard cardboard or a plastic card**, ideally with slightly rounded corners. An old loyalty or credit card is perfect for the job.

For cutting out shapes or sharpening pencils, a **craft knife** is very handy to have.

A **hairdryer** is an optional bit of equipment, and care should be taken when you're a beginner, as it can blast paint in the wrong direction if it's still quite wet. However, it can be used to help speed up the drying process between stages of painting, or making the glue of masking / painter's tape tacky again for easier removal.

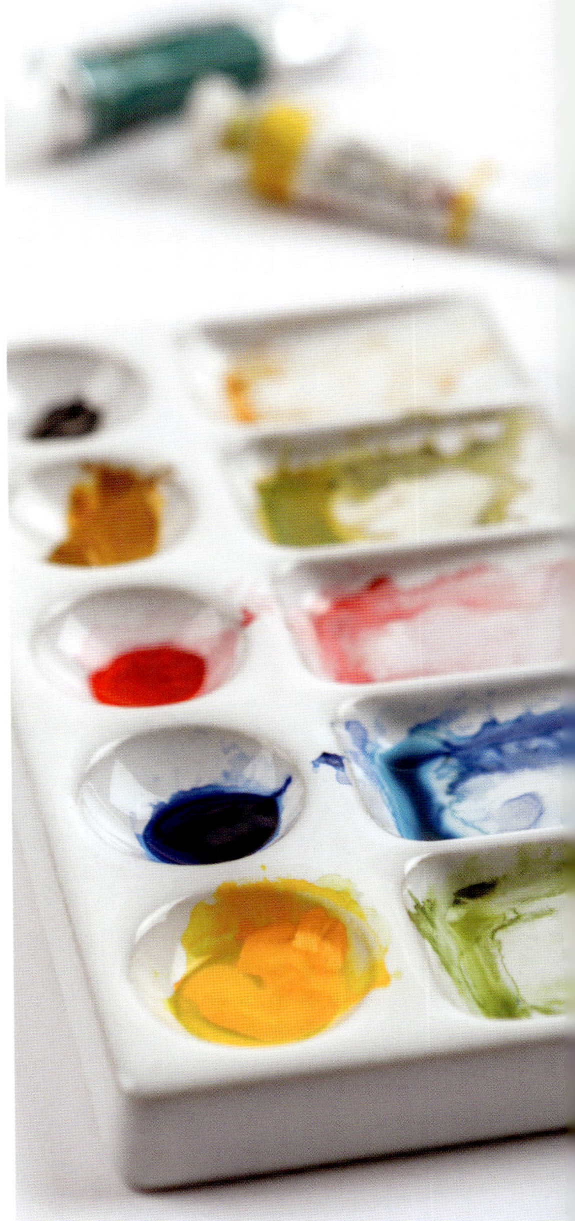

COLOUR MIXING

Learning how to mix watercolour paint as a beginner can be tricky, as you need not only to work out the amounts of each colour to mix together, but also to consider how much water to add to your mix too. For this reason, I've kept the process simple with my tried-and-true ratio approach.

HOW TO MIX

Ratios

In all the books I have published, I've tried to simplify the process of mixing paints by using percentages, indicating what quantity of each pure colour to add to the mix. For example, a 'shadow' grey is made up of 60% French Ultramarine, 20% Alizarin Crimson and 20% Aureolin or Cadmium Yellow.

Consistencies

Knowing how much water to add to your mixes is simpler than you think. I use a 'three levels' approach (see below). Pale, diluted shades are made by adding 2–3 brushloads of water to the palette first before adding your colours (level 3); a medium, mid-tone colour is 1–2 brushloads of water added in the well before adding your colours (level 2); and a strong tone is simply soaking up some water on your brush then adding your colours to the well (level 1).

Process

To pick up the paint, use a wet or slightly damp brush. If the paint dries on the palette, just 'wake it up' by adding a drop of water.

Unless stated otherwise, alway clean the brush when changing to a new mix; this stops you from muddying the colours as you paint.

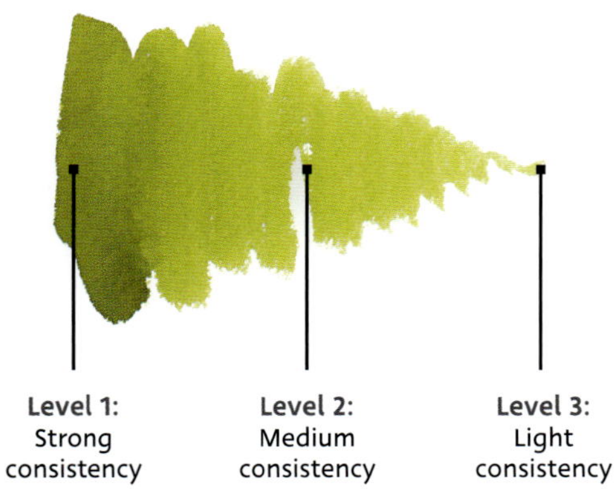

Checking the mix

It's important to know that watercolours tend look 20–30% lighter once the paint has dried. This is something you will get used to over time. However, I think it's always worth testing your colours on a scrap of paper first, then leaving the paint to dry, to see what the final shade will look like; you can then alter the amount of water you add to your mix, if needed.

PURE COLOURS

Below are the key pure watercolours you'll need throughout this book. If you are using paint tubes, squirt small blobs of each colour into its own small well on the palette.

Yellows

You can use **Cadmium Yellow**, **Aureolin**, **Lemon Yellow** or **Yellow Ochre**. All can be used interchangeably, but do create slightly different colour effects.

Cadmium Yellow and **Aureolin** are similar in shade, but Cadmium Yellow is more opaque and lightfast, and is on the bolder side. However, Cadmium Yellow can vary in shade across different brands. If you need help choosing the right shade of Cadmium Yellow, you're looking for a mustard yellow colour. Cadmium Yellow and Aureolin make nice, **mid-green mixes**, when combined with French Ultramarine.

Lemon Yellow is a bright yellow that, when mixed with French Ultramarine, makes punchy, **vibrant greens**.

Yellow Ochre is a brown-yellow shade, and together with French Ultramarine makes **earthier shades of green**.

Blues

I've used just one blue throughout this book – **French Ultramarine**. This is a bright blue that's used for almost all the mixes, from greens to greys.

Reds

I've used only one kind of red throughout this book: **Alizarin Crimson**. This is a bright red with a slightly cooler tone to it. I use it mainly to make up browns and greys.

Browns

Like the yellows, I alternate between different browns in this book – **Burnt Sienna** (a warm, reddish brown) and **Burnt Umber** (a dark, cool brown). They're used primarily for mixing your brown and orange shades.

They can be used somewhat interchangeably, but you'll find there are slight differences. **Burnt Sienna** is better for making oranges and browns that need a **warm, golden tone** to them; **Burnt Umber** is perfect if you're looking to mix up browns with a **cooler, greyer tone**.

White

For highlights, I sometimes use **Titanium White** gouache paint. As this is such a strong colour, you'll need to dilute it with water. You can mix in tiny amounts of other colours, to tailor your highlights to the shades used elsewhere in the painting.

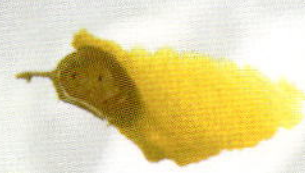

Cadmium Yellow / Aureolin

Lemon Yellow

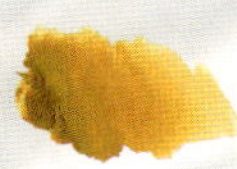

Yellow Ochre

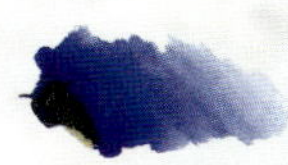

French Ultramarine

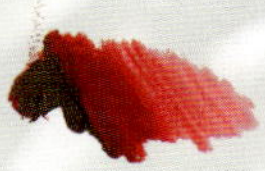

Alizarin Crimson

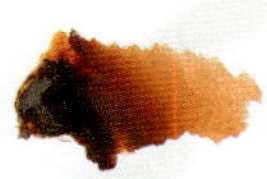

Burnt Sienna

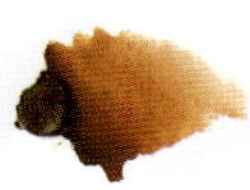

Burnt Umber

Titanium White (gouache)

MIXES

Throughout this book, there are 12 mixes you'll use frequently to paint your tree scenes, and to use as a reference. The mixes key is below, and is also on the inside cover flaps, for easy referencing while you paint. For each mix, I've given percentages of how much of the pure colours to use to achieve almost the exact shade.

(A) Bright green =
80% Lemon Yellow,
20% French Ultramarine

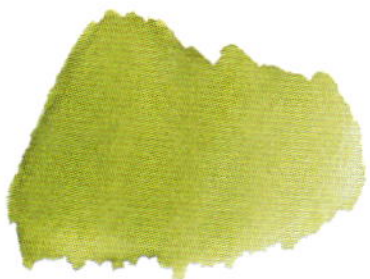

(B) Light Green =
80% Cadmium Yellow / Aureolin,
20% French Ultramarine

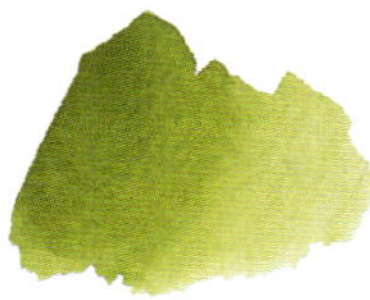

(C) Medium Green =
70% Cadmium Yellow / Aureolin,
30% French Ultramarine

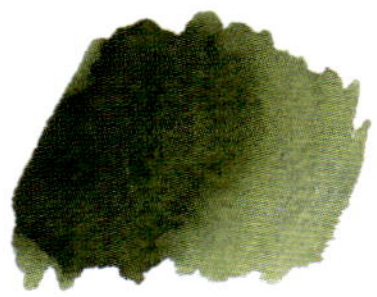

(D) Dark Green =
60% Cadmium Yellow / Aureolin,
30% French Ultramarine,
10% Alizarin Crimson

(E) Deep Shadow Green =
50% Cadmium Yellow / Aureolin,
40% French Ultramarine,
10% Alizarin Crimson

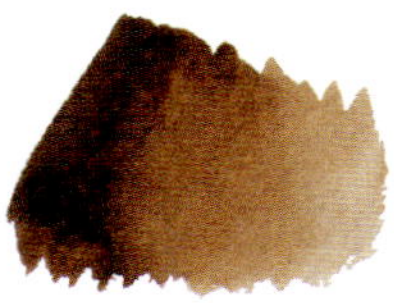

(F) Dark Brown =
70% Burnt Umber,
30% French Ultramarine

(G) Light Brown =
80% Burnt Sienna,
20% French Ultramarine

(H) Shadow Grey =
60% French Ultramarine,
20% Yellow Ochre,
20% Alizarin Crimson

(I) Dark Grey =
70% French Ultramarine,
30% Burnt Umber

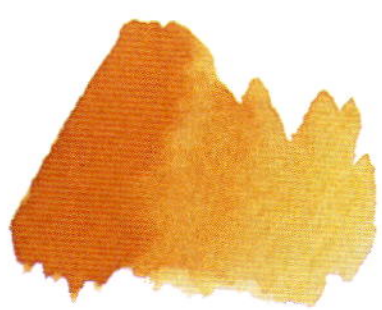

(J) Light Orange =
60% Burnt Sienna,
40% Cadmium Yellow / Aureolin

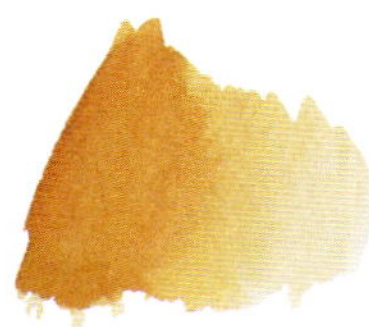

(K) Dark Orange =
50% Burnt Sienna,
40% Cadmium Yellow / Aureolin,
10% French Ultramarine

(L) Violet =
80% French Ultramarine,
20% Alizarin Crimson

TECHNIQUES

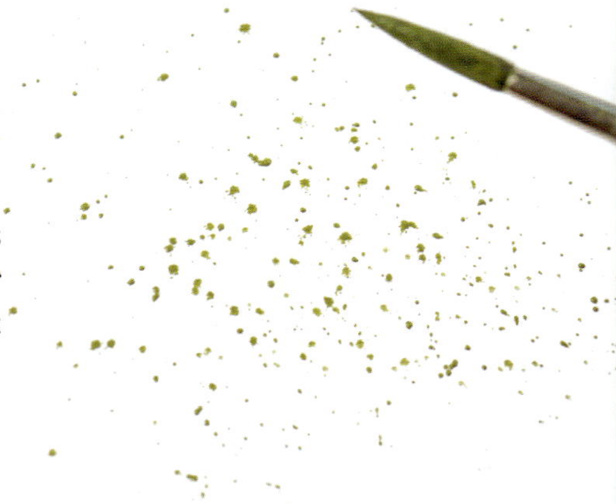

Below are the most common techniques that I use for the lessons and the final project in this book, and for most other watercolour paintings. Techniques that are specific to a lesson or the final project will be covered in its relevant steps.

Wet on dry

- This is applying wet paint to dry paper.
- You'll use this a technique about 90% of the time – from painting in basic elements to adding shadows and other details.
- The effect is a shape with hard edges.
- Typically you'll use a Round brush, but a Rigger is used for finer features.

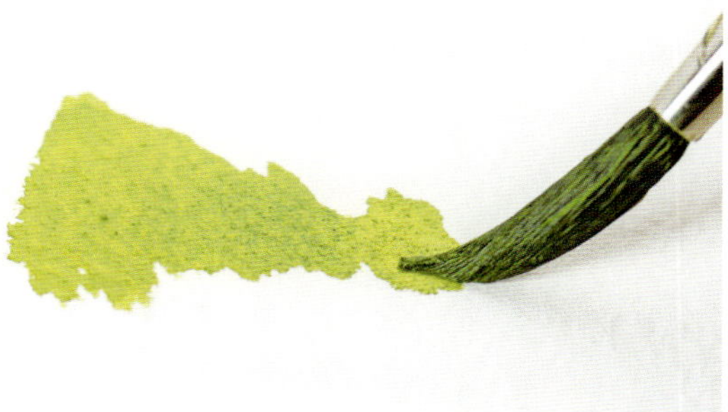

Wet in wet

- This is applying wet paint to wet paper, which could be wet with either paint or water.
- It's ideal for whenever you want to add washes for a background, or to create misty, blended effects – basically, anywhere you don't want clean, hard edges.
- I like to use a large Round brush for washes, but you could use a large Flat brush for this job too.
- For skies, I twist the brush as shown to suggest cloud shapes, and will work in from the edges of the painting towards the centre.

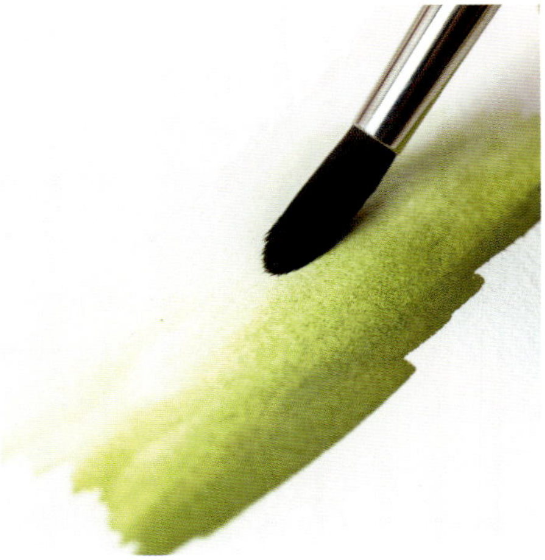

Blending

- This is a wet-on-dry technique, using the Round brush.
- It involves blending the edge of wet paint on dry paper, to create a graduation of colour.
- A decent amount of colour, of a medium strength, needs to be applied to the paper or else it won't blend well.
- Paint the shape to be blended. Clean the brush, lightly dab the brush head on a bit of kitchen paper to remove excess water, then run the brush along one edge. Keep cleaning and dabbing the brush head as you work, to create a clean, even blend.

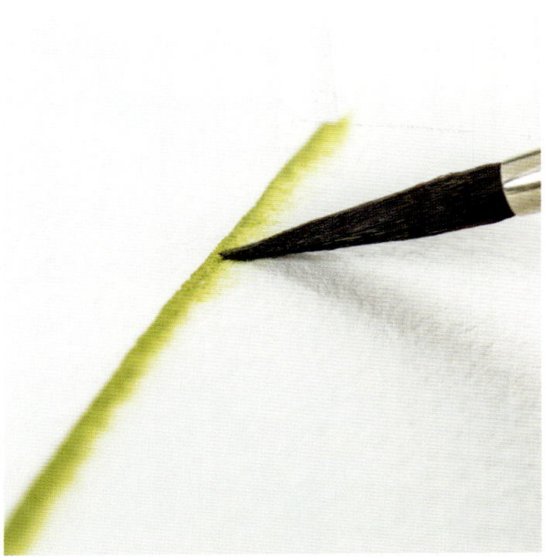

Feathering

- This is a wet-on-dry technique.
- This is similar to blending, but is much more subtle.
- As the area is usually small, you should use a finer brush like a size 6 Round, size 2 Rigger or 'Branch & Detail' brush.
- A decent amount of colour, of a medium strength, needs to be applied to the paper or else it won't blend well.
- After painting the feature, clean the brush, dab it onto kitchen paper until it's nearly dry, then carefully 'tickle' the edge to soften.

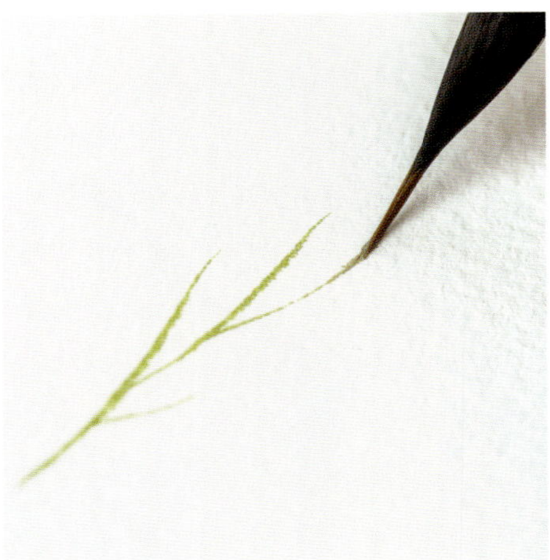

Fine branches

- This is a wet-on-dry technique, using either the Rigger or the 'Branch & Detail' brush.
- Work in the direction of 'growth', so painting from the tree trunk outwards and towards you; you may need to rotate the paper as you paint to achieve this.
- Lift the brush off the paper as you come to the end of the stroke, to create a delicate, tapered end to the branch – a Rigger brush works well for the finest branches.
- Hold the brush like you would a pen, with the side of your hand resting on the paper.
- Ensure there's not too much paint on the brush; pick up the mix then dab off the excess onto kitchen paper before painting.

Stippling with a round brush

- This is a wet-on-dry technique, using a Round brush (example right features a size 6 Round).
- Squash the brush into the palette to spread out the bristles and make them spiky; holding the brush vertically, gently bounce the brush onto the paper to make several dots at a time.
- Rotate the brush occasionally to add variation and slightly more textural marks, and to use up all the paint on the brush, too.

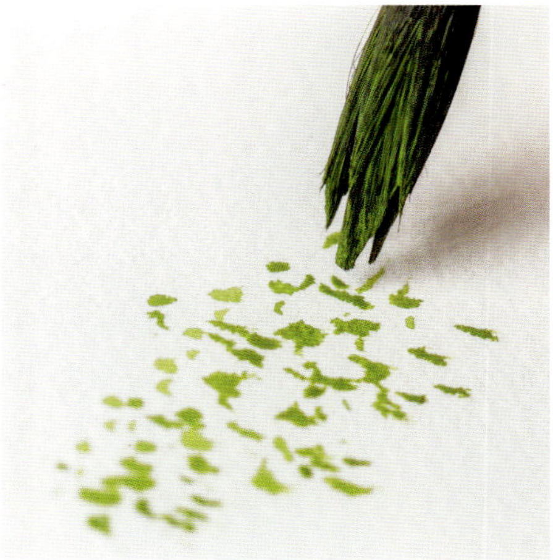

Stippling with a fan brush

- This is a wet-on-dry technique, using a Fan brush.
- Squash the brush into the palette to ensure all the hairs of the brush are covered in paint; tap the brush onto kitchen paper to knock off some excess paint.
- Holding the brush vertically, gently bounce the brush onto the paper to make several finer dots at a time.

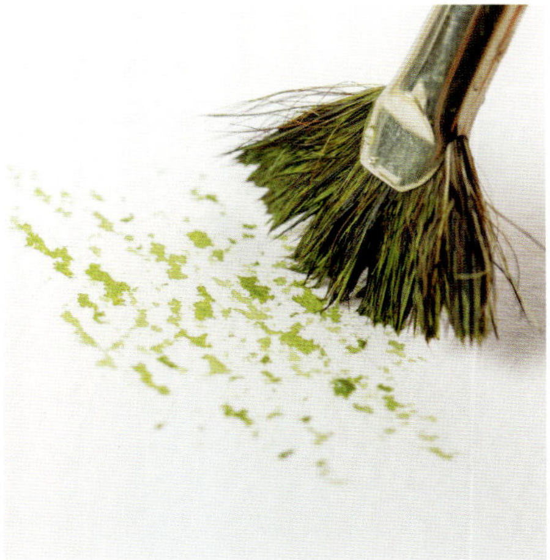

Dotting and dabbing

- This is a wet-on-dry technique, using the size 6 Round brush.
- Simply 'tap' the tip of the brush on the paper to create a single dot on the paper. Rotate the brush occasionally to add variation and slightly more textural marks.
- Hold the brush like a pen, with the side of your hand resting on the paper.

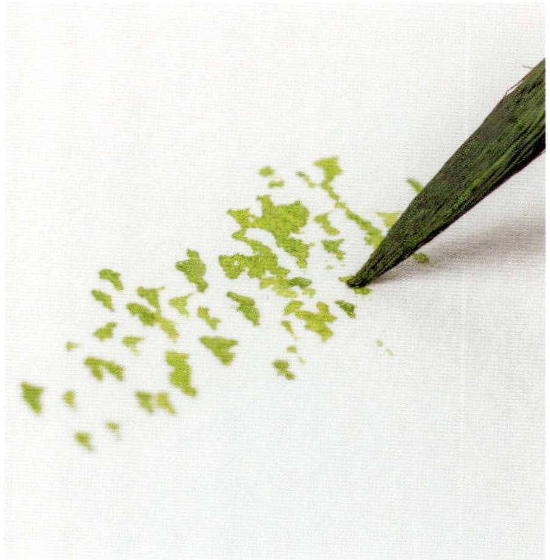

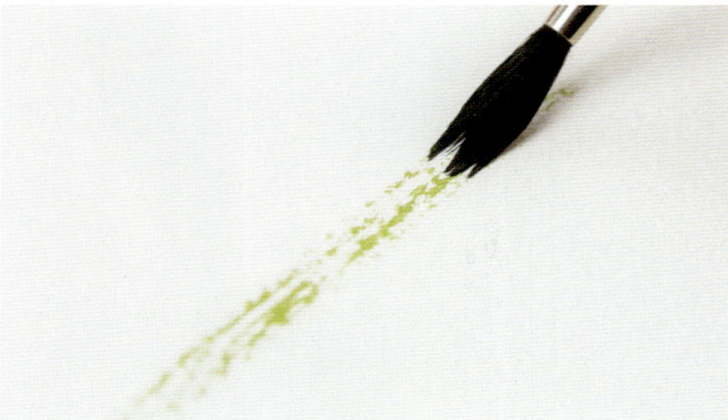

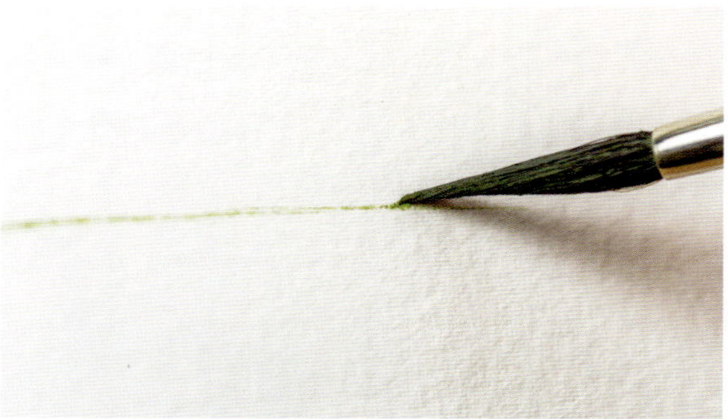

Dry brushing

- This is a wet-on-dry technique.
- For larger surface textures, use the pinch method (see the top image, left); for finer rough lines, keep the tip of the brush fine (see the bottom image, left).
- **Pinch method:** Dip the tip of the brush into the paint. Pinch the brush head between your index finger and thumb to make a flat spiky edge. Holding it at a low angle, pull the brush across the paper.
- **Fine-tip method:** Dip the tip of the brush into the paint. Tap off the excess onto kitchen paper. Holding it like a pen, and with a slightly higher angle, pull the brush across the paper.

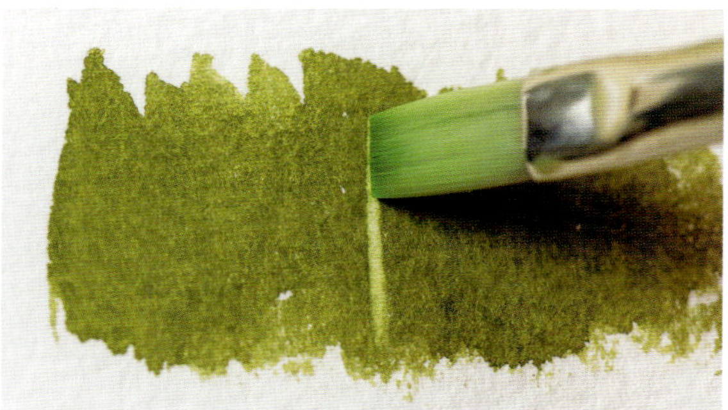

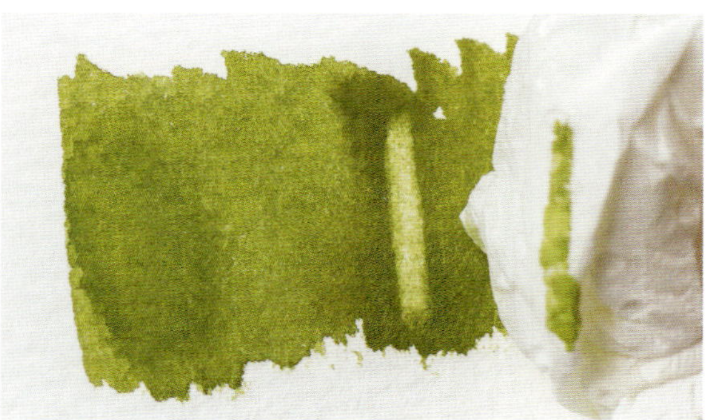

Lifting out

- This is used mainly for creating highlights in your painting, but it's handy for removing mistakes too!
- You can use a Round or Flat brush for this job; the example on the left shows a 6mm (¼in) Flat.
- Ensure the paper and paint are dry. Wet the brush with clean water, tap on kitchen paper to remove excess water, then 'scrub' the area with the brush a couple of times. Immediately press the kitchen paper over the area to lift out the paint.
- **Tip:** To remove excess water without distorting the brush head, after cleaning the brush run it between your thumb and index finger, from ferrule to tip.
- **Note:** Certain colours, like blue, are harder to remove; you may need to repeat the process a few times to lift out the paint. This won't affect the paper.

Scratching out

- Use a piece of hard cardboard or plastic for this – an old loyalty or bank card is perfect.
- The paint should still be damp when scratching out – but not too wet, or else the marks don't appear.
- With just the corner of the card touching the paper, simply pull it across the damp paint. Don't hold the card vertically; the corner in contact with the paper should be angled almost flat to the paper.
- Wipe the card before each 'scratch', so it's always clean – this stops older paint getting into the scratch marks, and affecting the colours in the painting.
- It's worth practising on a test painting before committing to the final artwork, to familiarize yourself with the process and ensure you're happy with the results.

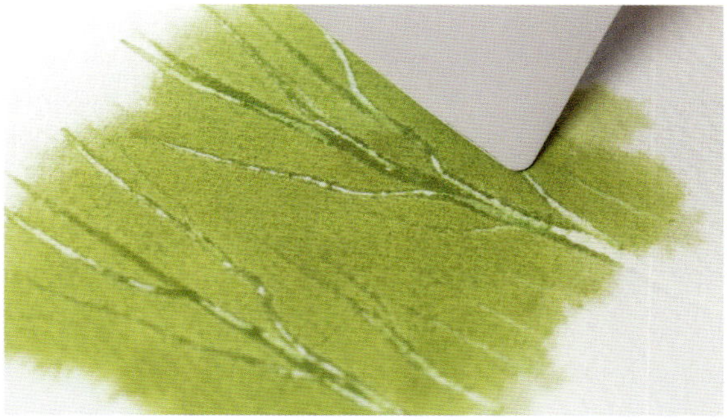

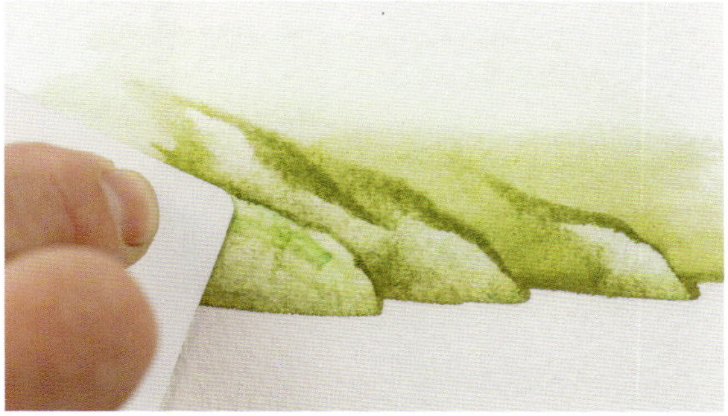

Flicking

- This involves tapping a brush's ferrule (the metal casing below the brush head) against your finger, to flick paint onto a surface.
- The brush head should be damp and half full of paint so that a good amount of paint comes off the brush, but isn't too much or too wet or you won't achieve distinct, tiny dots of colour.
- Changing the position of your finger changes the results of the flicks. Moving your finger closer to the brush head creates subtle flicks; placing your finger closer to the brush handle results in larger, stronger spots of colour.
- It's worth practising on a scrap of paper before committing to the final artwork, to experiment with finger and brush placement, and ensure you're happy with the results.

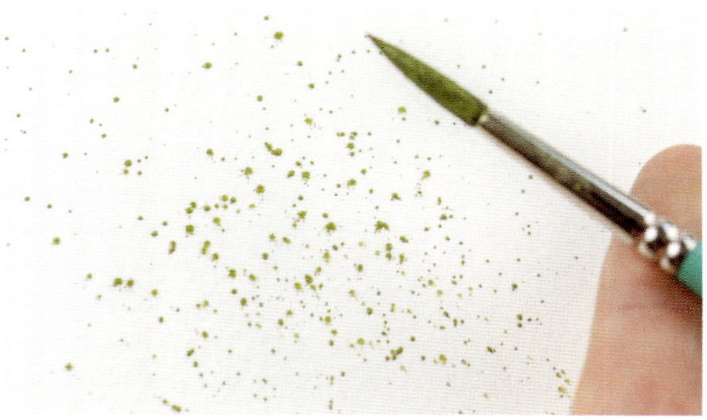

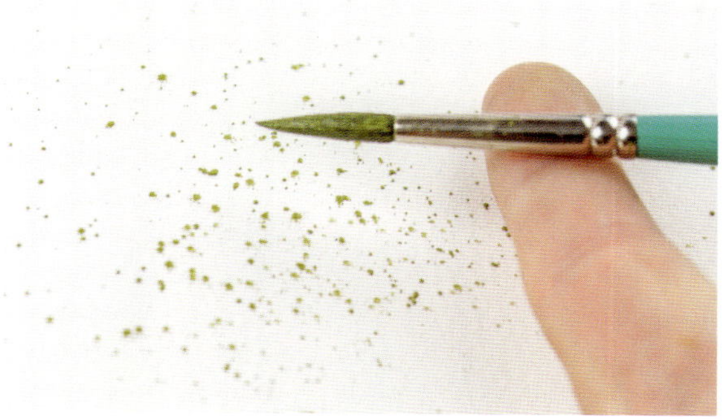

THE LESSONS

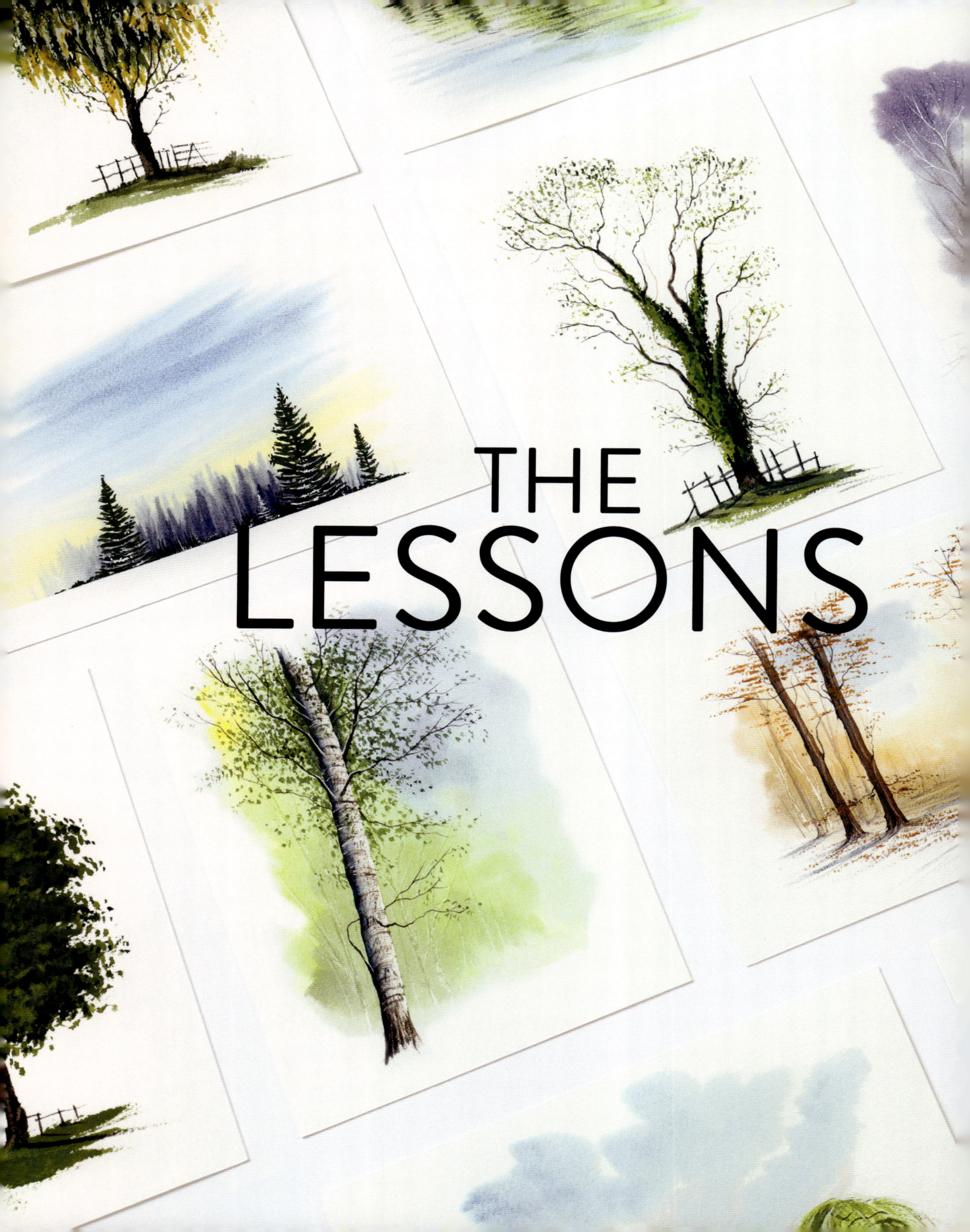

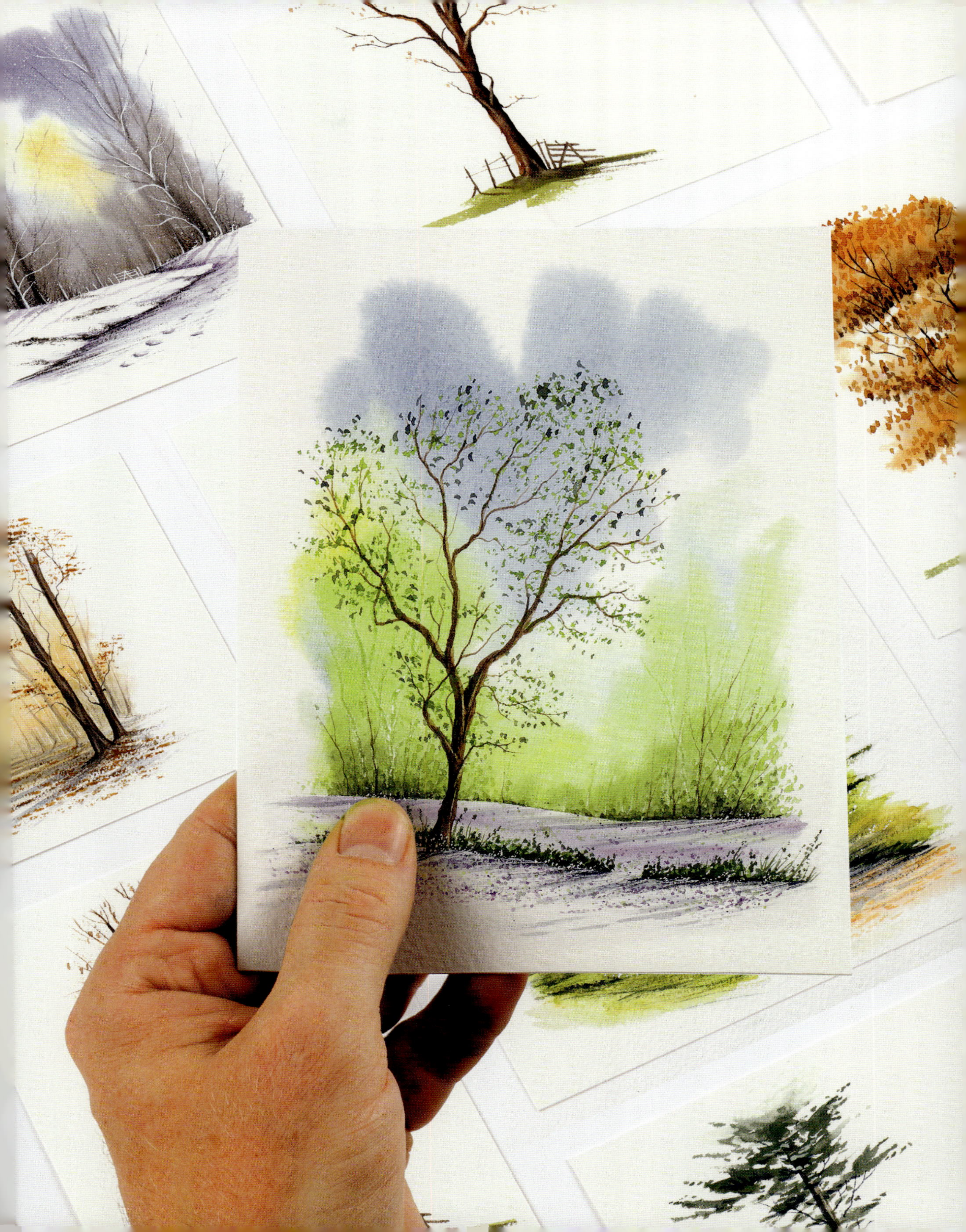

HOW TO READ THIS SECTION

1

2

Lesson #7
FIR TREE FOREST

3

1. Start off with a strip of masking / painter's tape that's longer than the width of the painting. Slide the length between your fingers to remove some of the tape's stickiness. Lay it horizontally over the paper, about a third of the way up from the bottom edge. The top edge of the tape will be your horizon line. Note: if the paint leaks underneath the top edge later, don't worry: any accidental paint can be worked into the painting later.

2. With the size 10 or 12 Round, wet the paper from the top edge down to the masking / painter's tape. Wet the paper a couple of times to ensure there's an even spread of water, and spread out any puddles that have gathered on the surface.

3. As soon as you've finished wetting the paper, pick up and sweep in a light-strength pure Yellow Ochre mix from the masking / painter's tape upwards, **wet in wet**, to add a warm colour to the bottom of the sky area. While the paint is still wet, clean the brush, pick up a light-strength pure French Ultramarine mix and sweep this in from the top of the paper downwards, into the yellow. Allow the two colours to mix around the centre, creating a graduated wash.

3

Adding blue at a slight angle adds interest to the sky

4

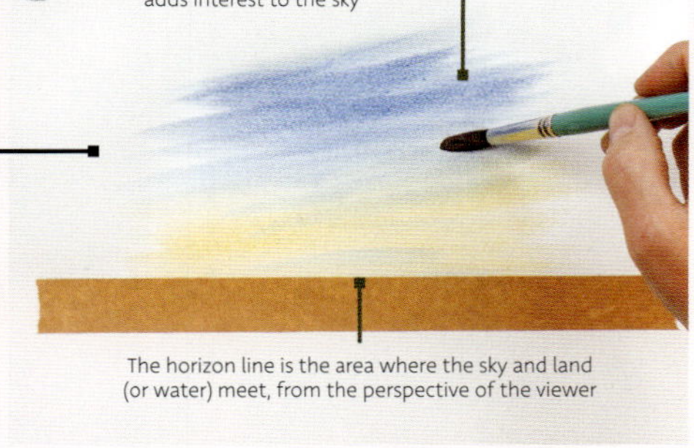

The horizon line is the area where the sky and land (or water) meet, from the perspective of the viewer

PURE COLOURS

Yellow Ochre

French Ultramarine

MIXES

See page 14 or the cover flaps for details.

H

D

BRUSHES

- Size 10 or 12 Round
- Size 6 Round
- Size 2 Rigger or Detail

EXTRAS

- Masking / painter's tape
- Titanium White gouache
- Optional: hairdryer

TECHNIQUES

- Wet in wet
- Wet on dry
- Dotting and dabbing

1. LESSON

This shows what number lesson you're on, and what you'll be learning in this lesson. There are 12 lessons in total.

2. INFORMATION PANEL

The panel contains lists the pure colours and mixes used in the lesson, as well as the brushes, extra equipment and techniques you'll use. Combined-colour mixes have been assigned a letter; a key can be found on page 14 and on the inside cover flaps.

3. INSTRUCTIONS

These take you step by step through the process of creating the painting.

Underlined text highlights which equipment and mix to use.

Bold text highlights the technique you'll use.

4. STEP IMAGES

Photographs of each significant stage are featured alongside the instructions. Annotations are included to share helpful tips.

5. USEFUL INFO BOXES

If you'd like to learn more about a technique or principle connected to the lesson, I've added some info boxes that contain extra details that will take your painting skills even further.

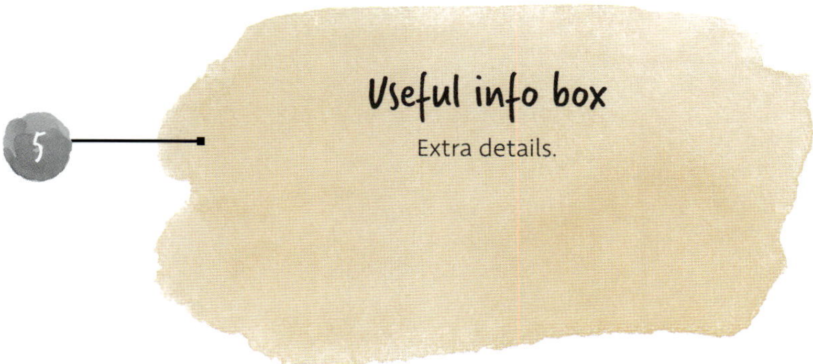

Lesson #1
SIMPLE SUMMER TREE

MIXES

See page 14 or the cover flaps for details.

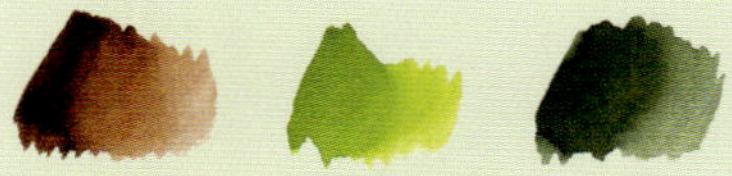

F A D

BRUSHES

- Size 6 Round
- Medium Fan

EXTRAS

- Kitchen paper

TECHNIQUES

- Wet on dry
- Fine branches
- Dotting and dabbing
- Lifting out
- Stippling with a Round brush

1. With a medium-strength F mix and the size 6 Round, and working **wet on dry**, paint in a tree shape: to start, paint in the main trunk, in one stroke from bottom to top; as you work towards the top of the tree, gradually lift your brush off the paper to taper off. Then add the **finer branches** along the length of the tree in a similar way, wobbling the brush to create more organic shapes, and again lifting the brush at the ends to taper off neatly.

2. While the trunk paint is still damp, create the basic background foliage on the tree using a medium-strength A mix and the medium Fan. With just one stroke, and working from top to bottom, zigzag the brush over the top of the tree trunk. Use the same method to add some land below the tree, to ground it.

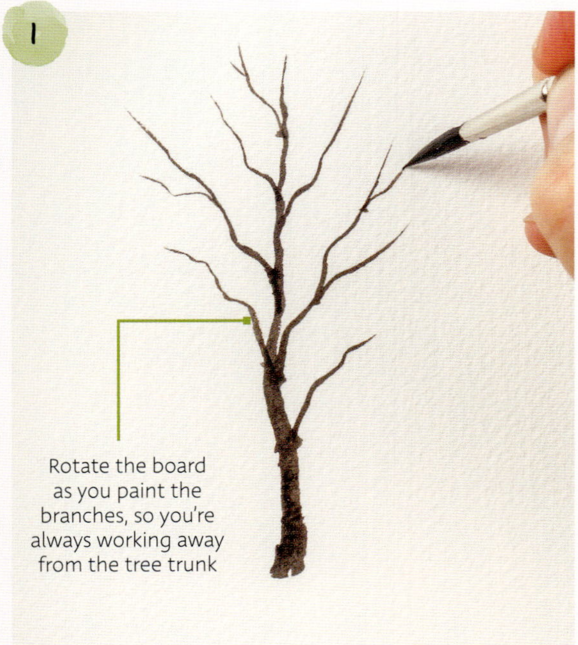

1

Rotate the board as you paint the branches, so you're always working away from the tree trunk

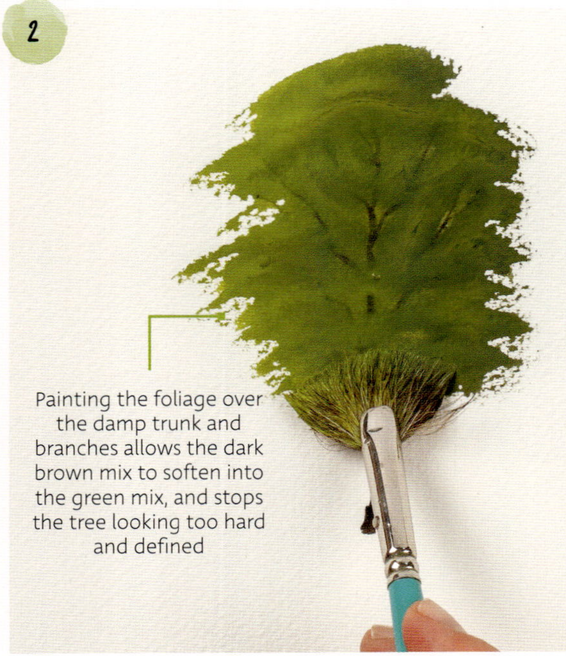

2

Painting the foliage over the damp trunk and branches allows the dark brown mix to soften into the green mix, and stops the tree looking too hard and defined

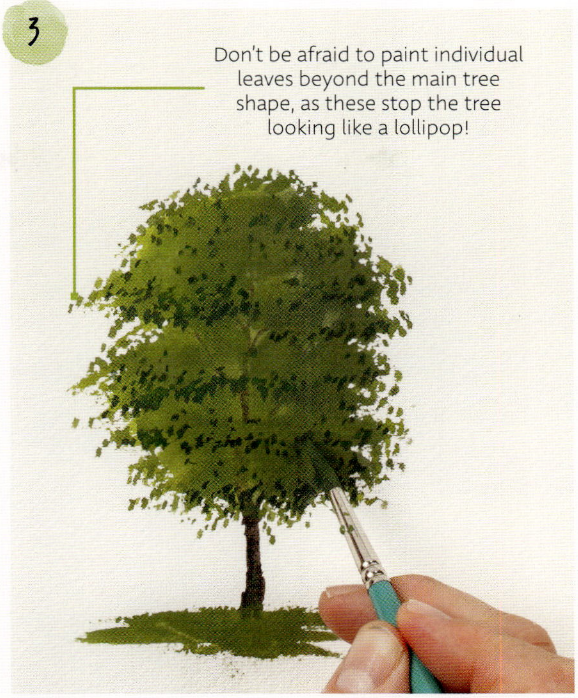

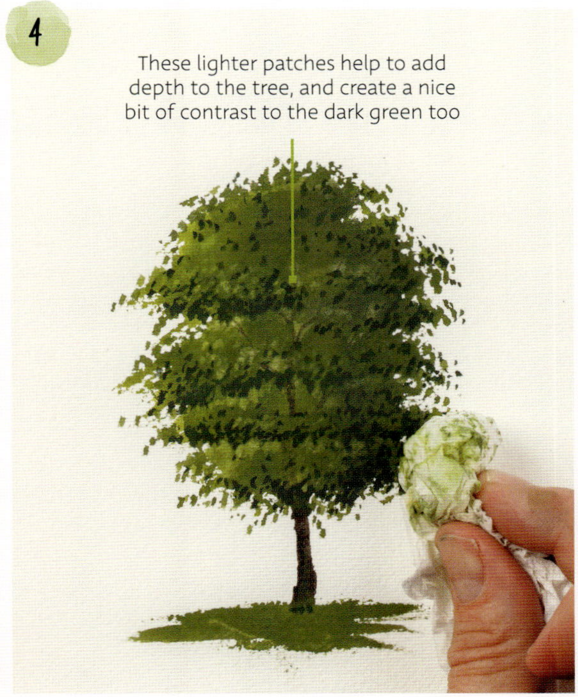

3. To add texture and foreground leaves, **dot and dab** in a medium-strength D mix with the size 6 Round. Work around the edge of the tree foliage first, then touch in further colour, suggesting shadow and indentations in the tree. Repeat with a medium-strength A mix to suggest lighter leaves. Leave the painting to dry.

4. **Lift out** lighter patches in the tree to create highlights: wet a clean size 6 Round, dab away the excess water on a piece of kitchen paper, then **stipple** the damp brush above and below the darker zigzagging lines of leaves. Immediately press clean kitchen paper onto the painting to lift out paint in these damp areas.

5. ***Optional details:*** with the size 6 Round and F mix, pull down a shadow to the right-hand side of the tree to 'attach' it to the ground. Add a fence and a farm gate for interest.

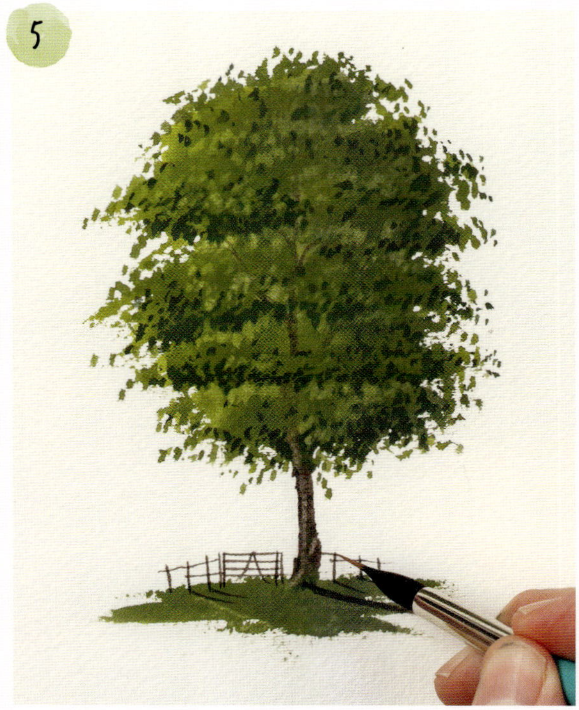

Lesson #2
SIMPLE WINTER TREE

MIXES

See page 14 or the cover flaps for details.

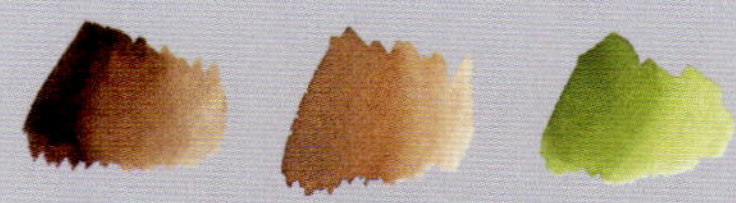

F G C

BRUSHES

- Size 6 Round
- Size 2 Rigger or Detail

EXTRAS

- Kitchen paper

TECHNIQUES

- Wet on dry
- Fine branches
- Dry brushing
- Dotting and dabbing
- Lifting out

1. With a medium-strength F mix and the size 6 Round, and working **wet on dry**, paint in what will be the darker, shadow sides of the main trunk and larger branches – for this tree, the shadows lie on the right-hand side. Paint in the main trunk first in one stroke from bottom to top; lift the brush off the paper as you work towards the top to taper off. Then add the branches along the length of the tree, wobbling the brush to create more organic shapes.

2. With the size 6 Round, and while the paint of the last mix is still wet, run a medium-strength G mix along the left-hand side of the tree and large branches, using the same process as in Step 1.

1

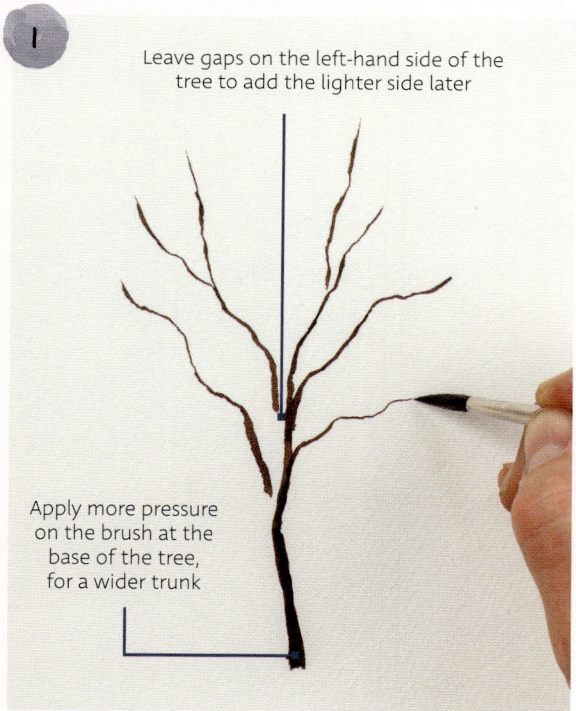

2

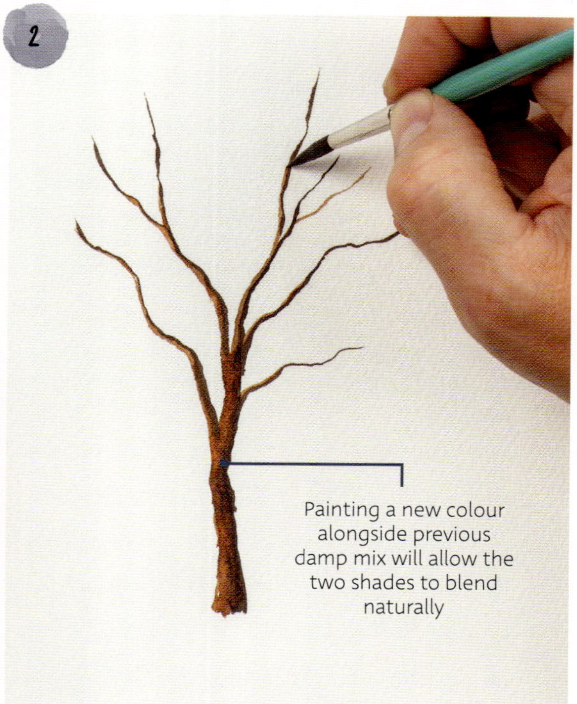

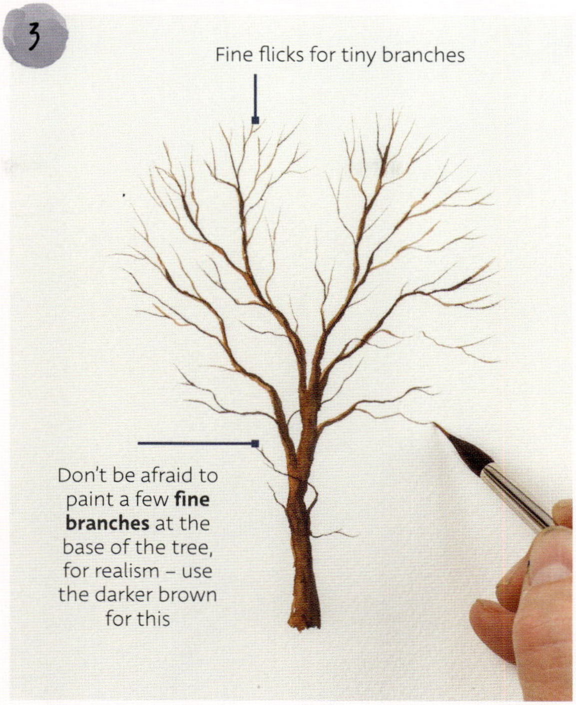

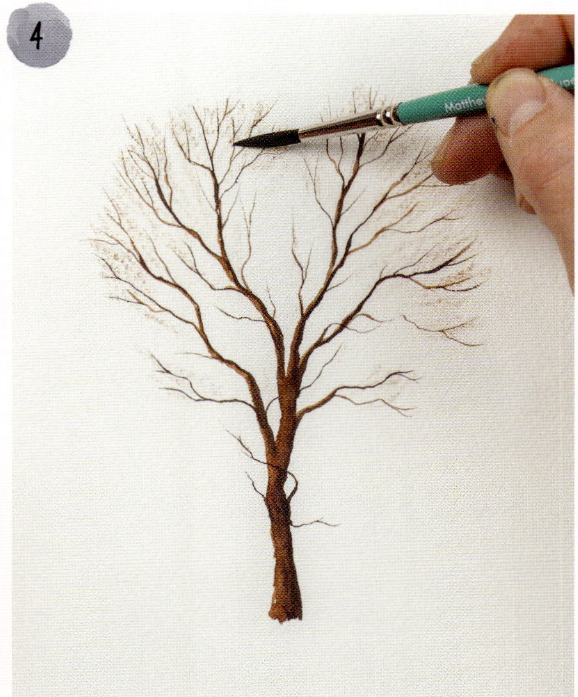

3. Switching between medium-strength G and F mixes and using a size 2 Rigger or Detail, paint in the **fine branches** on the tree. The F mix is great for suggesting tiny background branches. Hold the brush like a pen and rest the side of your hand on the paper, to ensure you're painting with just the tip of the brush and have greater control. Rotate the board as you paint, so you're always painting away from the trunk – i.e. in the direction of natural growth.

4. Dilute the G mix with clean water so it is a light strength. With a size 6 Round, stroke the colour over the tree branches using the **dry brush** technique, to suggest a few delicate leaves.

5. With the same mix and brush as before, **dot and dab** a few individual leaves amongst the branches.

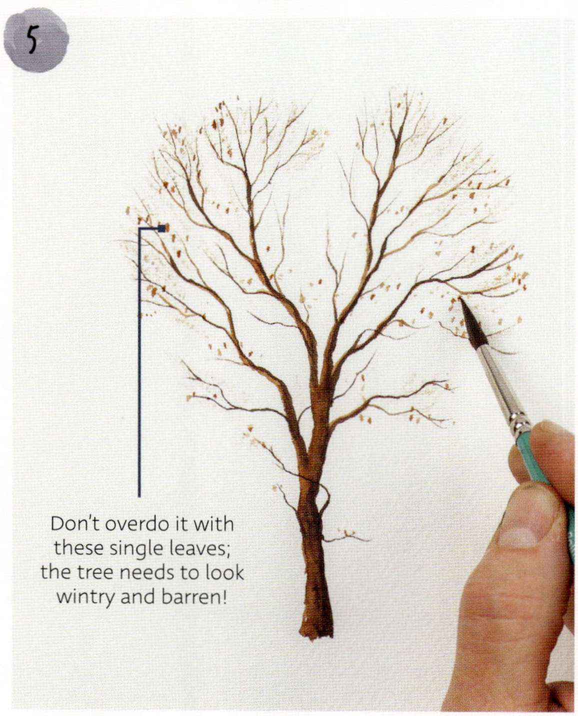

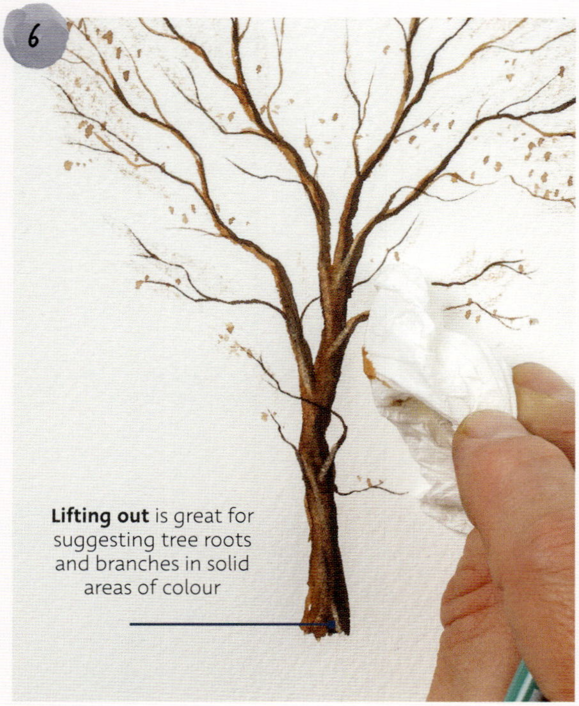

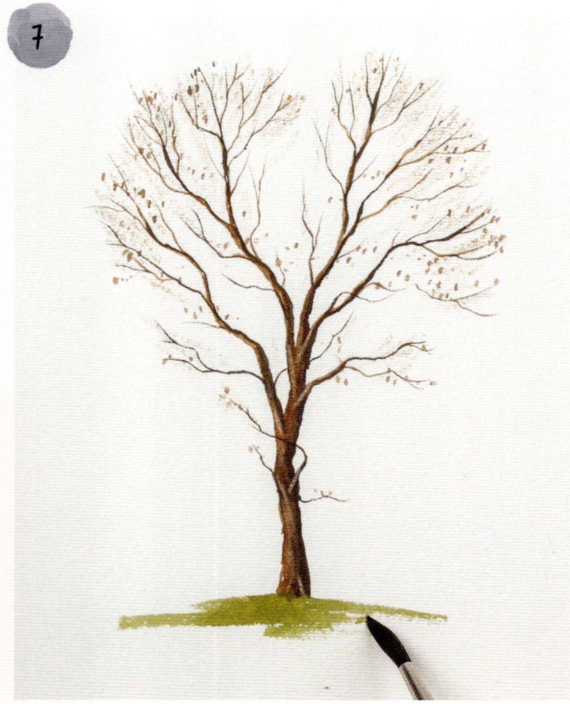

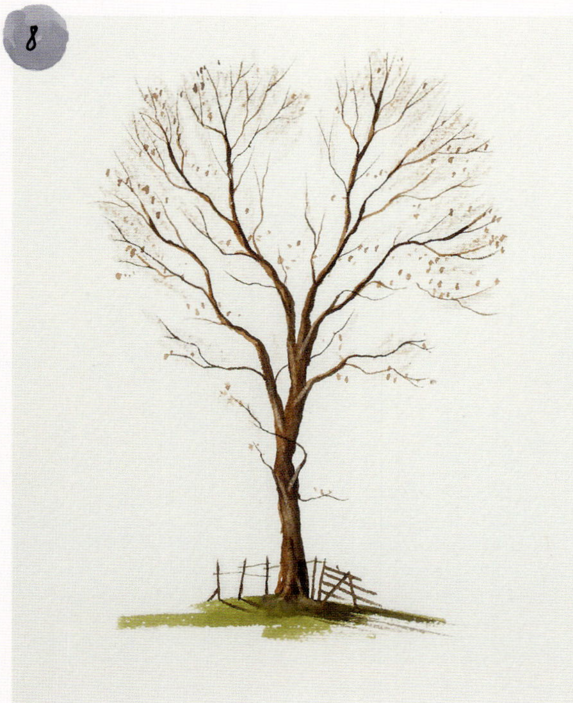

6. Clean the size 6 Round, dab it on a piece of kitchen paper to remove the excess water, then **lift out** a few highlights on the left-hand side of the trunk. Use the same process to add highlights to any of the branches with a dramatic angle, to make them more 3D.

7. Finish by sweeping a bit of land below the tree, working from top to bottom, using the size 6 Round and C mix.

8. ***Optional details:*** with the size 6 Round and F mix, pull down a shadow to the right-hand side of the tree to 'attach' it to the ground. Add a fence and gate, and perhaps a little bird sitting on it for interest.

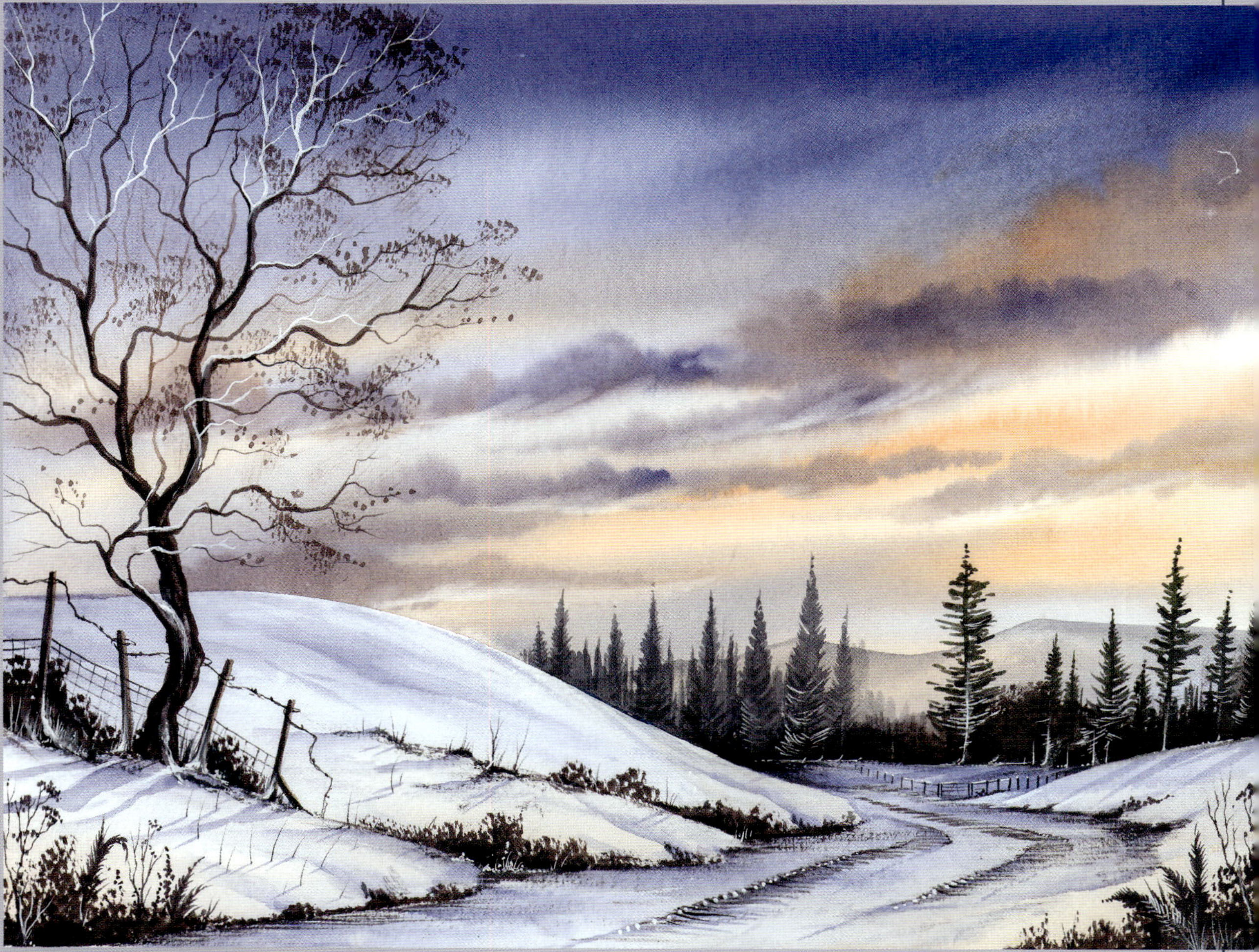

'A SNOWY LANDSCAPE'

35.5 x 28cm (14 x 11in)

This detailed winter landscape features a variety of watercolour techniques, from the masking-in of areas to wet-in-wet skies. The harsh contrast from the sky to the snow, as well as the dark shadow at the top of the trackway, makes for an interesting composition. The perfect colour for painting the shadows on snow is French Ultramarine with a touch of Alizarin Crimson. The large tree was painted using the same techniques described in Lesson #2; for the fir trees see Lesson #7. Titanium White gouache was used to add snowy details to the tree branches and other areas throughout.

Lesson #3
SIMPLE AUTUMN TREE

1. With a size 10 or 12 Round, wet the whole of the tree area. Wet the paper twice to ensure it's wet enough, and there's an even film of water across the surface. Sweep away any pooled areas of water by drying off the brush first on kitchen paper then using the dried bristles to 'suck up' the excess water.

2. With a medium-strength J mix and the size 10 or 12 Round, and working **wet in wet**, twist in some basic tree foliage. Work from top to bottom and in a zigzagging pattern, rotating the brush to create little swirling strokes. Deliberately leave little gaps here and there.

3. The tree shape and paper should still be damp. Using the same rotating brush stroke, and working mainly on one side of the tree shape (I decided the right-hand side), twist in a medium-strength K mix with the size 10 or 12 Round **wet in wet**. Again, leave little gaps here and there. Leave the painting to dry.

MIXES

See page 14 or the cover flaps for details.

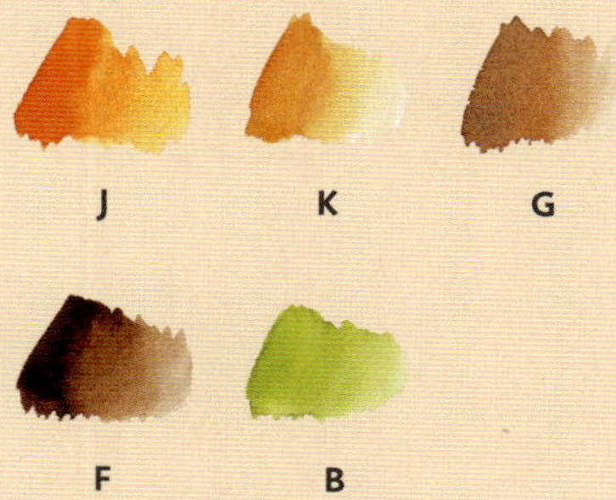

BRUSHES

- Size 10 or 12 Round
- Size 6 Round
- Size 2 Rigger or Detail

EXTRAS

- Optional: 2B pencil

TECHNIQUES

- Wet in wet
- Dotting and dabbing
- Fine branches
- Dry brushing

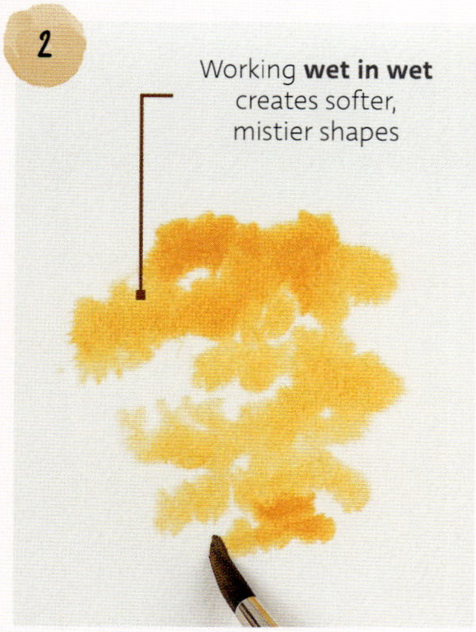

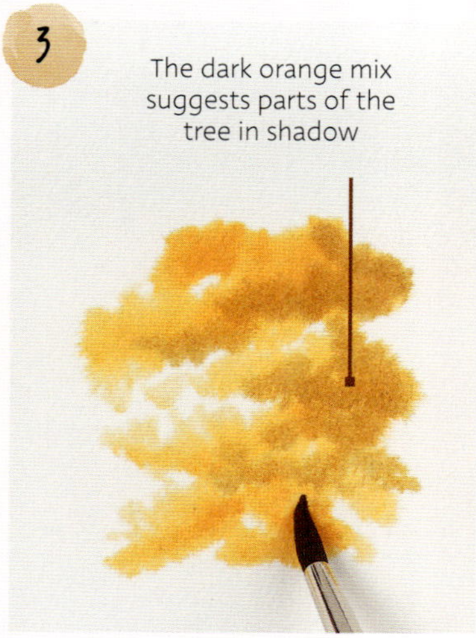

Paint drying too quickly?

Clean the brush, dab off the excess water onto kitchen paper then 'tickle' the drying areas to make them damp again.

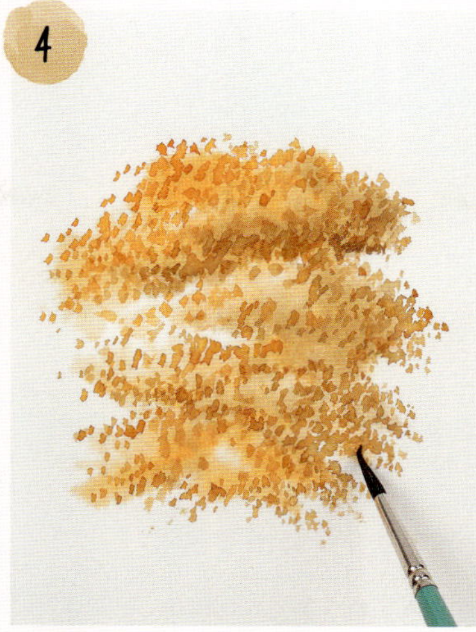

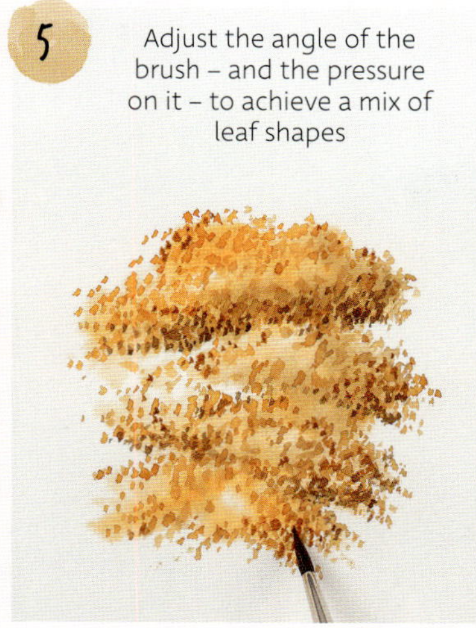

Adjust the angle of the brush – and the pressure on it – to achieve a mix of leaf shapes

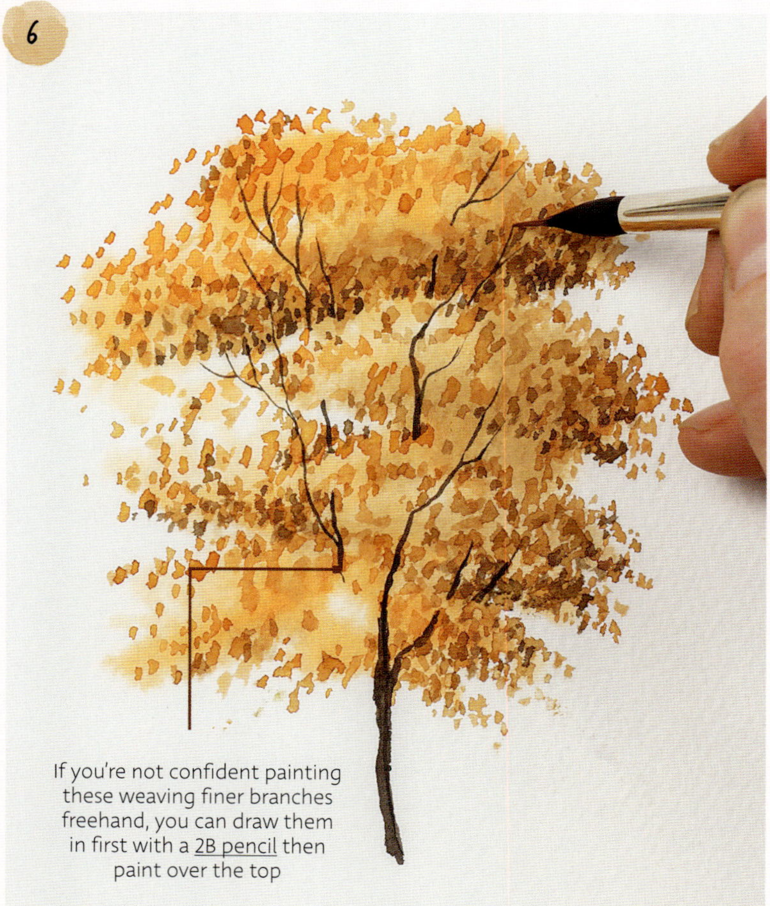

If you're not confident painting these weaving finer branches freehand, you can draw them in first with a 2B pencil then paint over the top

4. Water down both orange mixes to a light strength. To create some texture and darker foreground leaves, **dot and dab** over the basic tree shape with the K mix and size 6 Round. Work around the edge of the main tree foliage first, then touch in 'lines' of dots across the tree shape in a zigzag-like motion, suggesting shadow and indentations in the tree. Repeat with the light strength J mix to suggest lighter leaves. Don't paint too many leaves with either mix at this stage, as more leaves will be added later.

5. With a light-strength G mix and working over the orange leaves, **dot and dab** in a few darker leaves. Paint a few edge leaves, but add most of the darker leaves around the zigzagging shadow 'lines' in the tree. Leave the painting to dry.

6. Using the size 6 Round and with the F mix, paint in the 'dark' side of the tree trunk and branches first **wet on dry**, as per Step 1 on page 26. Work from the bottom of the trunk upwards, putting more pressure on the brush at the base of the trunk, then tapering off towards the top. Switch to the size 2 Rigger or Detail then add in some darker **finer branches** with the same mix. To create the impression of branches weaving in and out of the foliage, leave gaps in the branches.

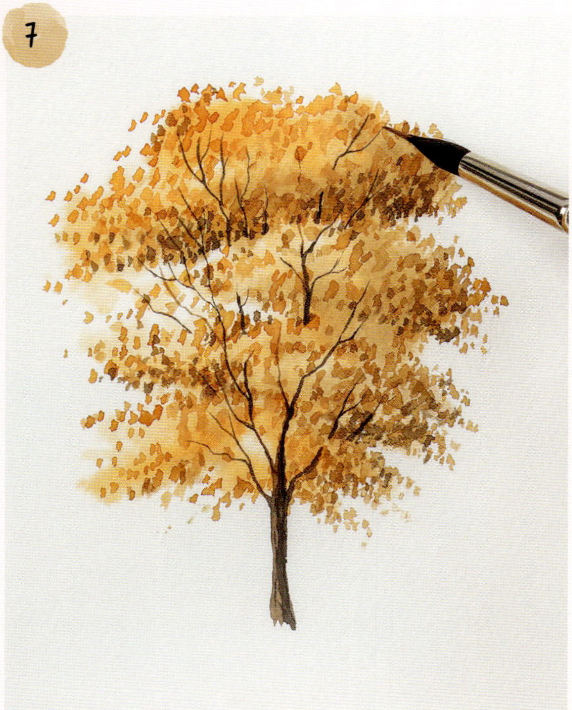

7. While the paint is still damp, run the G mix along the left-hand side of the trunk and branches, to add in the 'lighter' side of the tree. Use the size 6 Round for the trunk and the size 2 Rigger or Detail for the branches. Take the opportunity to add a few extra **fine branches** too, as the lighter-coloured mix will help to suggest some mid-ground and background branches.

8. To finish, sweep the B mix below the trunk of the tree, from top to bottom and in a slight zigzagging motion, using the size 6 Round and the **dry brush** technique. Again, with the **dry brush** technique, stroke little patches of J mix over the grass to suggest fallen autumn leaves. Pick up the F mix on the tip of the brush then stroke in a line from the base of the trunk out to the right-hand edge of the grass area to create the cast shadow of the tree. As optional additions, using the F mix and the size 2 Rigger or Detail, paint a fence and a gate with a tiny bird on top.

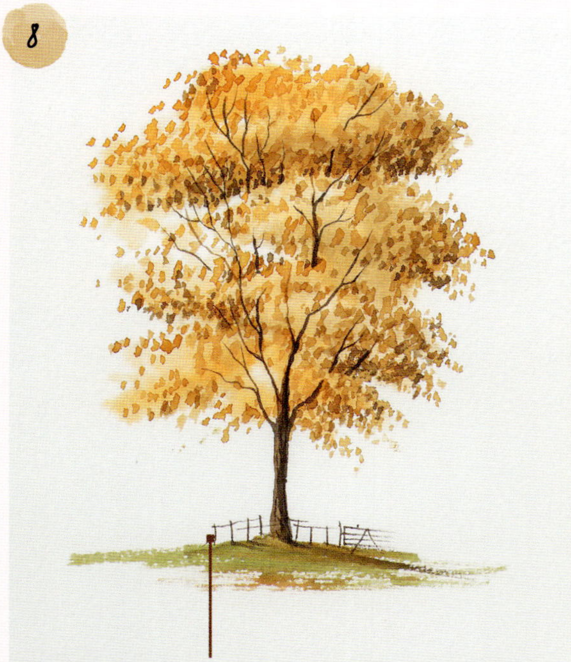

Adding a few features to a simple vignette like this not only adds interest but helps put the tree in context and gives a sense of scale too

Déjà vu?

You may have noticed the tree foliage is worked in a similar way to that of the Simple Summer Tree on page 25. Why not swap the oranges in this project to greens for an atmospheric spring or summer tree? Or, use Rose Madder mixes to create a cherry blossom tree: the lighter pink for this could be a light strength of pure Rose Madder, and the darker pink could be 80% Rose Madder, 20% French Ultramarine.

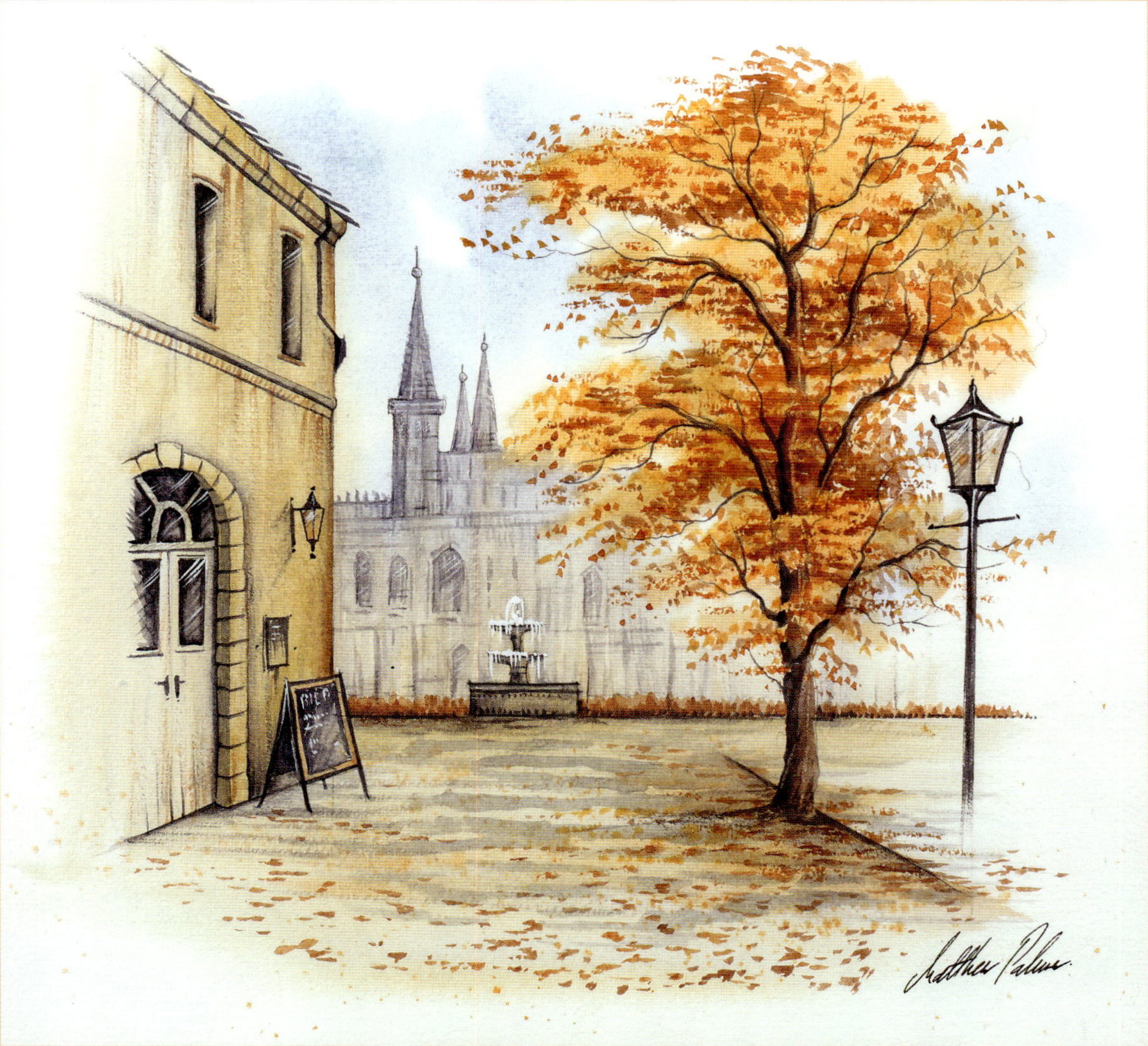

'AUTUMN IN VIENNA'

25.5 x 25.5cm (10 x 10in)

This is one of my favourite autumnal paintings of recent times, and was painted in the actual place. The tree in this painting uses mostly the same techniques described in Lesson #3; the only slight difference is when I used the dot and dab method to add the leaves, I laid the brush flat against the paper to create more textured, almost horizontal, leaves. Highlights were added to the trunk by lifting out colour with a Flat brush (see Step 6 on page 28). The pale grey shadow added to the ground gives a dappled light effect.

Lesson #4
SIMPLE SPRING TREE

1. Holding a medium Fan vertically, **stipple** a trunk-like shape that then branches off at the top of the shape: use a medium-strength C mix for this, **wet on dry**, to create the impression of ivy. I created two large branches at the very top, and a small branch halfway up.

2. Pick up a strong-consistency A mix then **stipple** this around and a little way into the still-wet tree shape. This adds volume and brighter green sections in and around the trunk.

3. Pick up and **stipple** a medium-strength H mix into the still-wet tree shape, focusing this mix on the right-hand sides of the branching ivy and trunk (the side of the tree in shadow).

MIXES

See page 14 or the cover flaps for details.

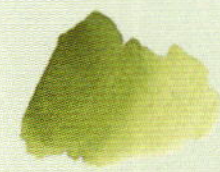
C

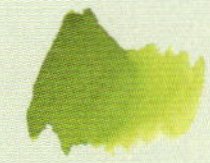
A

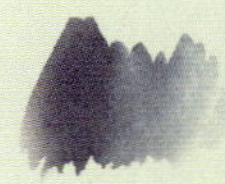
H

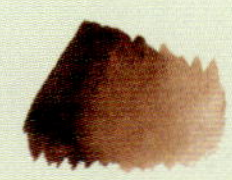
F

BRUSHES

- Medium Fan
- Size 6 Round
- Optional: Size 2 Rigger or Detail

TECHNIQUES

- Wet on dry
- Stippling with a fan brush
- Dotting and dabbing
- Fine branches

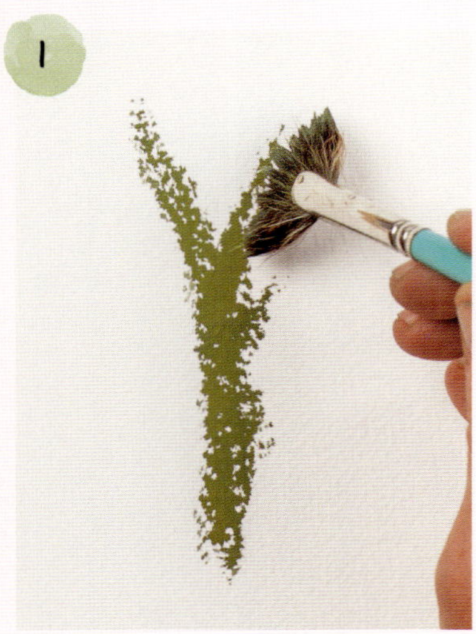

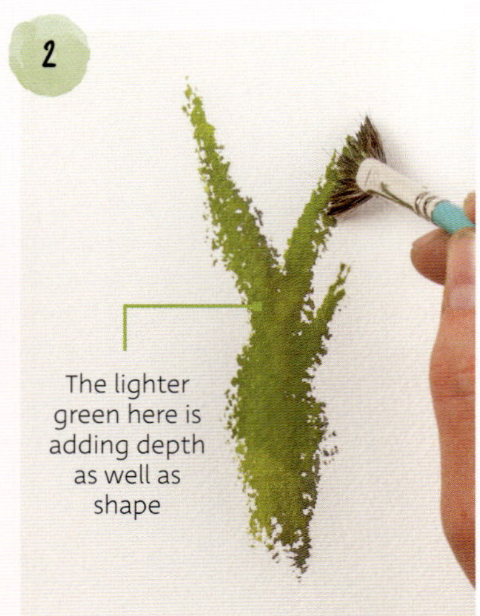

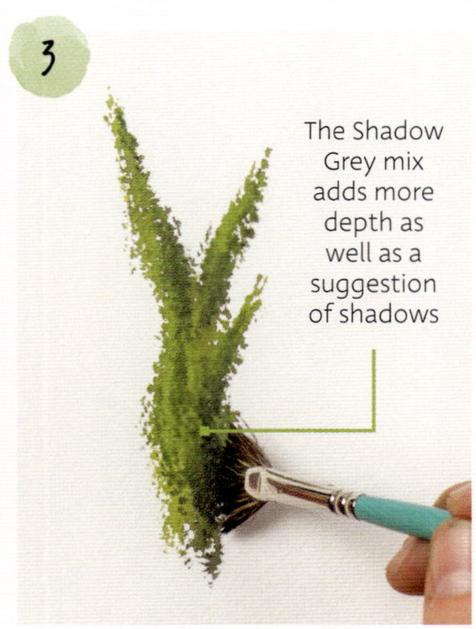

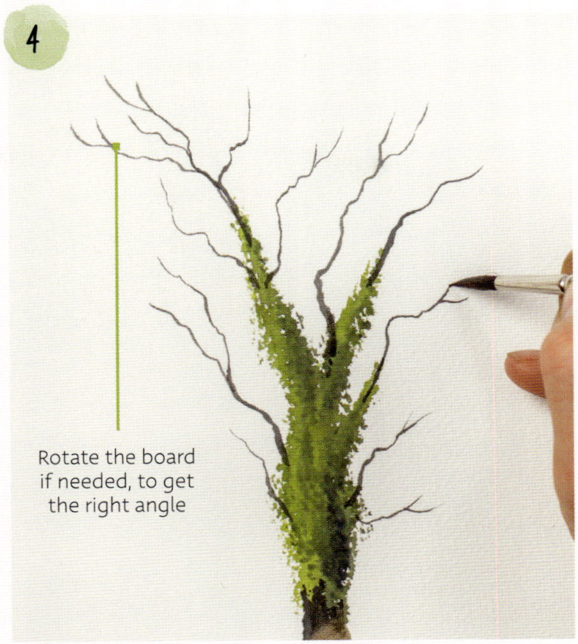

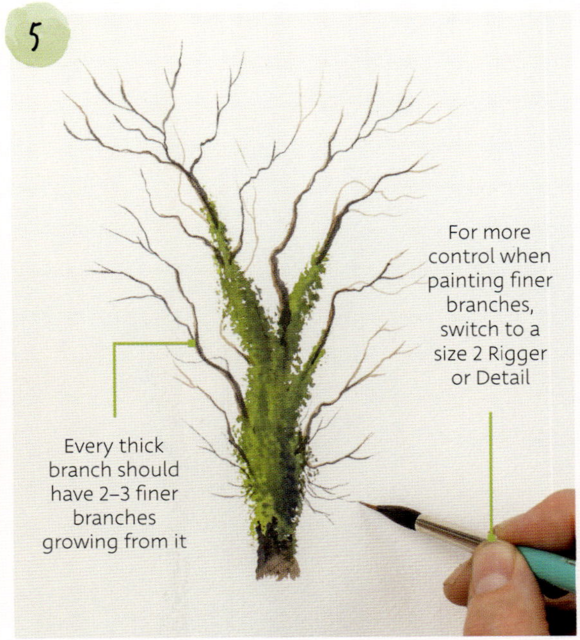

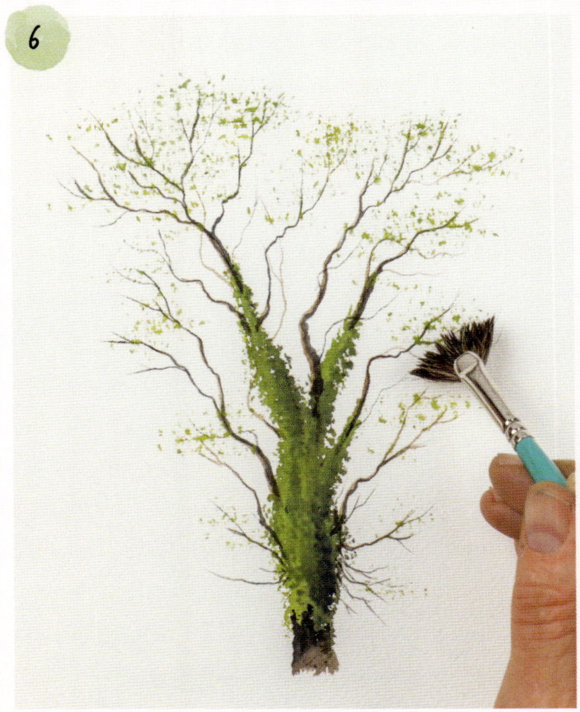

4. Switching to the size 6 Round but staying with the medium-strength H mix, paint in the trunk below the ivy and the larger tree branches. Remember to wobble the brush for more organic branch shapes, and to lift the brush off the paper at the end of each branch to taper off.

5. Clean the brush, pick up a medium-strength F mix then run this along the left-hand sides of the branches, to suggest they're in sunlight. Add some of the mix at the bottom of the trunk, to give the impression this area isn't in the shadow of the ivy. Add a few **fine branches** with the tip of the brush – typically tiny, stubby branches try to grow around the ivy at the base of a tree, which I've suggested here.

6. With the damp medium Fan, pick up the medium-strength A mix and **stipple** leaves around the ends of the branches. Spring trees don't have many leaves, so try not to stipple in too many. Repeat with the C mix.

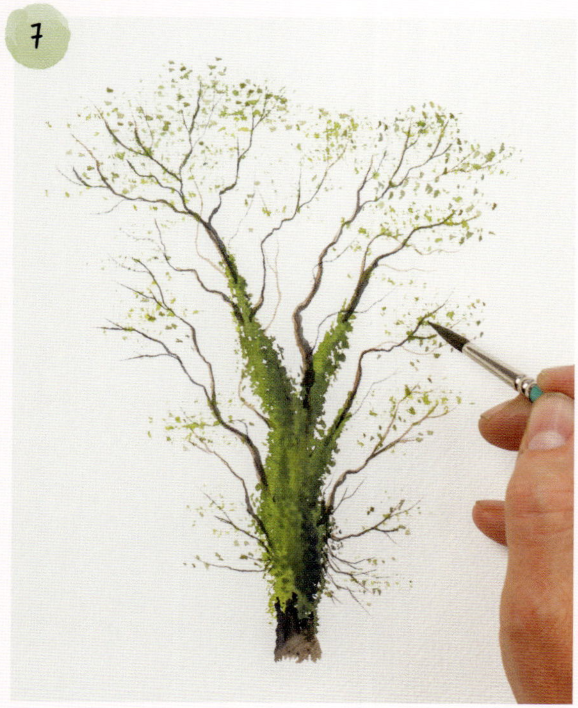

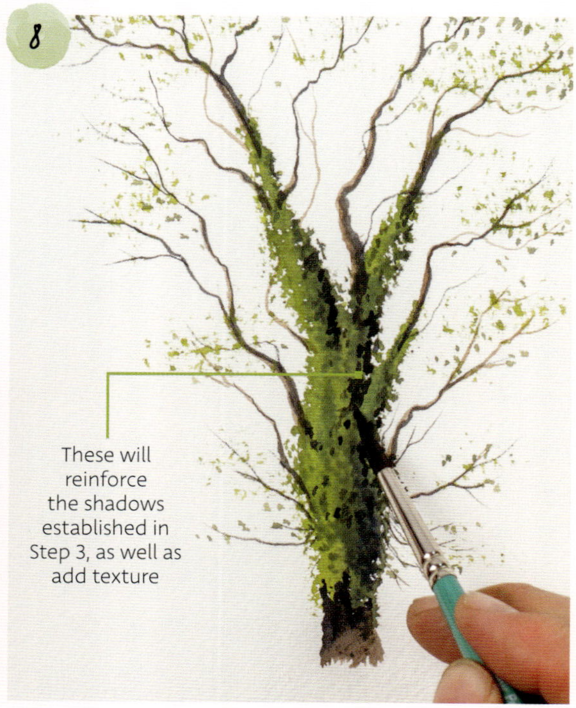

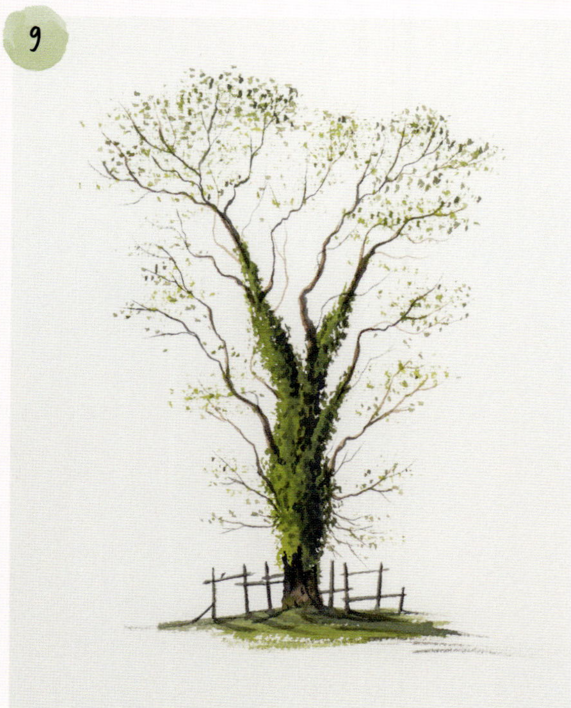

7. Switching between medium-strength A and D mixes, and with the size 6 Round, **dot and dab** in individual leaves. Less is more here, but these will give you the opportunity to fill in gaps or add shape to areas your fan brush missed.

8. Pick up the H mix and **dot and dab** this into the ivy on the tree, mainly on the right-hand side and between branches.

9. To finish, sweep in a grassy mound below the tree from top to bottom using whatever green you have left in your palette – I used the D mix at the top, then the A mix towards the bottom. Using the H mix, stroke in a cast shadow to the right of the tree. If you wish, paint in some fence posts and perhaps a gate to add a sense of scale to the final painting.

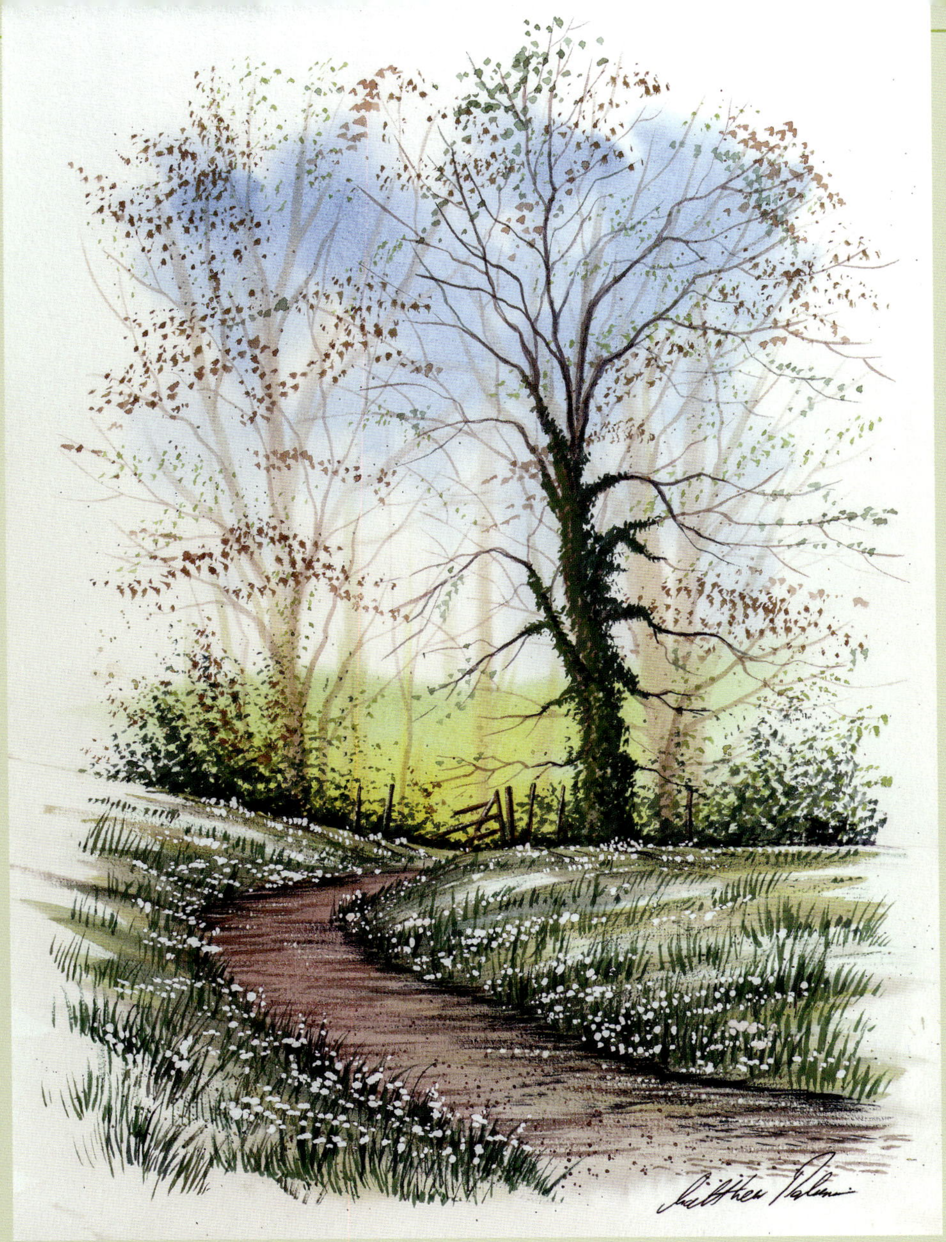

'SNOWDROPS IN THE WOOD'

35.5 x 28cm (14 x 11in)

This watercolour vignette of a wintry woodland features a similar ivy-covered tree to the one in Lesson #4. The background was painted wet in wet to create an out-of-focus effect, to suggest distant greenery. This involves wetting the paper first and applying the paint to the damp area – see Lesson #12 (page 78) for more details on how to do this. The snowdrops were added using Titanium White gouache. The broken gate helps to give a sense of scale, as well as creating atmosphere and interest in the middle distance.

Lesson #5
PINE TREE

1. Paint in the tree trunks with the size 6 Round and strong I mix **wet on dry**, working from bottom to top and wiggling the brush here and there for knots and texture. Clean the brush, pick up a strong F mix and run this along the right-hand side of the trunks, to suggest these sides of the trees are in sunlight.

2. Soften the tops of the trees by **feathering** them with a clean, damp size 2 Rigger or Detail. With the same brush, pick up the I mix and flick a few little twigs and **fine branches** along the lengths of the trunks.

MIXES

See page 14 or the cover flaps for details.

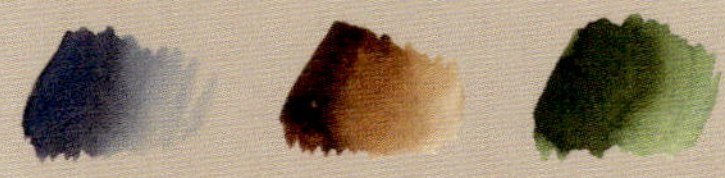

BRUSHES

- Size 6 Round
- Size 2 Rigger or Detail
- 6mm (¼in) Flat

EXTRAS

- Kitchen paper
- Titanium White gouache

TECHNIQUES

- Wet on dry
- Feathering
- Fine branches
- Dotting and dabbing
- Lifting out

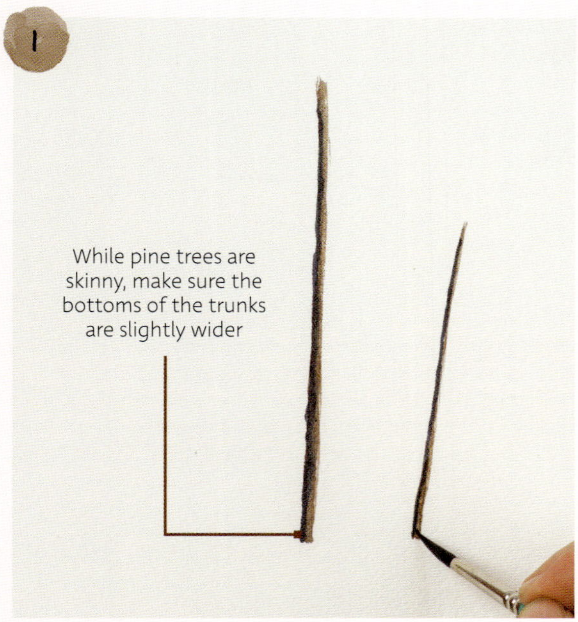

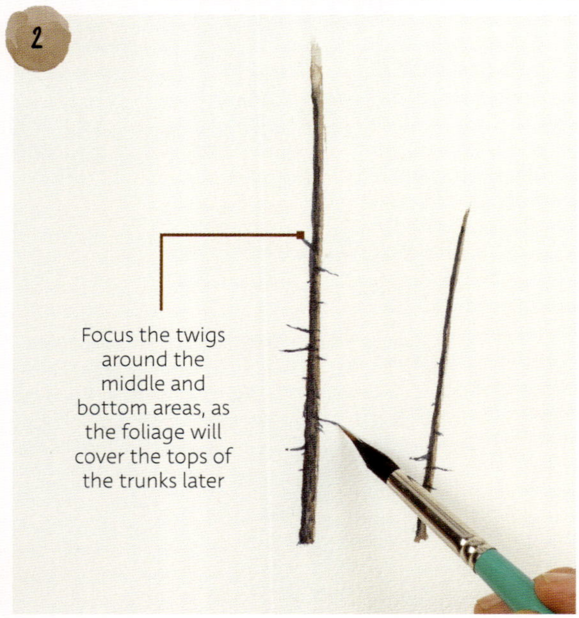

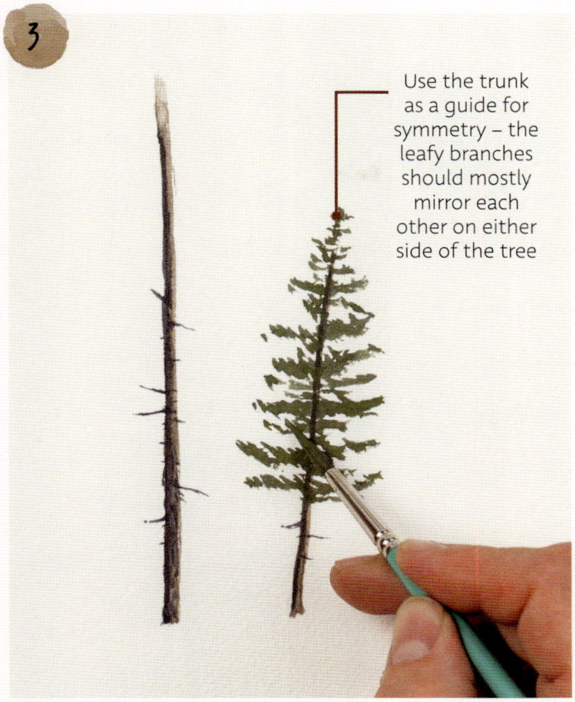

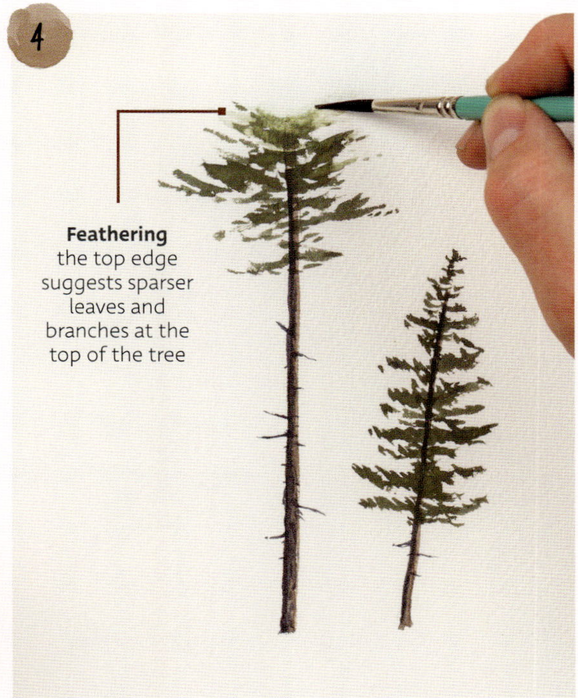

3. Switch to the size 6 Round. Pick up a medium-strength D mix then paint in the foliage for the right-hand tree: start with a few small spots at the top, then flick and **dot and dab** little leaves from the top of the tree downwards, making the leafy branches wider towards the base of the trunk.

4. With the same mix and brush, follow a similar process to paint in the foliage for the taller tree on the left. Use more flicks for this tree, and keep the bottom two-thirds quite sparse, for a wider and bushier treetop. Clean the brush, tap off the excess water then **feather** along the top edge with the tip of the brush head.

5. With a strong D mix, **dot and dab** a few darker leaves in the greenery, and on the end of branches for extra texture. Repeat with the I mix. Switch to the size 2 Rigger or Detail, and paint in some **finer branches** between the leafy sections of both trees.

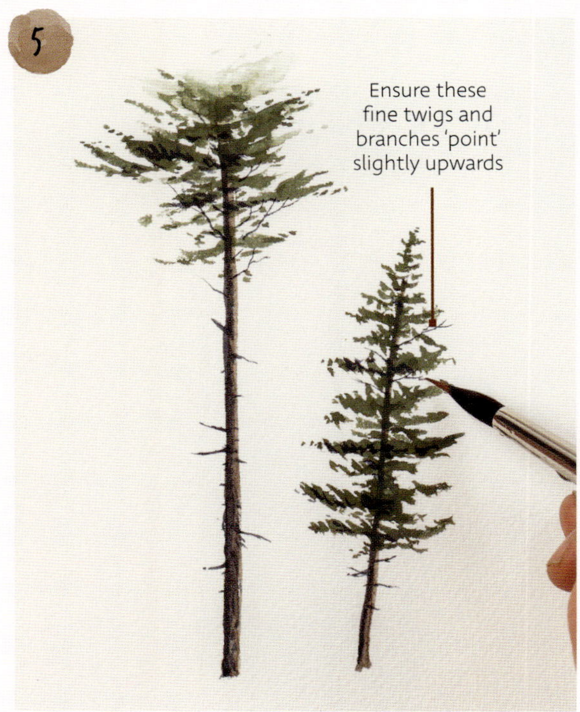

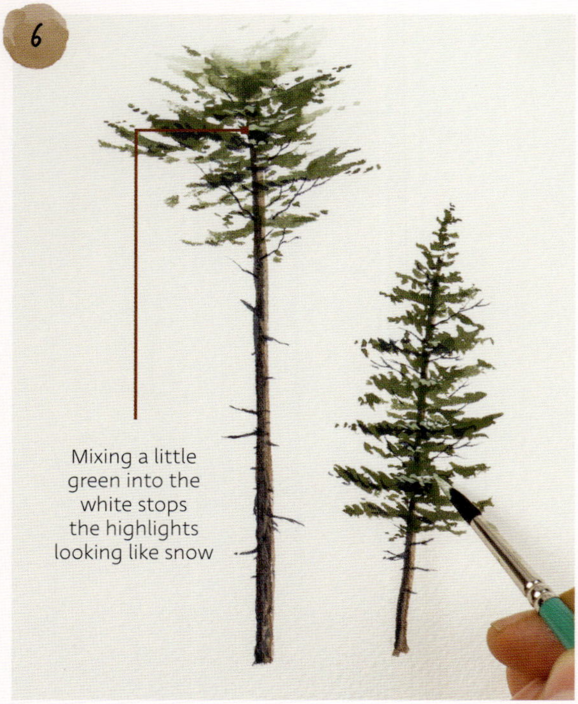

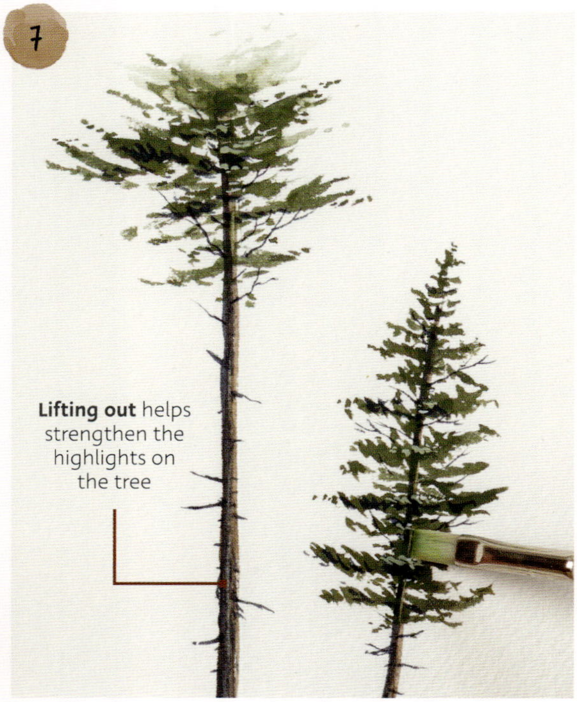

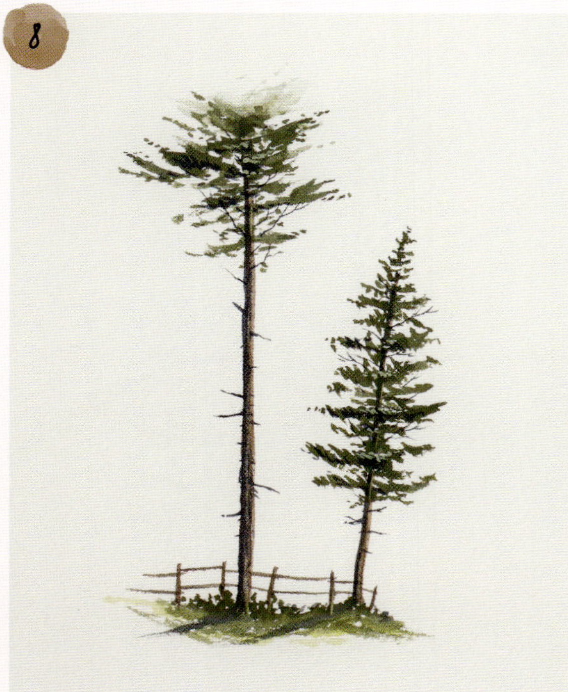

6. Squeeze a tiny amount of Titanium White gouache into the palette, then add a touch of the D mix to it to make a silvery green. With the tip of the size 6 Round, stroke this silver-green mix into the top sections of a handful of branches on the middle and right-hand sides of the trees, suggesting highlights.

7. With a clean, damp 6mm (¼in) Flat, **lift out** some highlights on the right-hand side of the tree trunks that aren't covered by leaves and branches.

8. ***Optional details:*** with the medium D mix and size 6 Round, **dot and dab** in some foliage at the bottom of the trees, then flick in a grassy area. **Feather** the bottom of the grass area. With the I mix, stroke in cast shadows from the bottom of the trees and out to the left. Add a rustic fence for scale with the remaining F mix and size 2 Rigger or Detail.

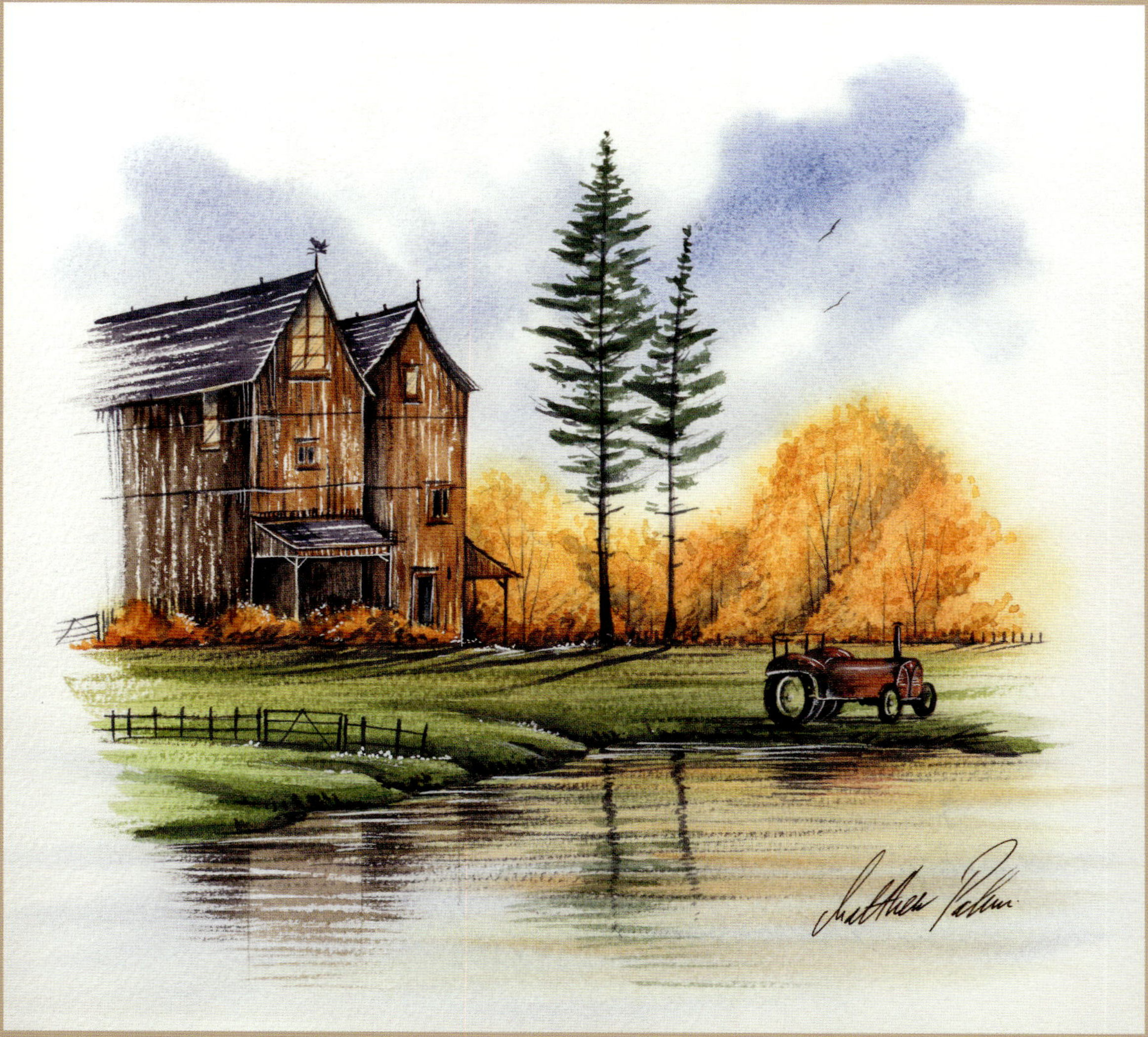

'AUTUMN DOWN AT THE FARM'

28 x 25.5cm (11 x 10in)

This warm and cozy scene features two pine trees painted in a similar way to those in Lesson #5. Notice the reflection of these trees has been added using the same colours. The important thing with reflections is to keep the lines horizontal and pick out the darker areas – for example, the shadow on the left-hand side of the barn.

Lesson #6
LABURNUM TREE

1. Paint in the darker, right-hand side of the tree first **wet on dry** with a strong consistency F mix and the size 6 Round, working from bottom to top and wiggling the brush a little for a gnarly shape. To start with, you just need to paint the trunk and larger branches.

2. Clean the brush, pick up a medium G mix then paint in the lighter side of the tree, along the left-hand sides of the trunk and the large branches. Paint in some **finer branches** that grow out from the thicker ones.

1

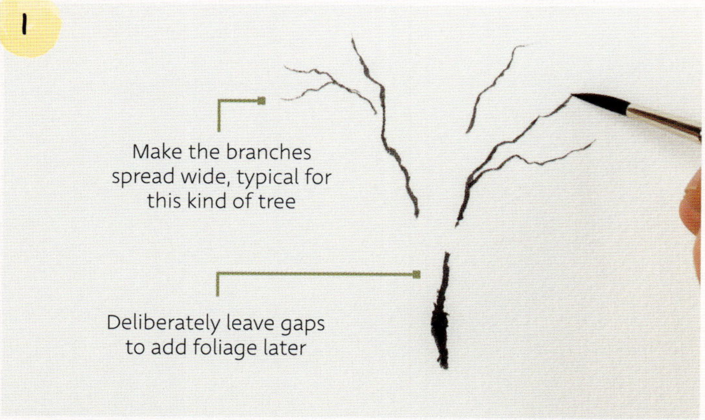

2

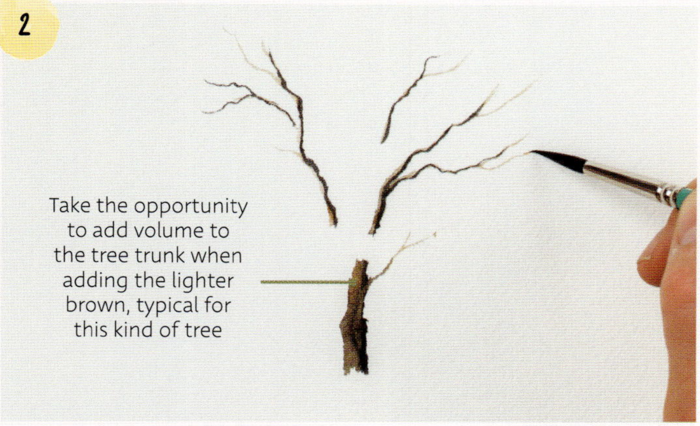

PURE COLOURS

Cadmium Yellow or Aureolin

MIXES

See page 14 or the cover flaps for details.

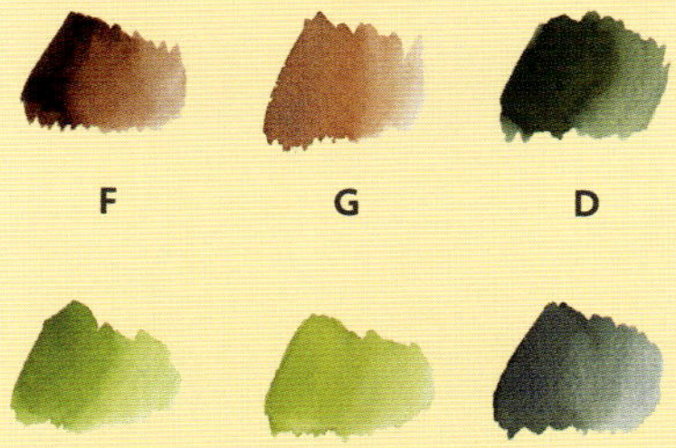

BRUSHES

- Size 6 Round
- Size 2 Rigger or Detail

EXTRAS

- Titanium White gouache

TECHNIQUES

- Wet on dry
- Fine branches
- Dotting and dabbing
- Optional: feathering

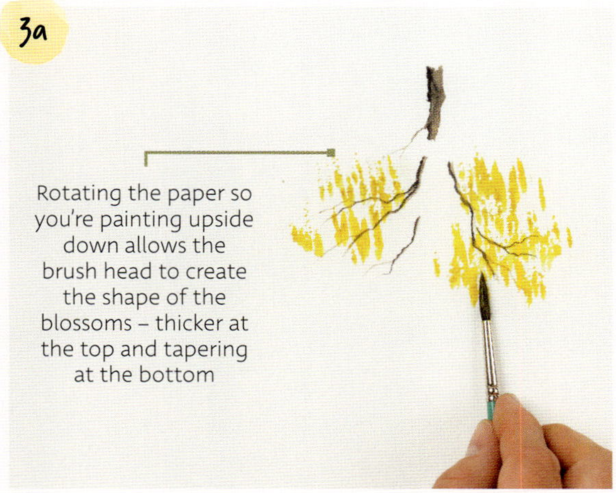

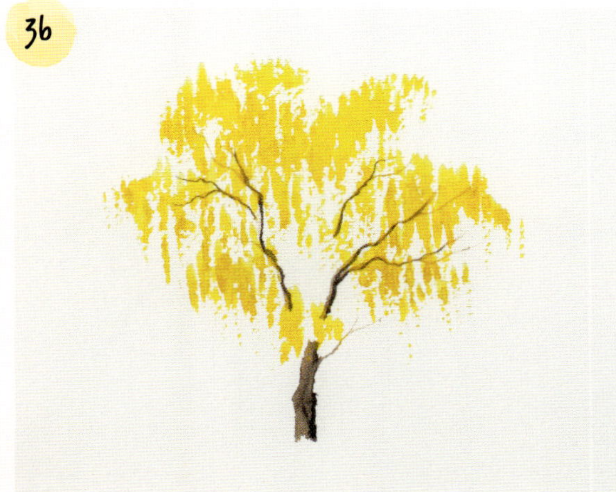

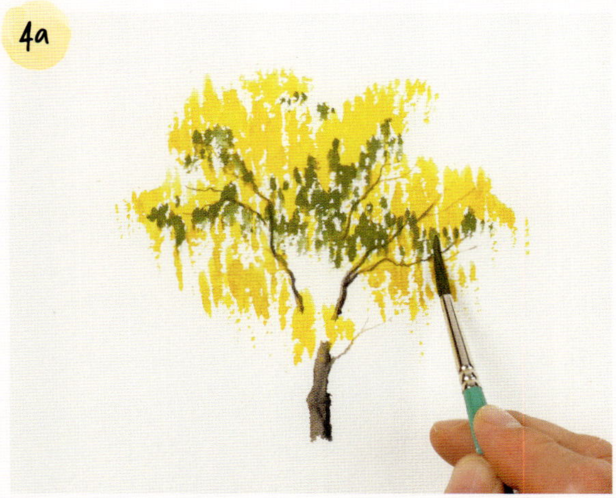

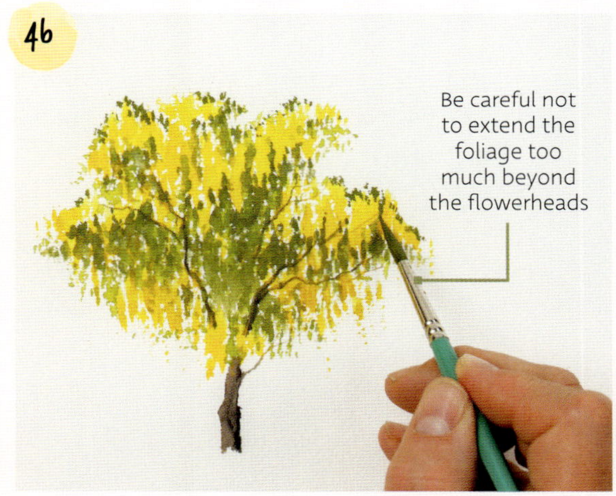

3. We're going to paint in the flower heads first, then add the leaves afterwards. With a size 6 Round, pick up a strong mix of pure Cadmium Yellow or Aureolin, tap some excess paint onto kitchen paper then tap long, flowerhead shapes on the painting in the gaps between the branches, using the side of the brush head (see 3a). Leave the top of the trunk / centre of the tree free of paint. Make sure you're starting to add the shape of the tree with these flowerheads (see 3b).

4. Clean the brush. Working around the flowerheads, **dot and dab** in a medium-strength D mix with a jittery motion for the foliage. Start at the top, with smaller spots of green, then work downwards (see 4a). Clean the brush again then repeat with the C mix around the centre of the tree, over the D mix (see 4b); follow the same process with the B mix, mostly around the bottom of the tree. Although you're adding depth here, leave some tiny gaps in the greenery to suggest sunlight shining through the tree. Leave to dry.

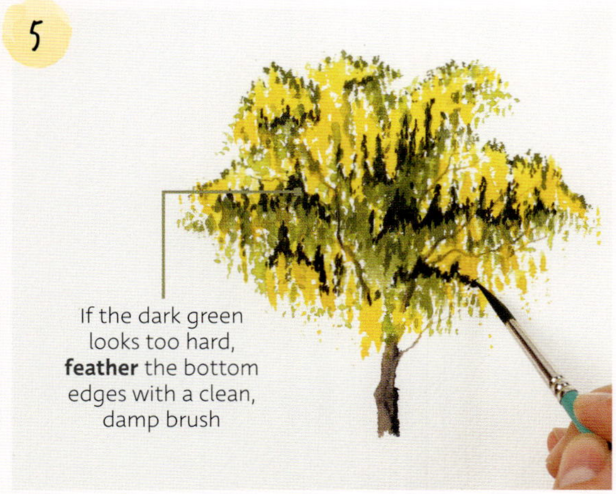

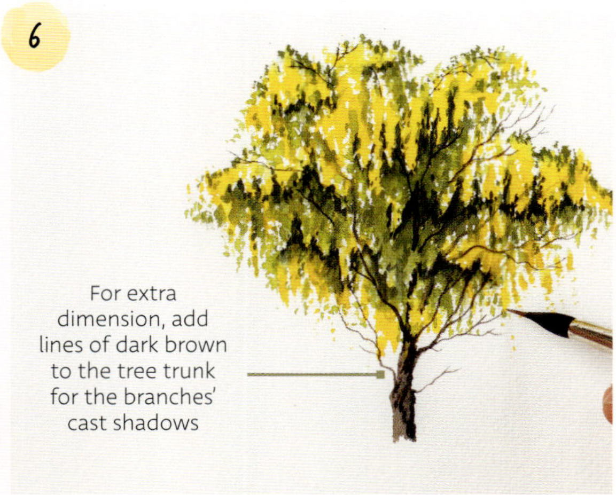

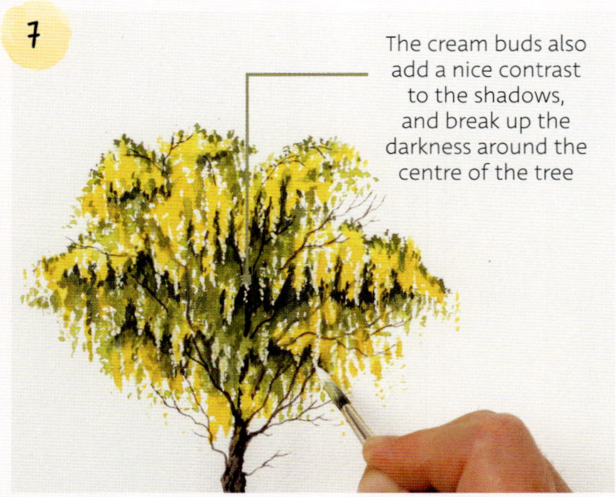

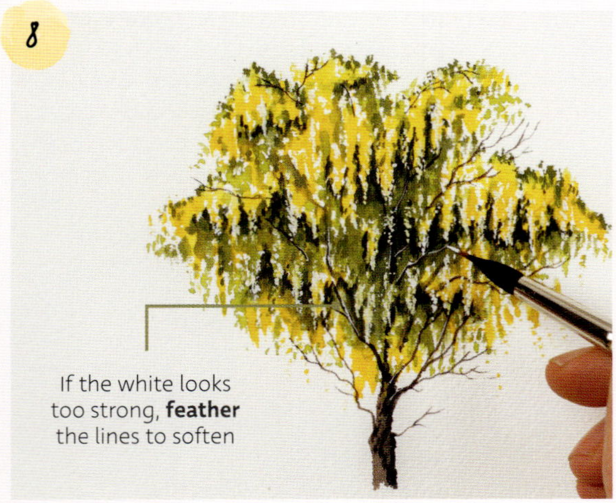

5. With the tip of the size 6 Round and using a strong E mix, **dot and dab** 'arches' of darker greenery **wet on dry** below the central flowerheads; this adds contrast and depth, and brings the flowerheads forward. Leave to dry.

6. With a strong F mix and size 2 Rigger or Detail, paint in some **fine branches** here and there, **wet on dry**, between the greenery, and at the top of the trunk. You can paint over the top of the darker areas, but you'll need to make sure your dark brown is a strong enough consistency to 'sit' over the dark grey-green shadows added previously.

7. Squeeze a tiny amount of Titanium White gouache on the palette then add a little pure Cadmium Yellow or Aureolin to it to make a creamy yellow mix. With the tip of the size 2 Rigger or Detail, **dot and dab** tiny cream 'spots' onto the flowerheads and the odd green leafy section, to suggest little hanging flower buds.

8. With diluted pure Titanium White gouache and the size 2 Rigger or Detail, delicately paint some highlights over the tops of the branches. The paint lines must be very fine, to stop the highlights looking like snow.

9

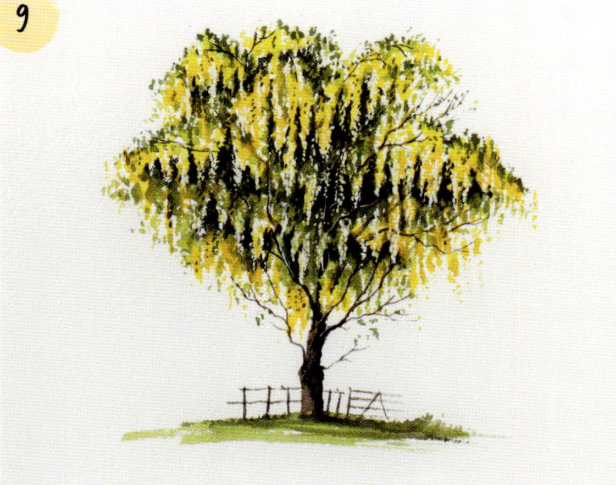

9. *Optional details:* using the green mixes remaining on your palette, sweep in a grass bank below the laburnum with the size 6 Round. Stroke in a cast shadow to the right with a light-strength E mix. If you wish, add some fencing and perhaps a gate for scale with a strong E mix and a size 2 Rigger or Detail.

'WISTERIA OVER A COTTAGE DOORWAY'

30.5 x 25.5cm (12 x 10in)

This pretty watercolour vignette of a simple doorway and window has been made more interesting by adding wisteria growing by the door. The strong grey shadow over the doorway, underneath the wisteria, is important to give depth. A tiny cast shadow has been added to the wisteria in a similar way to how the shadow was added to the laburnum. The technique for painting the wisteria is almost identical to the way the laburnum flowers were painted, including the use of Titanium White gouache. The colour used for the wisteria is a pale to medium violet shade, made from mixing 60% Dioxazine Violet and 40% French Ultramarine.

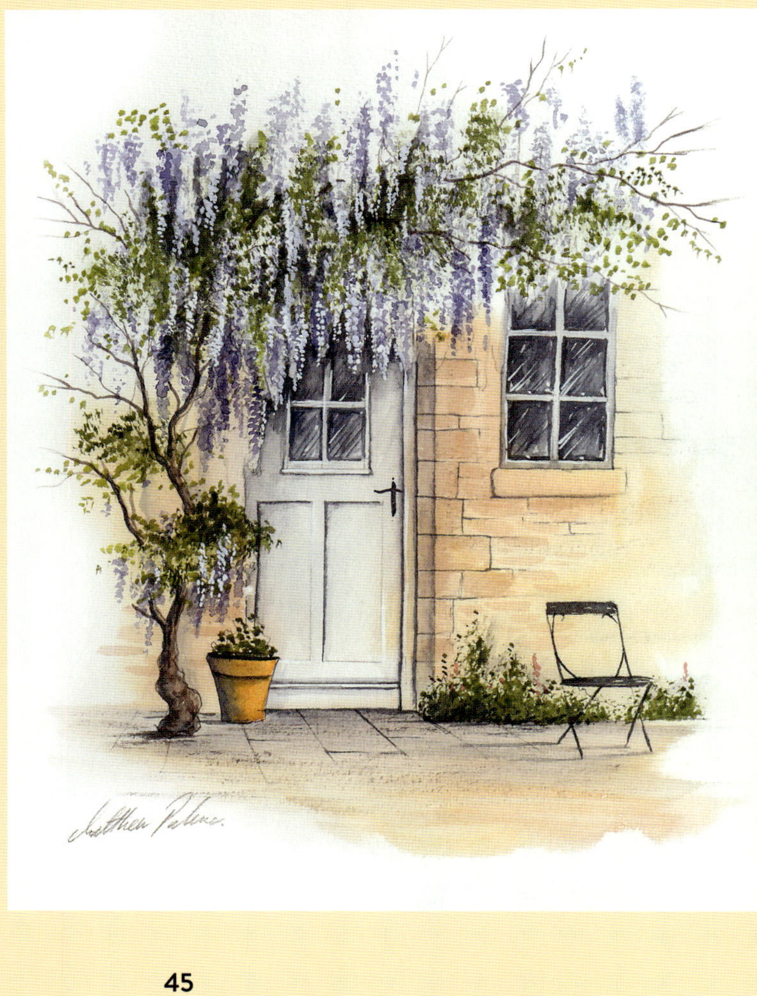

Lesson #7
FIR TREE FOREST

1. Start off with a strip of masking / painter's tape that's longer than the width of the painting. Slide the length between your fingers to remove some of the tape's stickiness. Lay it horizontally over the paper, about a third of the way up from the bottom edge. The top edge of the tape will be your horizon line. Note: if the paint leaks underneath the top edge later, don't worry: any accidental paint can be worked into the painting later.

2. With the size 10 or 12 Round, wet the paper from the top edge down to the masking / painter's tape. Wet the paper a couple of times to ensure there's an even spread of water, and spread out any puddles that have gathered on the surface.

3. As soon as you've finished wetting the paper, pick up and sweep in a light-strength pure Yellow Ochre mix from the masking / painter's tape upwards, **wet in wet**, to add a warm colour to the bottom of the sky area. While the paint is still wet, clean the brush, pick up a light-strength pure French Ultramarine mix and sweep this in from the top of the paper downwards, into the yellow. Allow the two colours to mix around the centre, creating a graduated wash.

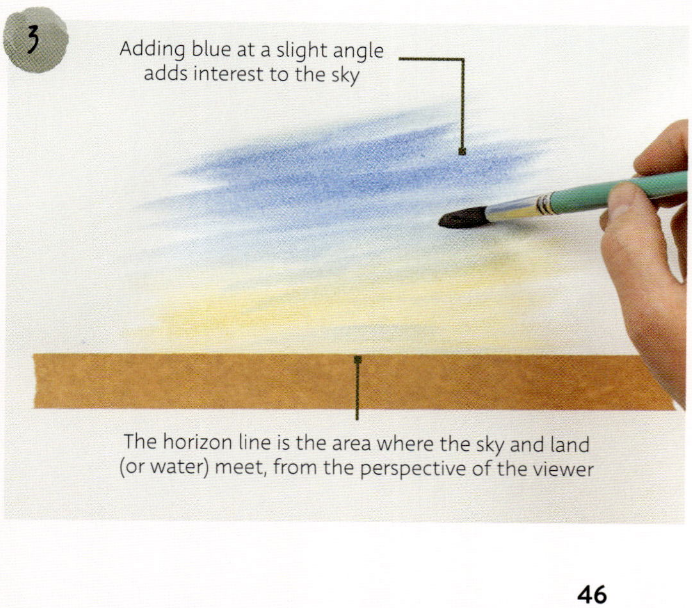

PURE COLOURS

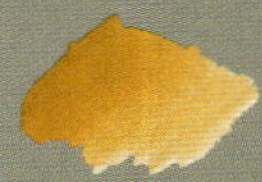
Yellow Ochre

French Ultramarine

MIXES

See page 14 or the cover flaps for details.

H

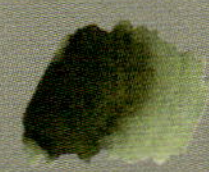
D

BRUSHES

- Size 10 or 12 Round
- Size 6 Round
- Size 2 Rigger or Detail

EXTRAS

- Masking / painter's tape
- Titanium White gouache
- Optional: hairdryer

TECHNIQUES

- Wet in wet
- Wet on dry
- Dotting and dabbing

4. Immediately clean the brush, pick up a medium-strength H mix and paint in vertical lines, from the top of the yellow down to the tape, to create distant trees. Work from the centre of the paper outwards, lightly dabbing the brush on kitchen paper as you paint, to make the trees 'fade' at the edges of the tree line.

5. While the painting is still damp, pick up a strong H mix and add more trees in front of the tree line with the size 6 Round. Leave the painting to dry.

6. Now for the foreground trees, which you'll paint **wet on dry**. Using the size 6 Round and a strong D mix, start off with a long vertical line with a few spots at the top. Using the line as your guide and working from the top of the tree downwards, 'rock' the brush from side to side to create branches.

7. As you get lower down the tree, add in a little medium-strength H mix over your D mix branches to darken the base of the tree, and help it blend into the misty background. **Dot and dab** at the ends of the branches with the D mix to suggest the individual leaves and add textures. Repeat with the H mix.

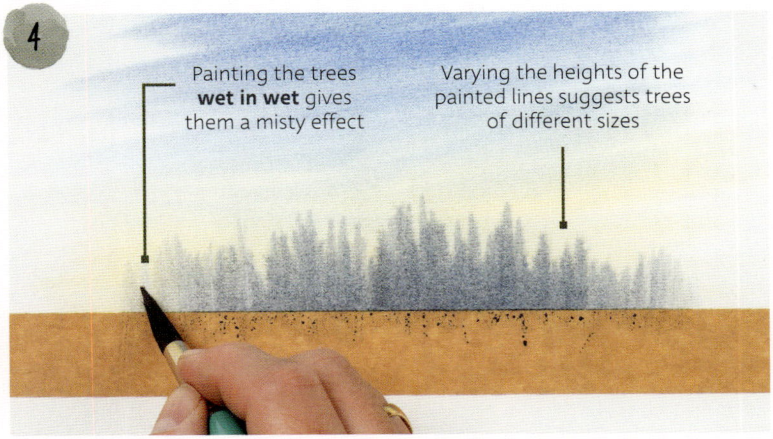

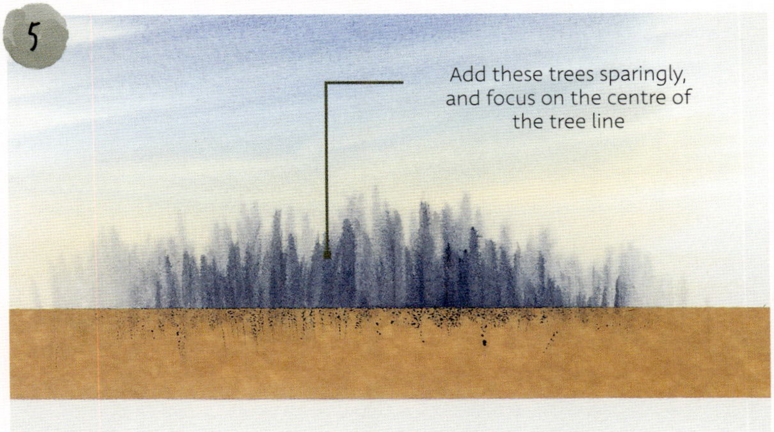

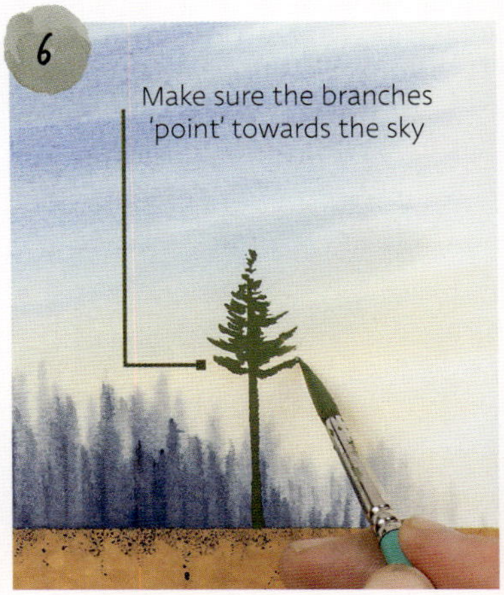

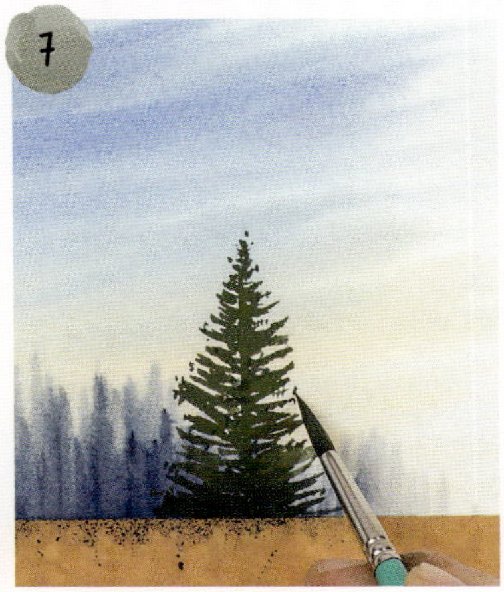

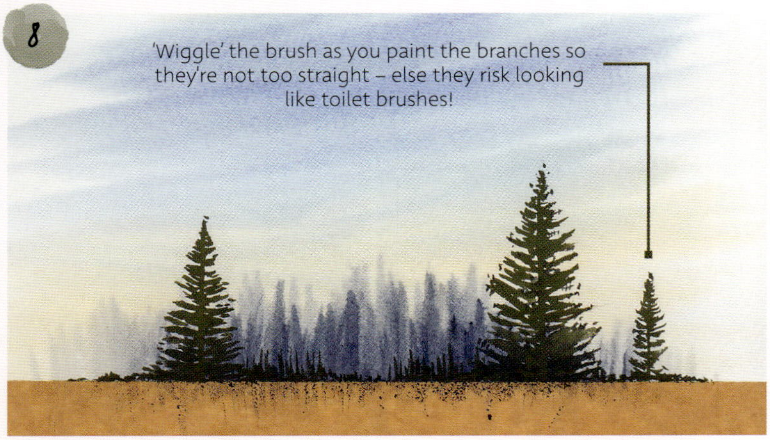

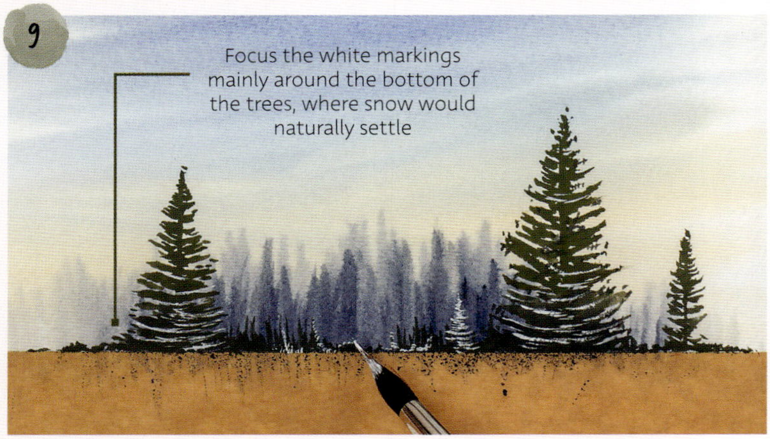

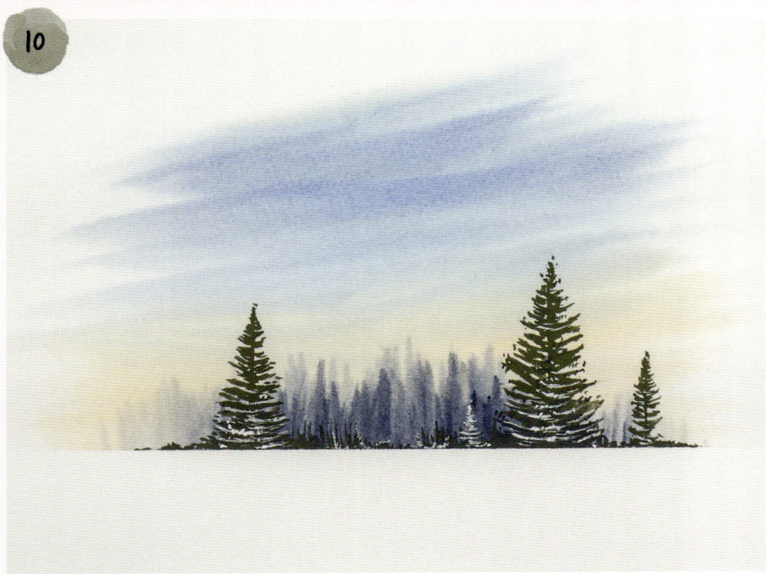

8. Continue in the same way to add a few more trees at different heights. Once you're happy with the number of trees in the painting, **dot and dab** the medium-strength D mix from the base of each tree a little of the way outwards, to help it connect and blend into the background. With the tip of the brush and the same mix, you can also add tiny vertical lines between the trees to suggest distant trees.

9. Dampen the size 2 Rigger or Detail with clean water, pick up a tiny amount of Titanium White gouache then run thin, gently curving lines of white along the tops of some of the branches of the largest trees for snow. **Dot and dab** a few textures with the same mix and brush over a few of the mid-ground trees too, to pull them and the larger trees at the front together.

10. Remove the tape to finish. Take care with this, in case you rip the paper – heating the tape with a hairdryer will help soften the glue so you can remove it. If any paint has seeped under the tape, tidy it up by adding more paint to blend it into the line of foliage under the trees.

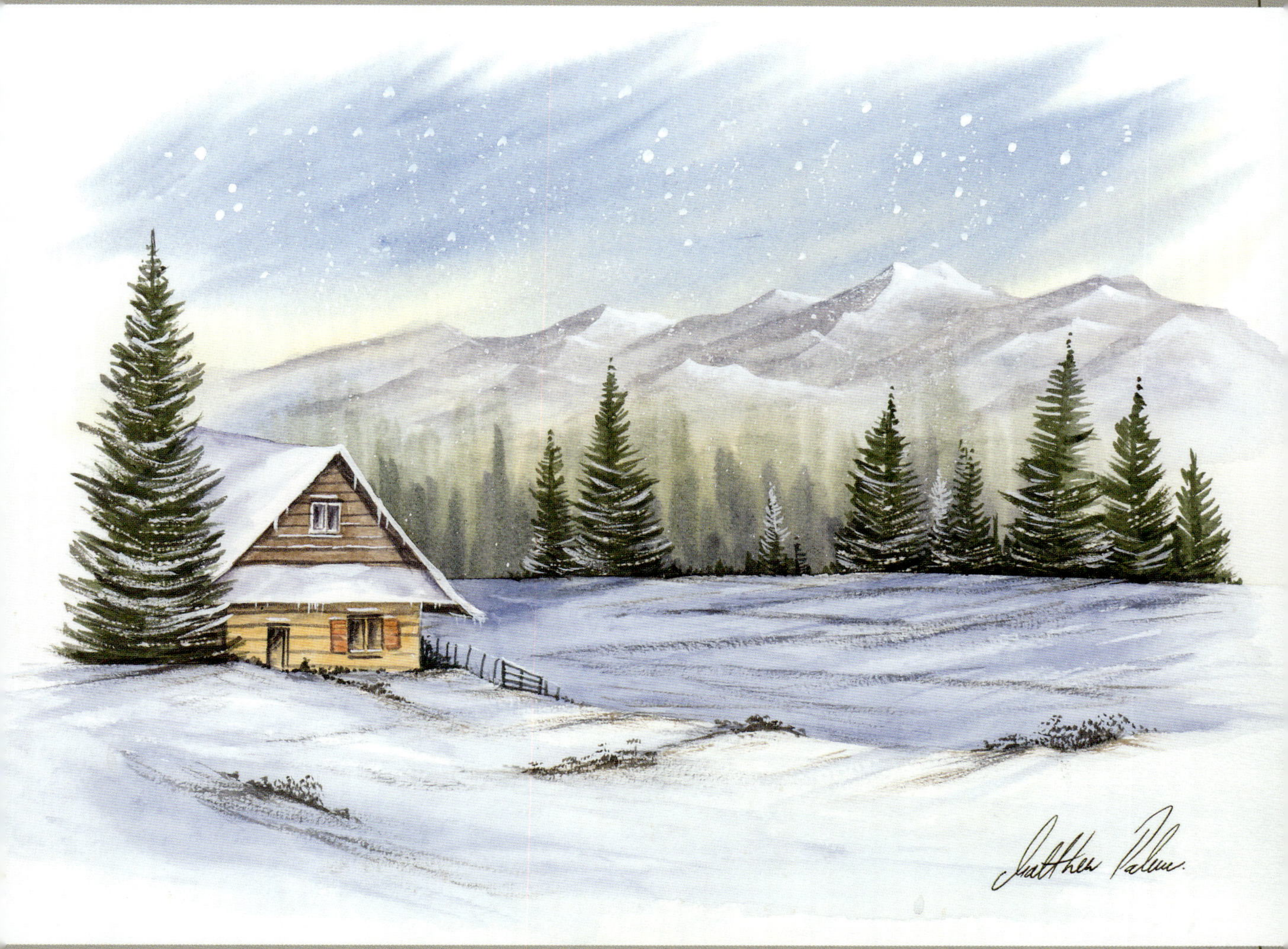

'MOUNTAINSIDE CHALET'

35.5 x 28cm (14 x 11in)

The trees in this scene are painted in the same fashion as in Lesson #7. The distant mountains were painted in after washing in the sky. While the paint for the mountains was still damp, background fir trees were painted in over the top (wet in wet), giving them a 'misty' appearance. The chalet was added in the foreground to give the scene a focal point, and a sense of scale. The perfect colour for the shadows on snow is French Ultramarine with a touch of Alizarin Crimson.

Lesson #8
SILVER BIRCH TREE

1. Establish the shape of the birch tree: tear off a long length of <u>masking / painter's tape</u> then narrow it by cutting it in half lengthwise with a <u>craft knife</u>. Slide the length between your fingers to remove some of the tape's stickiness. Loosely stick it onto the paper, about a third of the way in from the left-hand edge, so it's lying at a slight angle but relatively vertical. Shape the tape in places by pinching it with your fingers. When you're happy with the positioning, press the tape in place firmly.

2. Wet the paper all over with a <u>size 10 or 12 Round</u>, wetting it two or three times evenly to ensure there are no dry patches. Work over the tape as well. Then, pick up medium-strength <u>pure Cadmium Yellow or Aureolin</u> and twist the brush **wet in wet** around the tape in a triangular shape.

3. Clean the brush, pick up a light-strength <u>pure French Ultramarine mix</u> and twist this into the top-right part of the painting, bringing it down and into the yellow. Clean the brush, then twist a medium-strength <u>B mix</u> into the bottom-left part of the painting.

Rule of Thirds

This relates to composition. By mentally dividing your watercolour paper into nine equal sections (as shown by the dashed grid lines opposite), you can identify 'hot spots' where – if placed over them – elements in your painting will look the strongest compositionally. In the case of our tree, it will be placed over the first vertical line of the grid.

PURE COLOURS

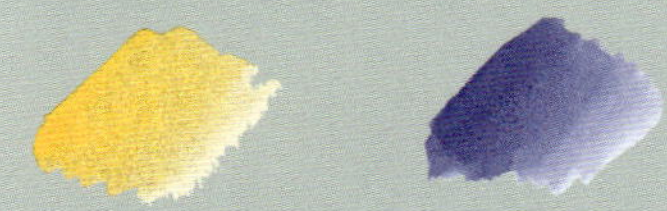

Cadmium Yellow or Aureolin — French Ultramarine

MIXES

See page 14 or the cover flaps for details.

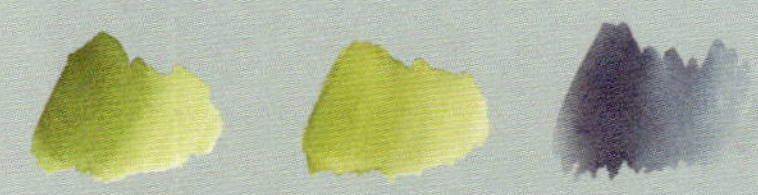

C — B — H

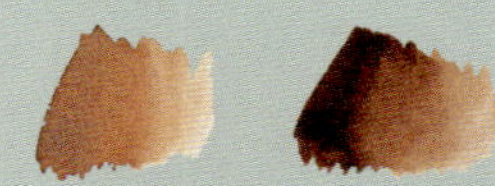

G — F

BRUSHES

- Size 10 or 12 Round
- Size 6 Round
- Size 2 Rigger or Detail
- 6mm (¼in) Flat

EXTRAS

- Masking / painter's tape
- Craft knife
- Piece of hard card
- Titanium White gouache
- Kitchen paper
- Optional: hairdryer

TECHNIQUES

- Wet in wet
- Feathering
- Scratching out
- Stippling with a round brush
- Wet on dry
- Blending
- Fine branches
- Dry brushing
- Lifting out

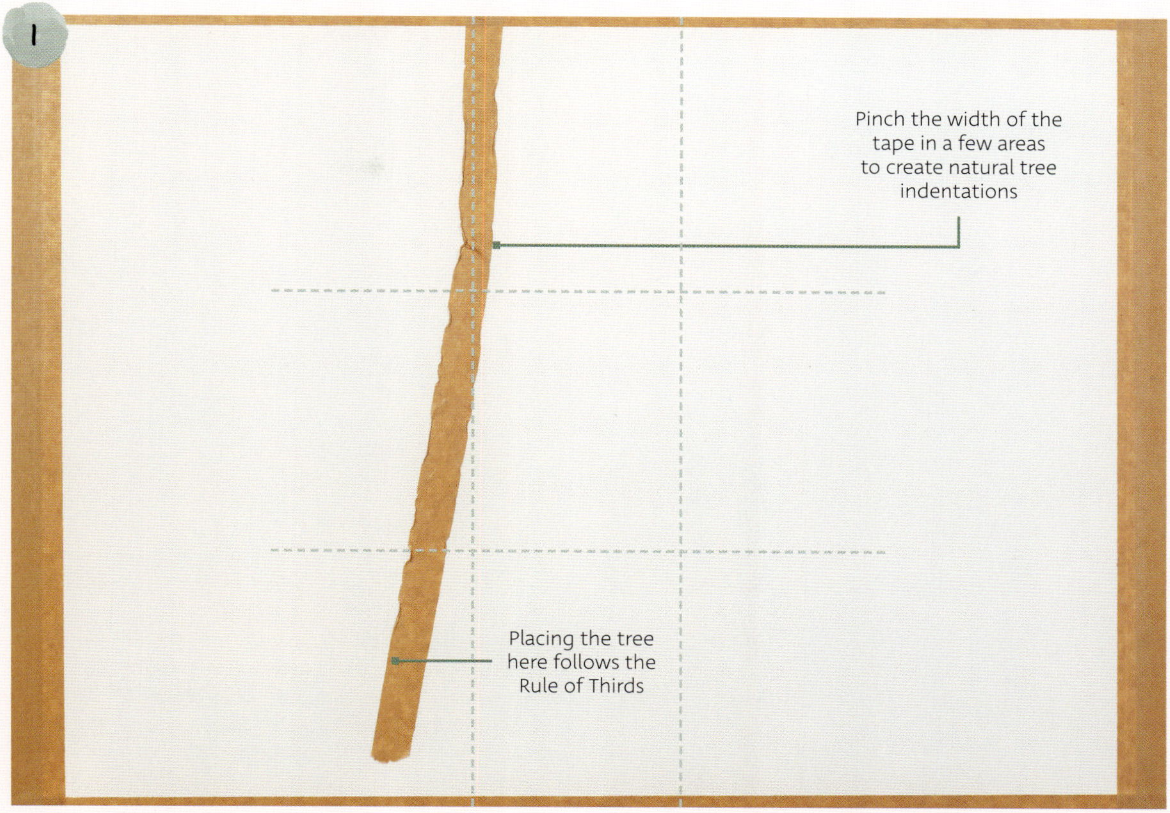
1
Pinch the width of the tape in a few areas to create natural tree indentations
Placing the tree here follows the Rule of Thirds

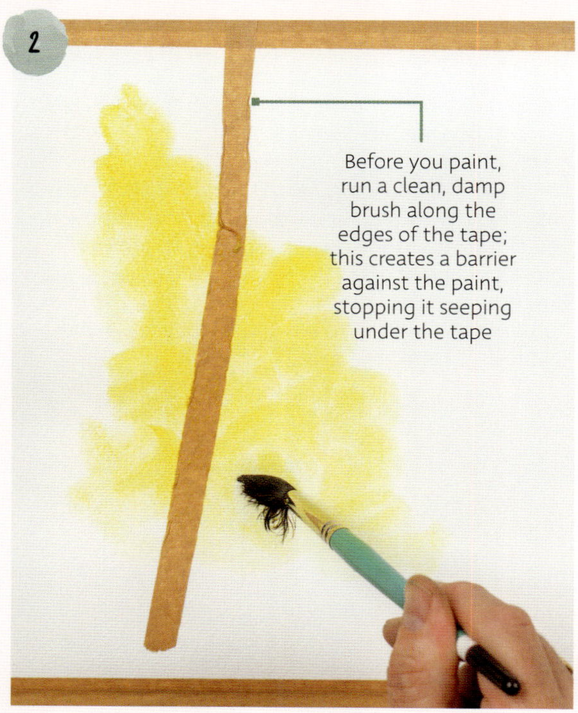
2
Before you paint, run a clean, damp brush along the edges of the tape; this creates a barrier against the paint, stopping it seeping under the tape

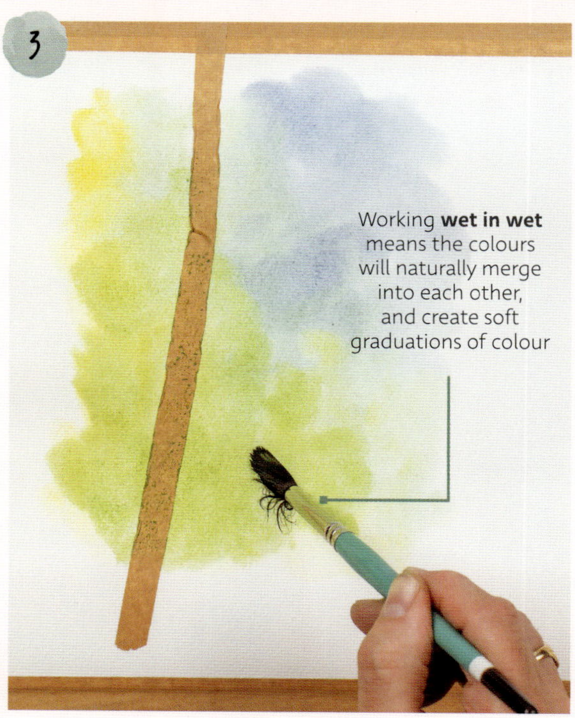
3
Working **wet in wet** means the colours will naturally merge into each other, and create soft graduations of colour

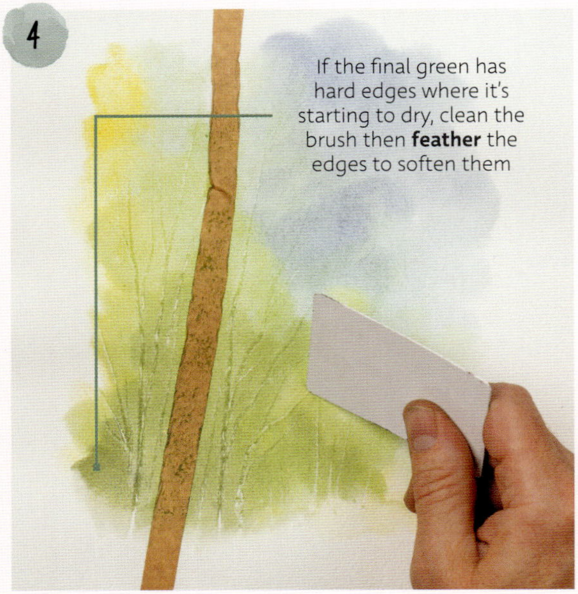

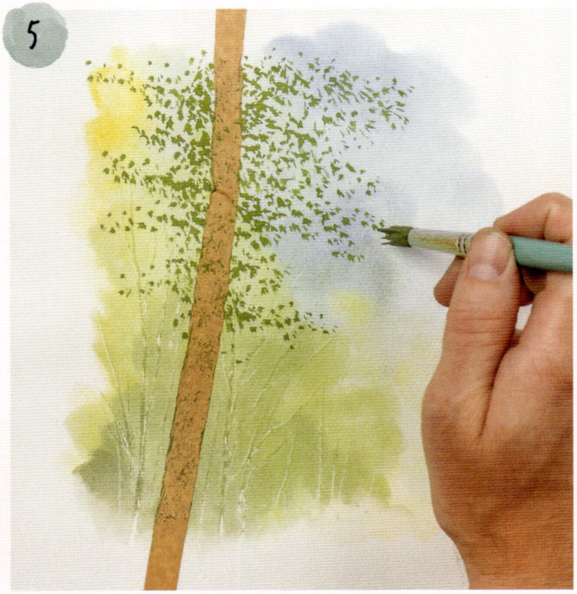

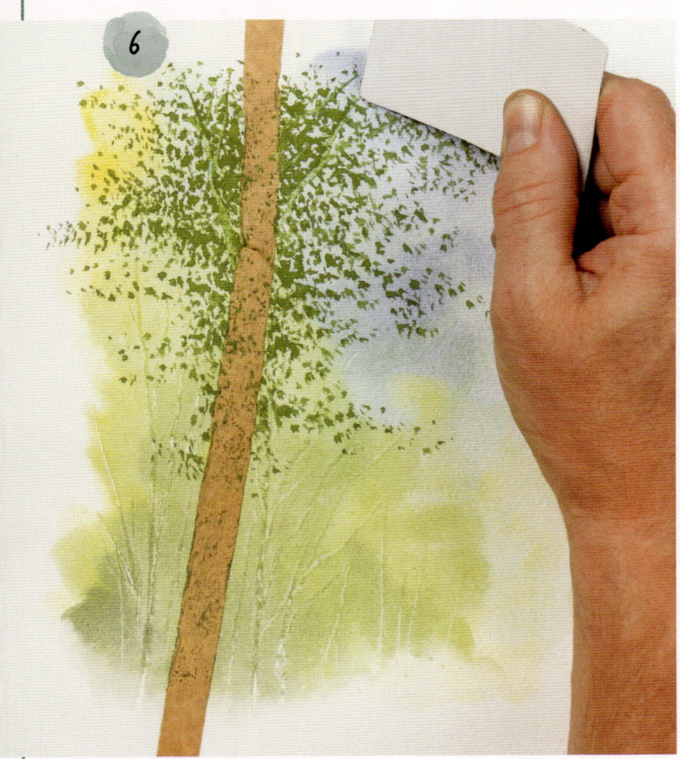

4. Twist a medium-strength C mix into the bottom of the painted area, focusing around the base of the tree. Leave the painting for a minute or so to dry, until it's only slightly damp, then **scratch out** some tree shapes with a piece of hard card. Leave to dry.

5. Squash the size 10 or 12 Round into a medium-strength B mix, flattening the bristles, then **stipple** in some leaves **wet on dry** around the upper part of the masking / painter's tape. Hold the brush vertically as you stipple, and work from the tape outwards, so the paint is concentrated around the trunk.

6. Repeat with the C mix, focusing around the masking / painter's tape 'trunk'. Leave the paint for a minute or two so it dries until slightly damp, then **scratch out** some upper branches in the foliage with a clean piece of hard card as shown. Remove the tape then leave to dry – if the tape is difficult to remove, try heating it with a hairdryer to soften the glue.

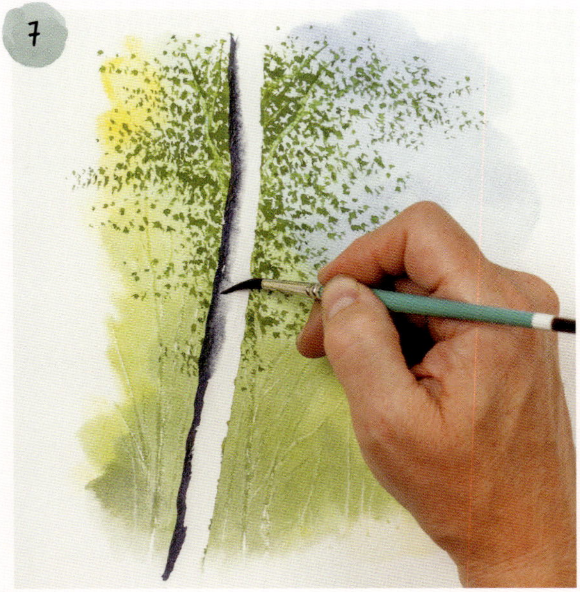

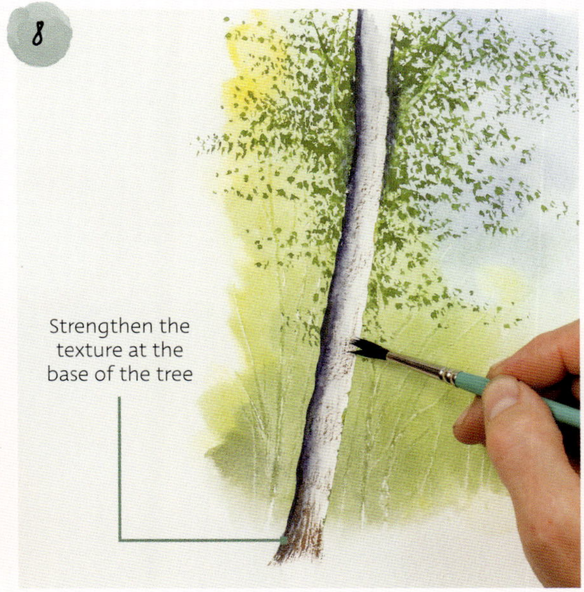

7. With the medium-strength H mix and size 6 Round, run a thin line of grey along the left-hand side of the tree, working from top to bottom. Clean the brush, then **blend** the line towards the right-hand side of the tree, creating a graduation of colour, as shown. Around the top of the tree, run a little more of the H mix along the edges of the trunk to add texture; **blend** if needed. Leave to dry.

8. Now to introduce some brown colour. Pick up a little of some medium-strength G mix, pinch the bristles flat with your index finger and thumb, then stroke the mix randomly here and there on the tree with the **dry brush** technique for that silver birch texture, working from bottom to top.

9. Pick up a little more of the G mix, pinch the bristles flat once again for a **dry brush** then paint little arch shapes along the length of the trunk. Adding fewer markings this time, clean the brush then repeat the process with the F mix.

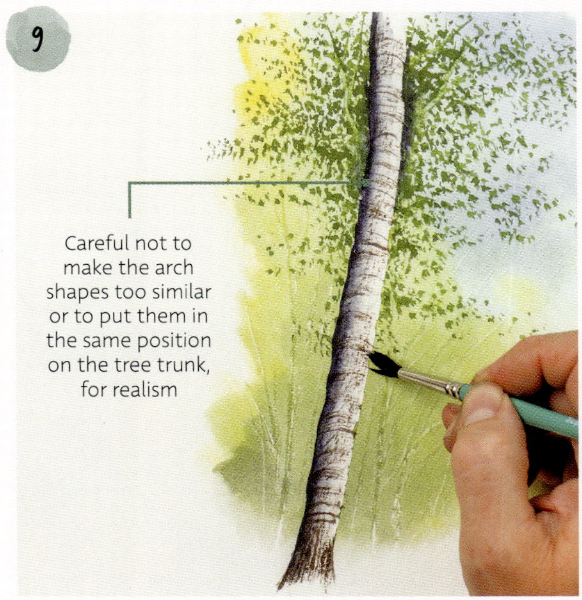

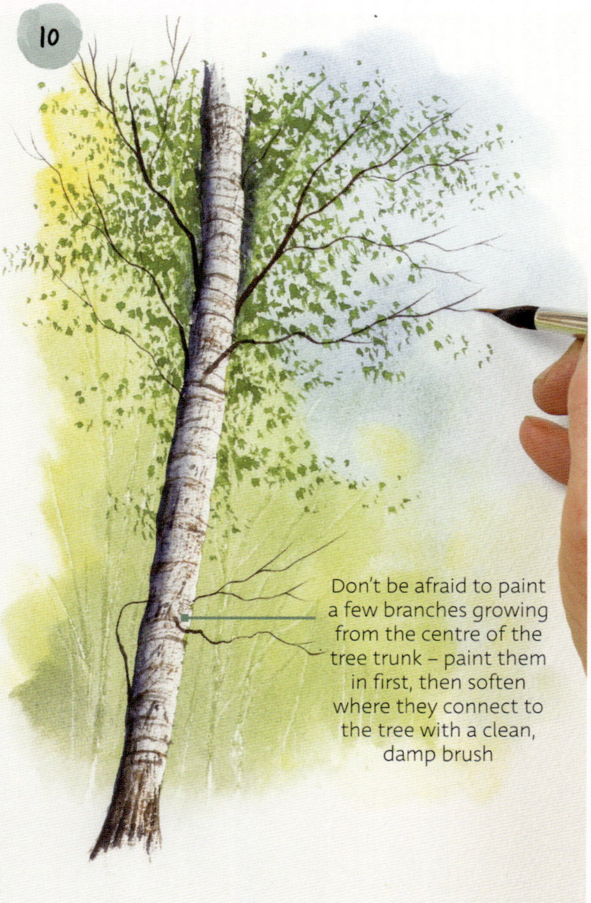

10. Squeeze the brush tip back into its original shape. Pick up more of the F mix then paint little upside-down V-shapes and 'eyes' here and there on the trunk. Change to a size 2 Rigger or Detail then paint in some **fine branches** on the tree with the F mix, working from the trunk outwards. Don't pick up too much paint for these, to keep them delicate and fine. Leave to dry.

11. With a clean, damp 6mm (¼in) Flat and kitchen paper, **lift out** highlights along the tops of some of the branches and into the tree, to bring them forward.

12. Add a little of whatever green is left on your palette to a tiny amount of diluted Titanium White gouache, making a silvery green shade. With a size 10 or 12 Round, **stipple** the silver-green mix here and there around the top of the tree, over the leaves. Pop a few 'dots' of leaves over the trunk too.

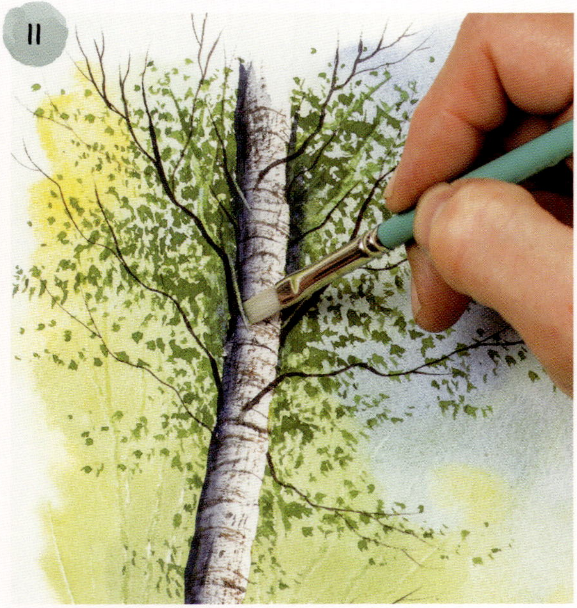

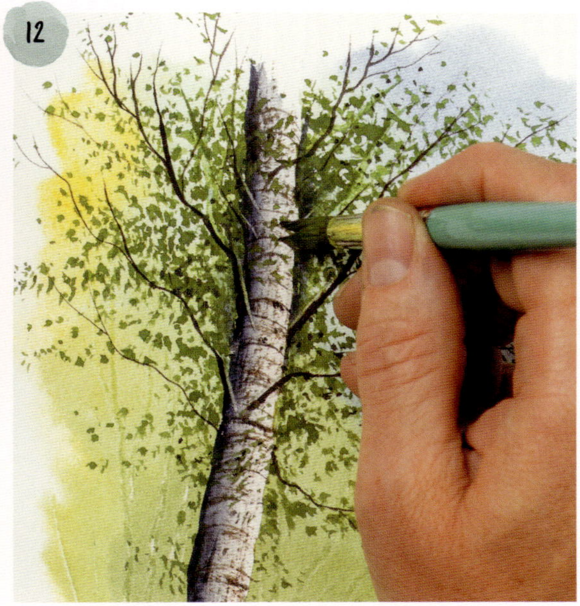

13

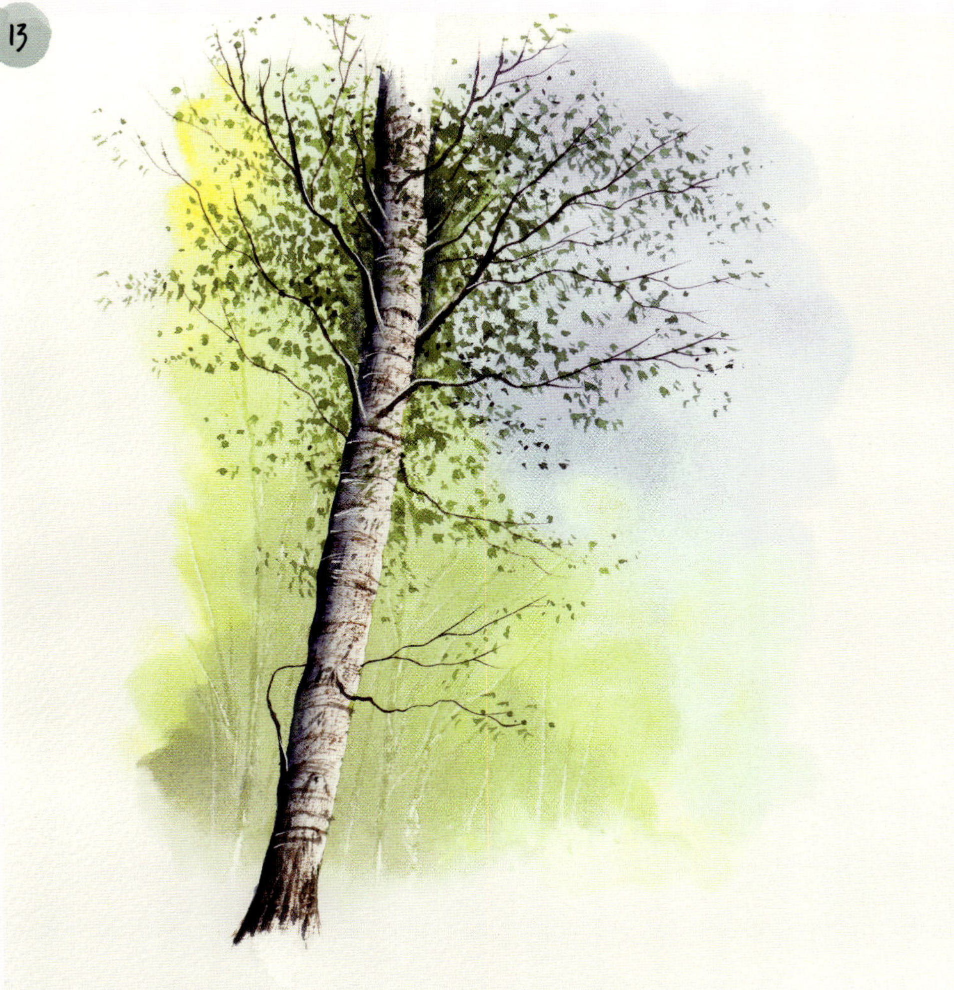

13. To finish, run a little diluted pure Titanium White gouache under some of the dark arches and rings on the left-hand-side of the tree with the size 2 Rigger or Detail, to make them look more 3D. If some of your lifted-out highlights from Step 11 need reinforcing, you can take the opportunity to strengthen them while the white paint is on your brush.

Lesson #9
WILLOW TREES

1. You'll need to do a bit of sketching for this one, with a 2B pencil. Roughly sketch a zigzagging line to represent the far edge of the water, about a third of the way up from the bottom of the paper. Then draw the general outline of the willow trees – these are basically lumpy waterfall shapes, which increase in size as they 'travel' towards the right-hand side of the paper.

2. Wet the whole paper with clean water using a size 10 or 12 Round. Make sure to brush the paper with water all over a couple of times for an even finish – but don't oversoak. Mix a light-strength pure Alizarin Crimson mix in your palette. Twist this **wet in wet** into the bottom of the sky area (just above the trees) upwards, then work horizontal strokes of the same mix just below the willow trees and downwards; this will be the river below the trees. Repeat with a light-strength pure French Ultramarine mix, this time twisting into the top of the sky downwards and stroking the colour horizontally from the bottom of the paper upwards – you'll eventually be sweeping into the Alizarin Crimson mix; this is correct.

3. While the paper and paint are still damp, twist the B mix into the tree shapes **wet in wet**. Immediately work horizontal brush strokes of the same mix directly below the trees, and along the top of water area. Allow the mix to merge with the red and blue clouds.

PURE COLOURS

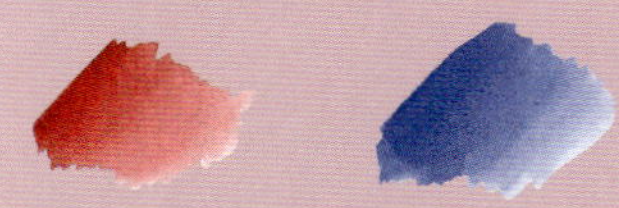

Alizarin Crimson   French Ultramarine

MIXES

See page 14 or the cover flaps for details.

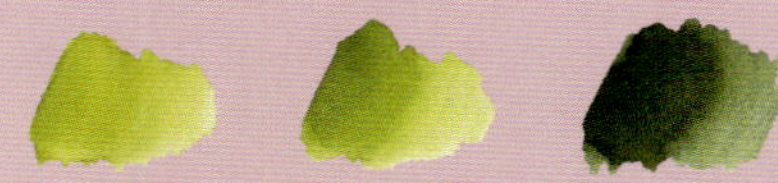

B   C   D

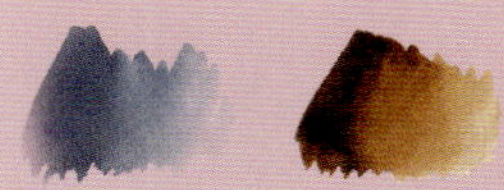

H   F

BRUSHES

- Size 10 or 12 Round
- Size 6 Round
- Size 2 Rigger or Detail
- Optional: 6mm (¼in) Flat

EXTRAS

- 2B pencil
- Titanium White gouache
- Kitchen paper

TECHNIQUES

- Wet in wet
- Wet on dry
- Dry brushing
- Feathering
- Fine branches
- Dot and dab
- Optional: Lifting out

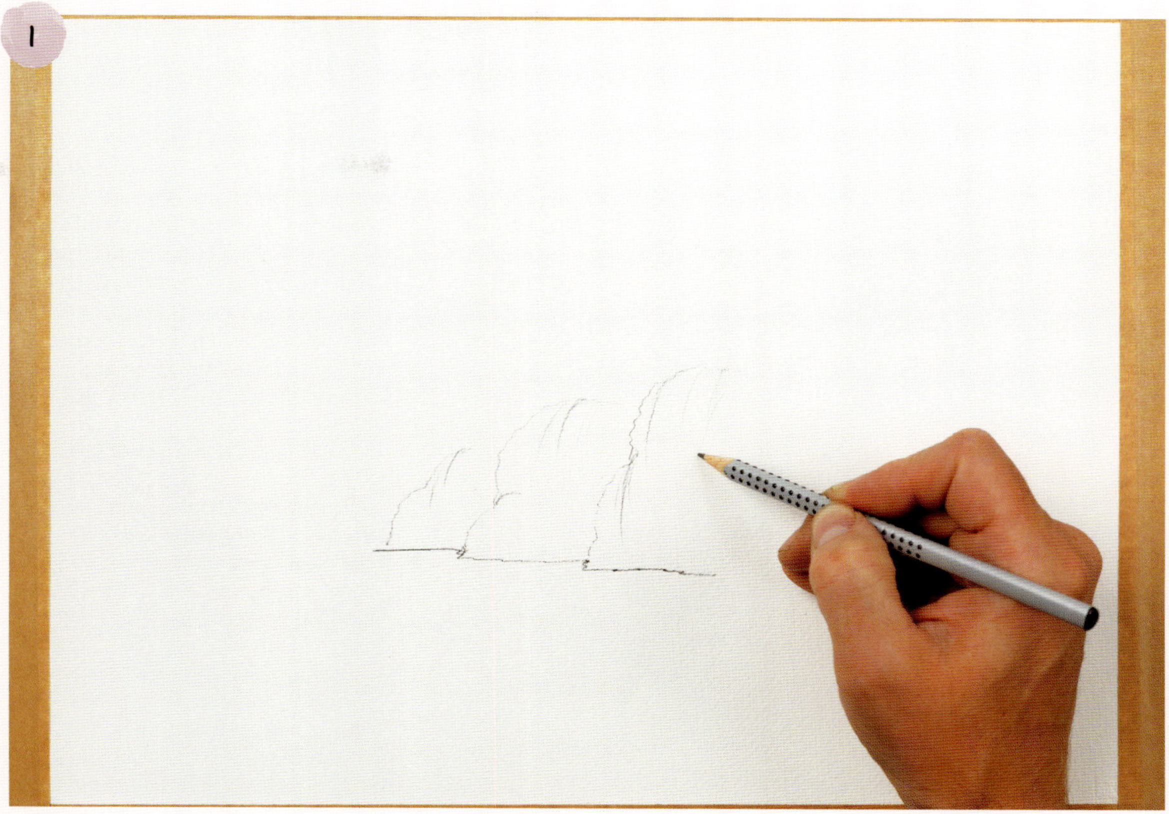
1

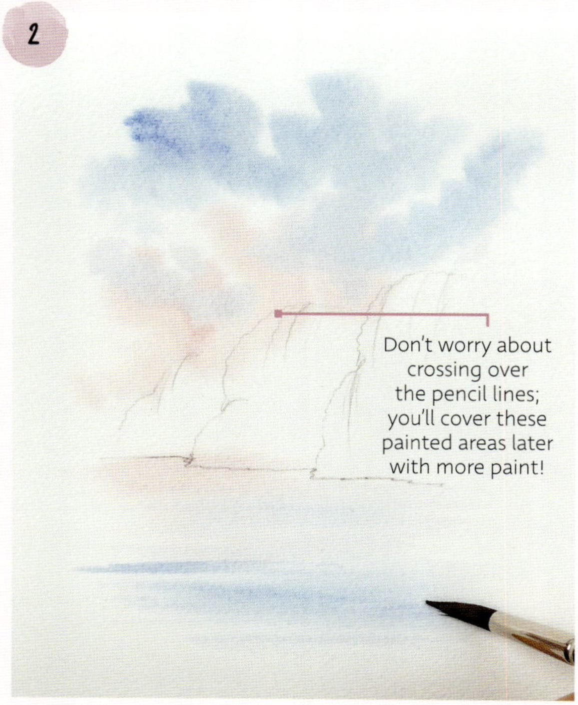
2
Don't worry about crossing over the pencil lines; you'll cover these painted areas later with more paint!

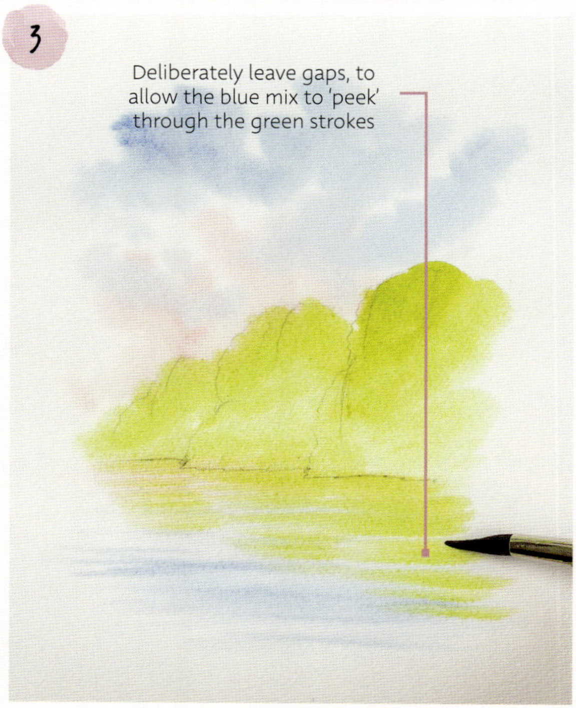
3
Deliberately leave gaps, to allow the blue mix to 'peek' through the green strokes

4a

4b

5

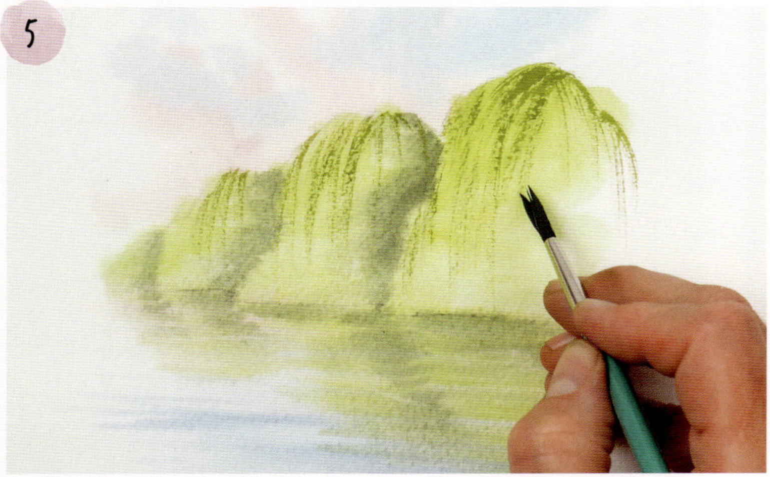

6

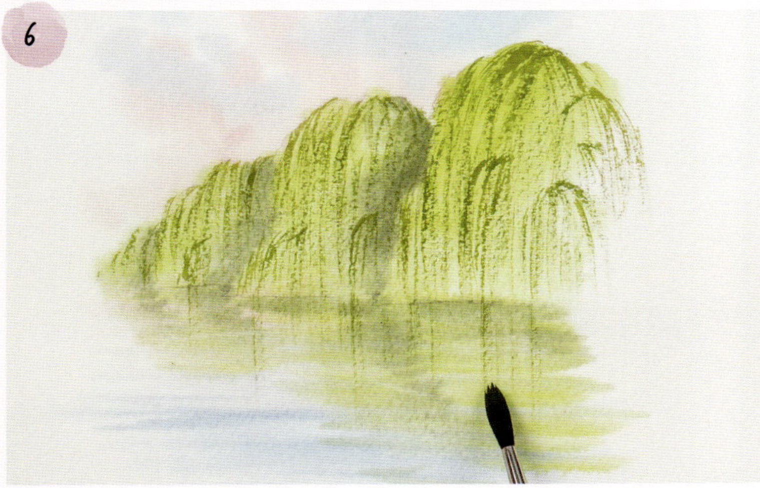

4. **Wet in wet**, twist medium-strength C mix in between the trees. Work horizontal strokes of the same mix just below the trees and downwards into the water area (see 4a). If your paper and paint are starting to dry out, like mine has, clean the brush, flatten the bristles by pinching the brush head between your index finger and thumb, then flick the clean, damp brush sideways over the edges of the darker green to soften it (see 4b). Leave the painting to dry completely.

5. Pick up some medium-strength C mix with the size 6 Round, tap off the excess onto kitchen paper, then with a **dry brush** sweep in the mix from the top of the tree to the bottom with an arching shape, working **wet on dry**.

6. Continue to add more **dry brush** strokes to the willow trees with the size 6 Round and C mix. To add shape within the trees, sweep stronger curving lines here and there to suggest protruding branches beneath the leaves. With the same mix and a **dry brush**, drag strokes into the water area to suggest the reflection of the trees in the water.

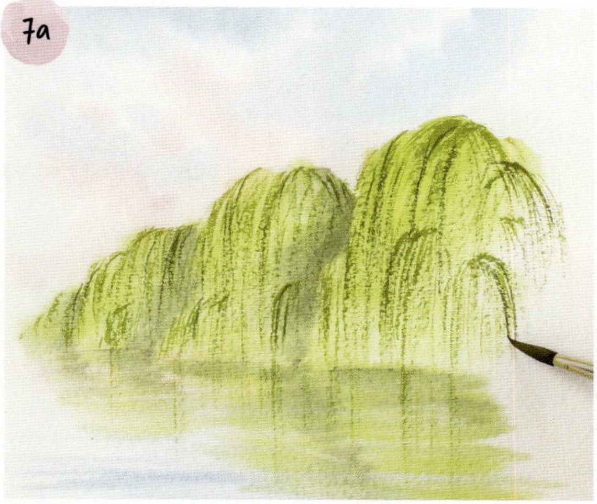

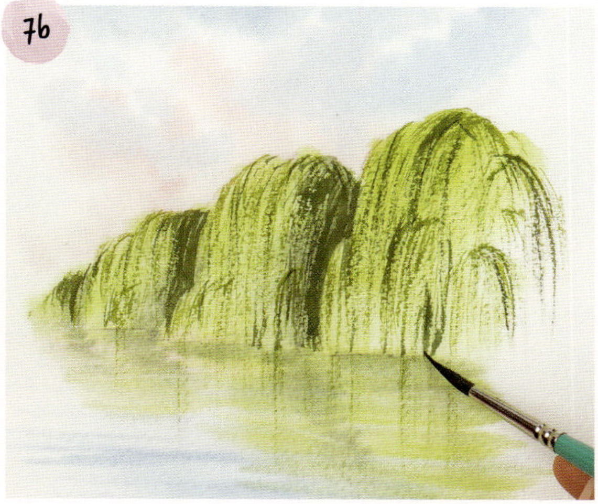

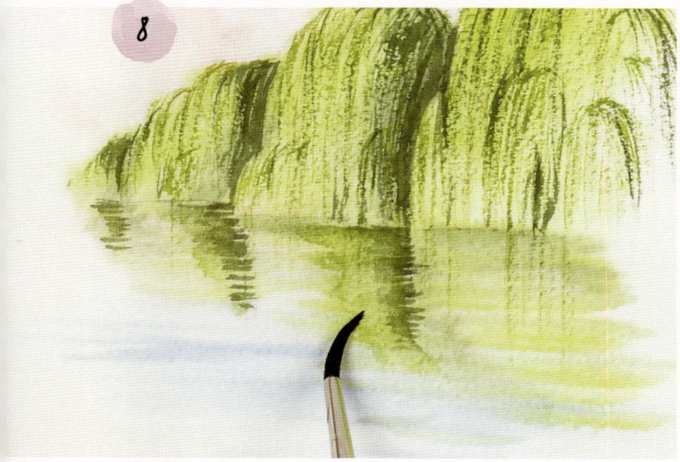

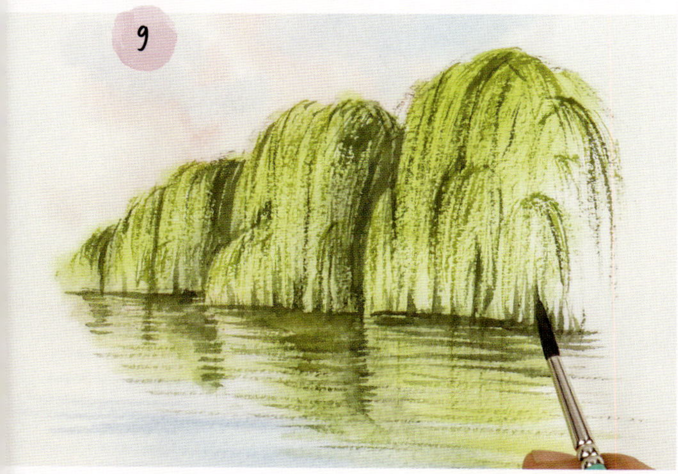

7. Using the medium-strength D mix and size 6 Round, repeat Steps 5 and 6 with a slightly damper **dry brush** to add textures and details to the trees. Add another layer of arching strokes from the tops of the trees downwards to suggest more trailing leaves (see 7a); then, work in between the willow trees to create more definite edges and emphasize the tree shapes (see 7b).

8. With a slightly damp **dry brush** add horizontal strokes of the D mix in the water to suggest the reflections of these darker tree sections. If the strokes look too strong, clean the brush, tap off the excess water onto kitchen paper then **feather** the edges with the brush tip.

9. 'Scribble' darker patches under the trees downwards with a slightly damp **dry brush**, into the water area, tapering off. **Feather** into the scribbles with a clean, damp brush to blend the colours and soften. Flick vertical lines from the water's edge up into the trees above, to suggest shadows and shape.

10

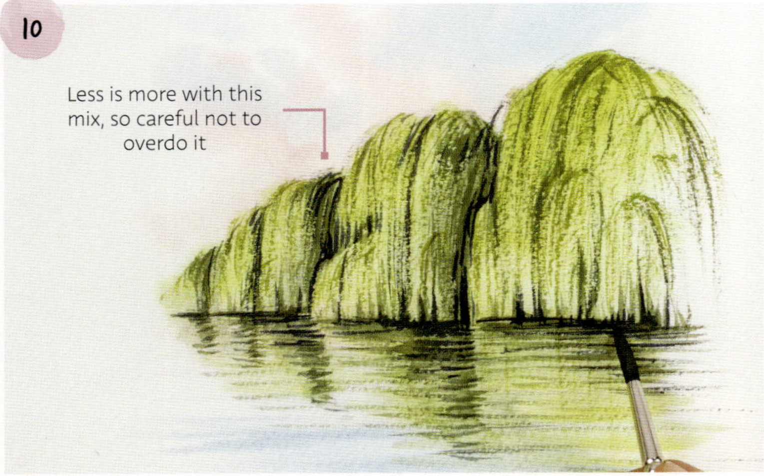

11

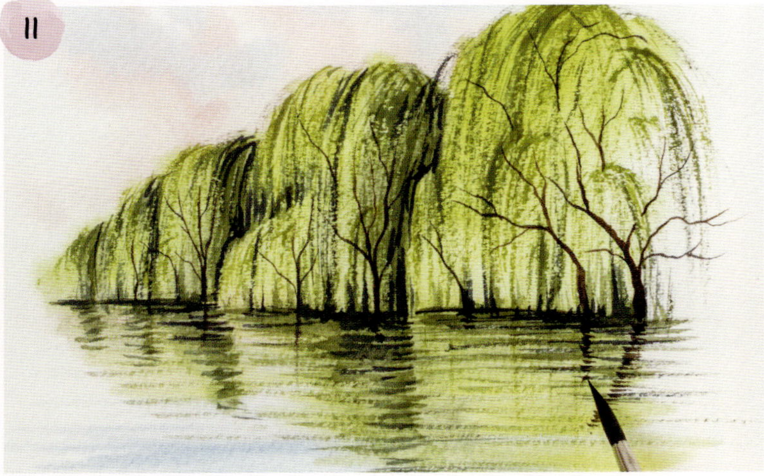

12

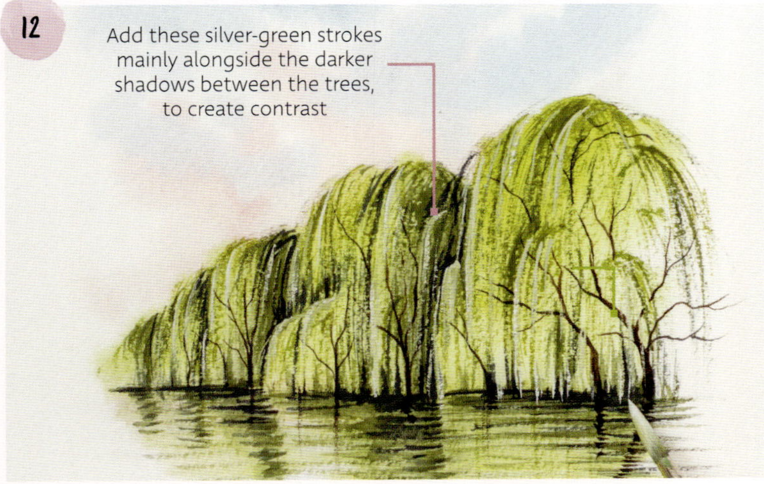

10. Repeat Steps 7–9 with a medium-strength H mix, to strengthen the shadows in the overall painting.

11. With a medium-strength F mix and a size 6 Round, paint in some tree trunks and larger branches within the green willow-tree shapes. (For a reminder on how to paint tree shapes, see page 24.) Work from bottom to top, and slightly curve the branches towards the upper section of the trees. Switch to the size 2 Rigger or Detail to paint in **fine branches**, ensuring you use the tip of the brush and taper off at the ends. With the same mix and the size 2 Rigger or Detail, 'wiggle' reflections of the trunks in the water area, working from the bottom of the trees downwards.

12. Now for highlights. Mix a tiny amount of diluted Titanium White gouache with the D mix to create a pale, silvery green colour. With the size 2 Rigger or Detail, stroke the pale silver-green shade over the tree shapes, from the top down. Drag a few highlights down into the water, in vertical strokes, from the top of the water downwards.

13. Run a few short horizontal lines of the silver-green shade in the water to suggest sunshine hitting the water.

13

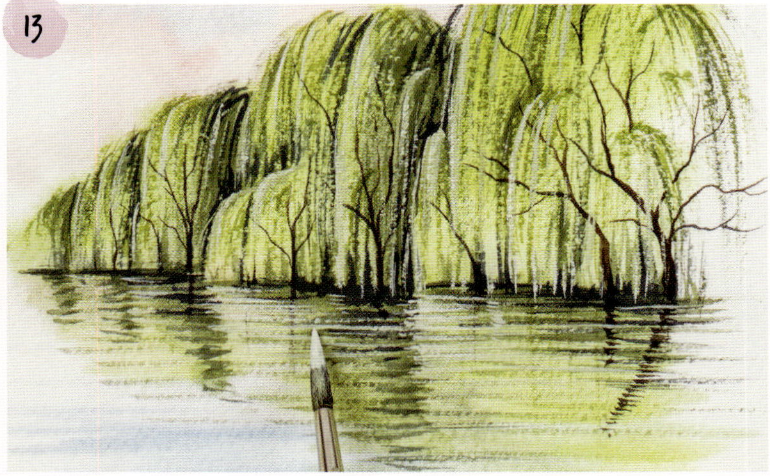

14

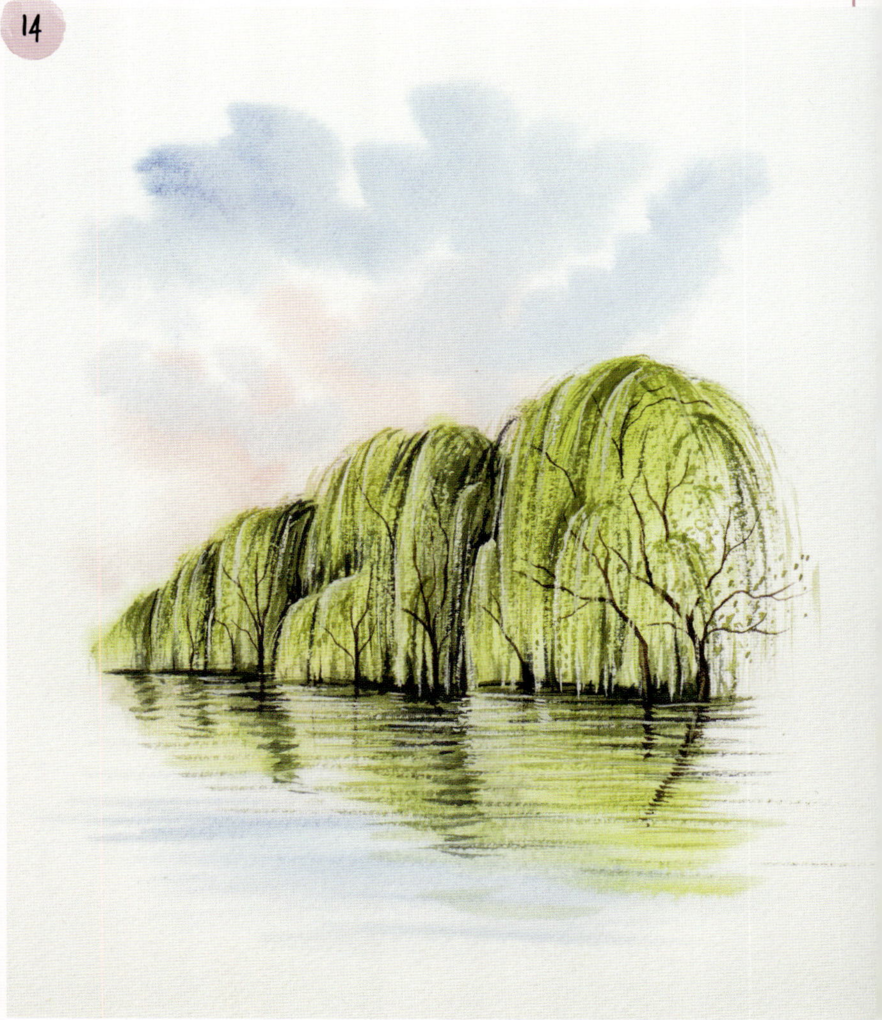

Highlights not strong enough?

If you're finding the green-white mix isn't strong enough, leave the painting to dry completely then **lift out** some highlights using a clean, damp 6mm (¼in) Flat.

14. To finish, with the size 6 Round and C mix, **dot and dab** a few individual leaves around the branches of the large foreground tree.

Lesson #10
AUTUMN WOODLAND

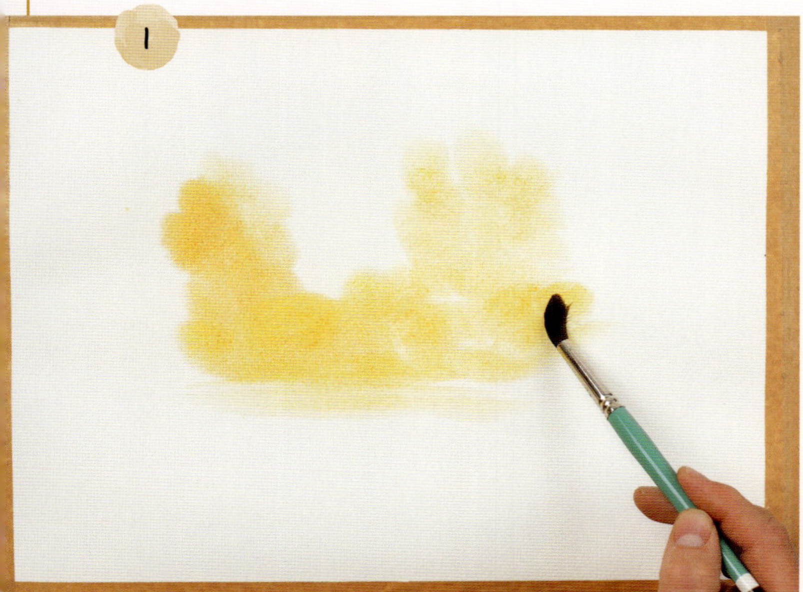

1. Start off by wetting the whole paper with clean water using a size 10 or 12 Round. Make sure to brush the paper all over a couple of times for an even finish, but careful not to add too much water. Using the same brush and a medium-strength J mix, sweep in a few horizontal strokes **wet in wet** around the middle of your paper for a horizontal line, then directly above this twist in clouds in a U-shape, from the horizon line upwards.

PURE COLOURS

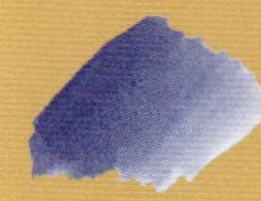

French Ultramarine

MIXES

See page 14 or the cover flaps for details.

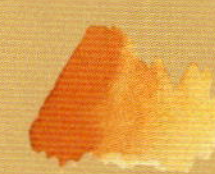

J

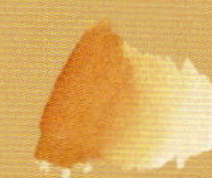

K

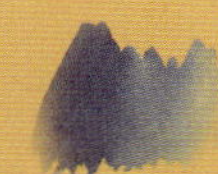

H

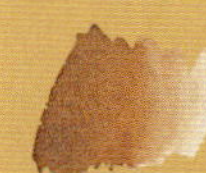

G

F

BRUSHES

- Size 10 or 12 Round
- Size 6 Round
- Size 2 Rigger or Detail
- 6mm (¼in) Flat

EXTRAS

- Piece of hard card

TECHNIQUES

- Wet in wet
- Feathering
- Scratching out
- Wet on dry
- Fine branches
- Dry brushing
- Lifting out
- Stippling with a round brush
- Dotting and dabbing

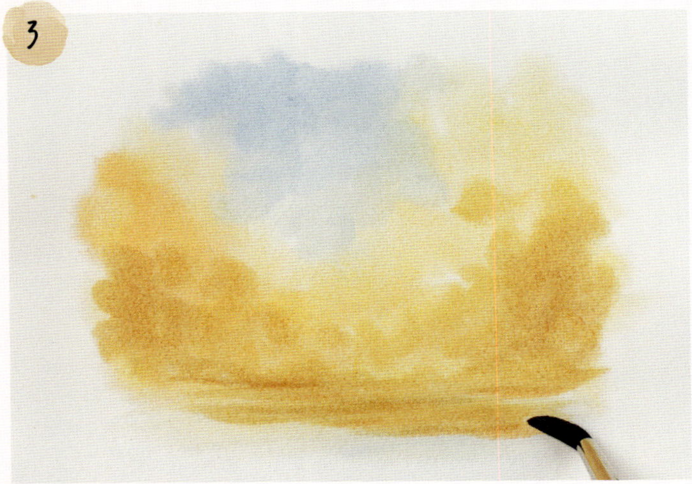

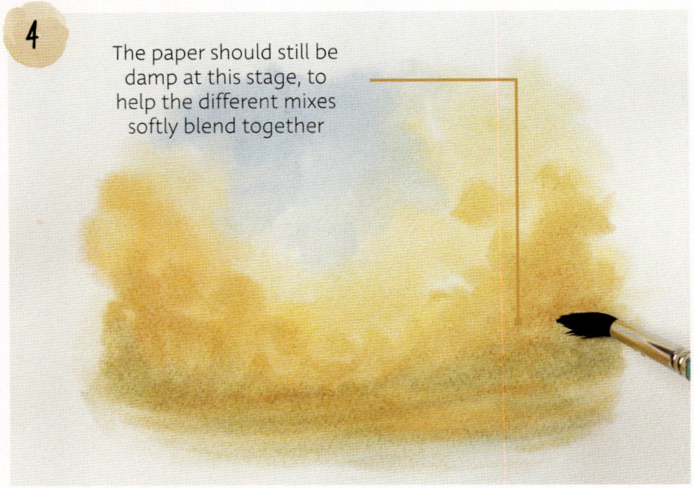

2. Repeat with a light-strength pure French Ultramarine mix, this time twisting in from the top of the sky area downwards. From the bottom of the paper upwards, sweep in a few horizontal strokes of blue, working into the horizontal strokes of the J mix.

3. While the paper and paint are still damp, twist patches of K mix into the bottom section of the U-shaped clouds. Stroke in a few horizontal lines of this shade below the horizon line, working mainly where the J mix and pure French Ultramarine mix meet. Any hard lines can be **feathered** with a clean, damp brush.

4. Pick up some of the K mix and place it in another spot on the palette. Add a touch of the pure French Ultramarine mix to it to make the K mix greyer. Twist this shade into the darker cloud shapes, just above the horizontal lines, working from the outer corners and work inwards, making these patches of grey-orange smaller towards the centre of the painting. Stroke in a few horizontal lines of this colour at the bottom, below the horizon line.

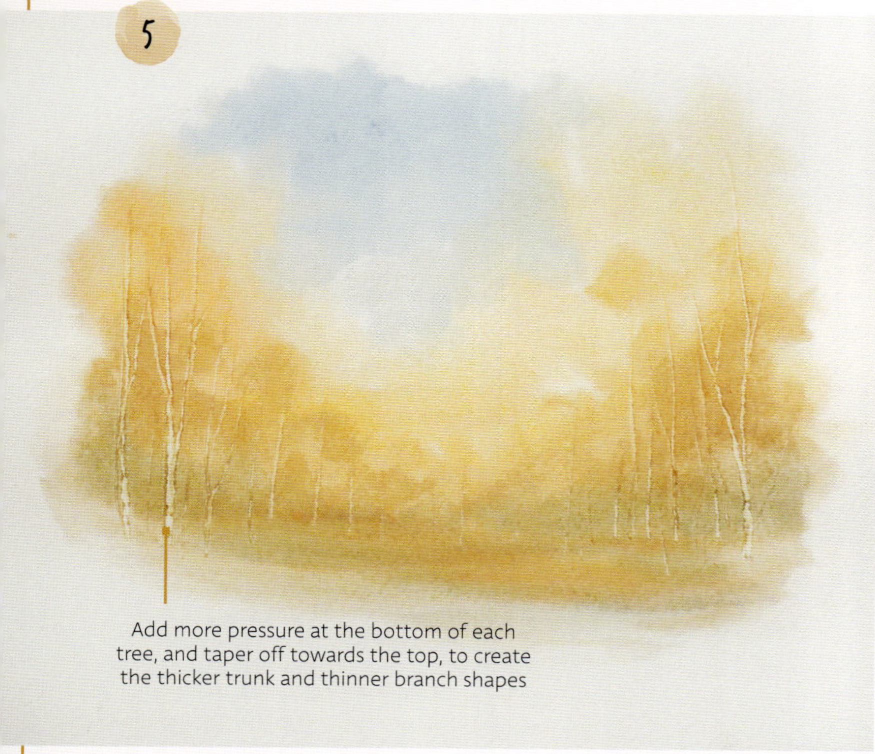

Add more pressure at the bottom of each tree, and taper off towards the top, to create the thicker trunk and thinner branch shapes

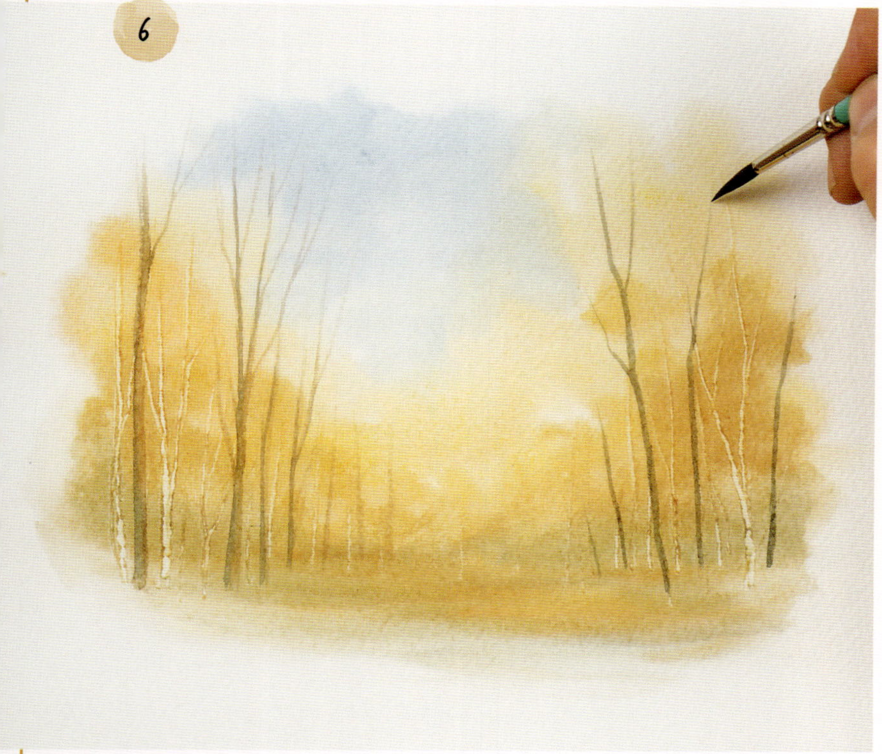

5. While the paint is slightly damp, **scratch out** tree shapes with the corner of a clean piece of hard card. Leave the painting to dry completely.

6. Next, the mid-ground trees. With the size 6 Round and a light-strength H mix, paint in some larger tree shapes **wet on dry** – focus on adding just the darker left-hand sides (see page 26 for more details). To create **fine branches**, paint with the very tip of your brush and taper off.

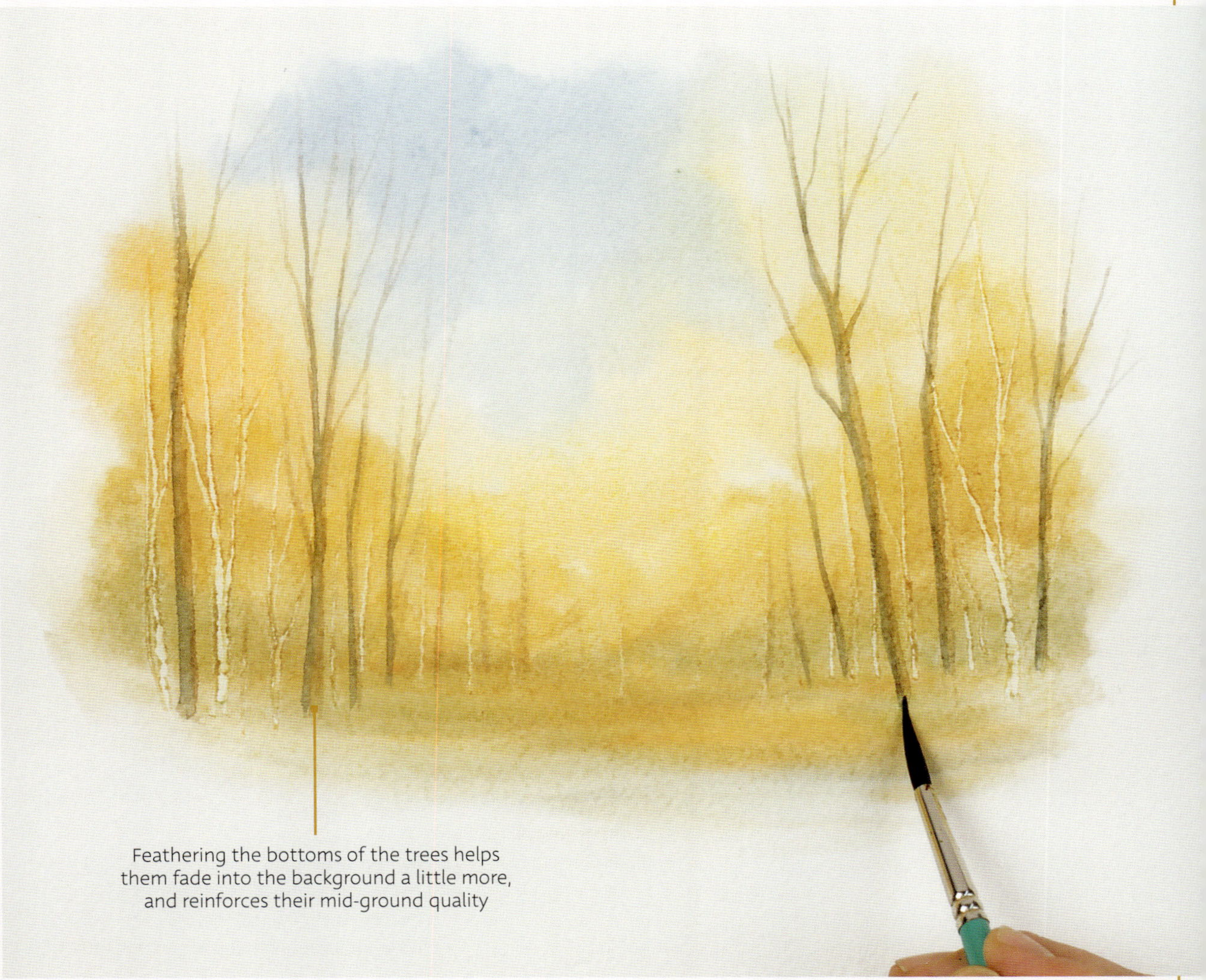

Feathering the bottoms of the trees helps them fade into the background a little more, and reinforces their mid-ground quality

7. With a light-strength G mix and the same brush, paint the warmer and paler right-hand sides of the tree shapes in the same way. Clean the brush, tap off the excess water onto kitchen paper then **feather** the bottom edges of the tree shapes, as shown. Leave the painting to dry completely.

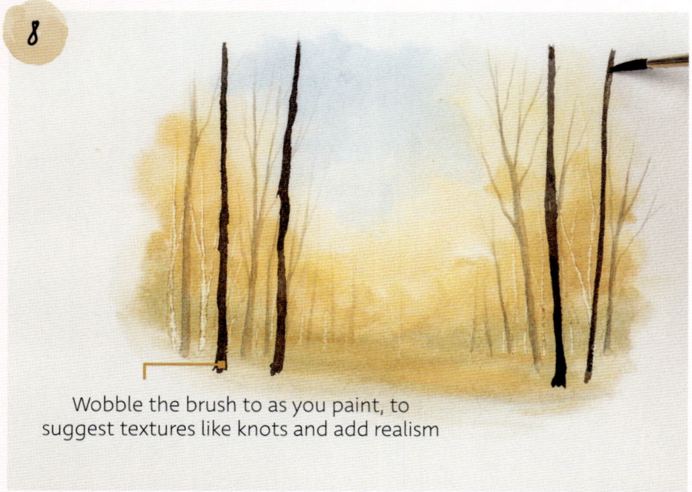

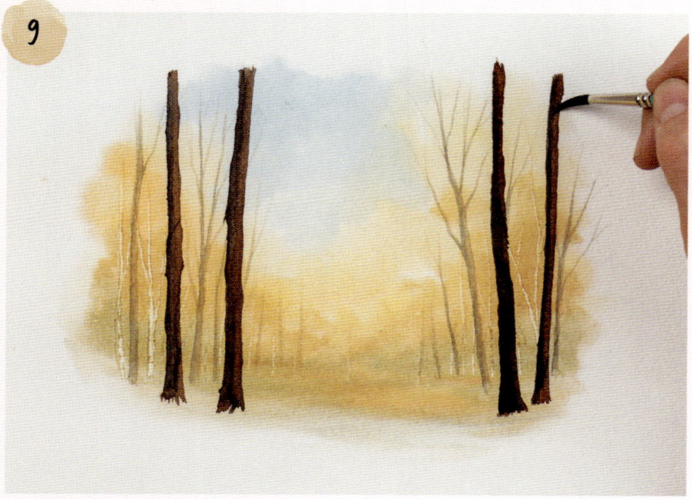

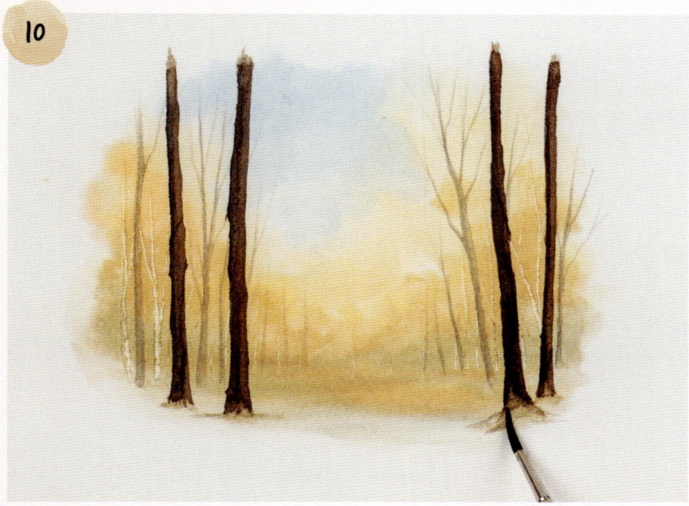

8. Now for the foreground trees. Using a strong F mix, paint in the darker, in-shadow, left-hand sides of the foreground trees from bottom to top (see page 26 for help with this). You can work a little over the background and mid-ground trees, so there's a little overlap, but try not to cover them too much.

9. Repeat Step 8 on the right-hand sides of the same tree shapes, this time using a medium-strength G mix to create the lighter sides of the trees.

10. Clean the brush, tap off the excess onto kitchen paper then **feather** the top and bottom edges of the trees, so they fade off a little and are grounded into the landscape.

11. Using a size 2 Rigger or Detail and a medium-strength F mix, paint in the **fine branches** of the foreground trees. Rest your hand on the paper as you paint for greater control, use just the tip of the brush, and ideally work towards you. To represent the closeness of the trees to the viewer, add the branches mainly around the top of the trees.

12. With the same brush and a medium-strength G mix, paint in a few paler 'background' branches using a **dry brush**. Add a few tiny branches at the ends of branches painted in Step 11, too.

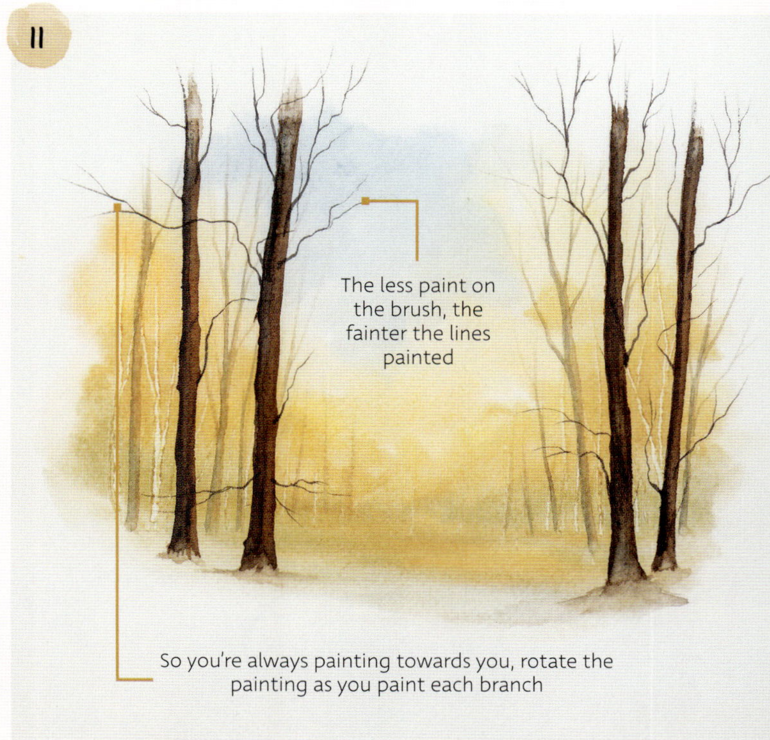

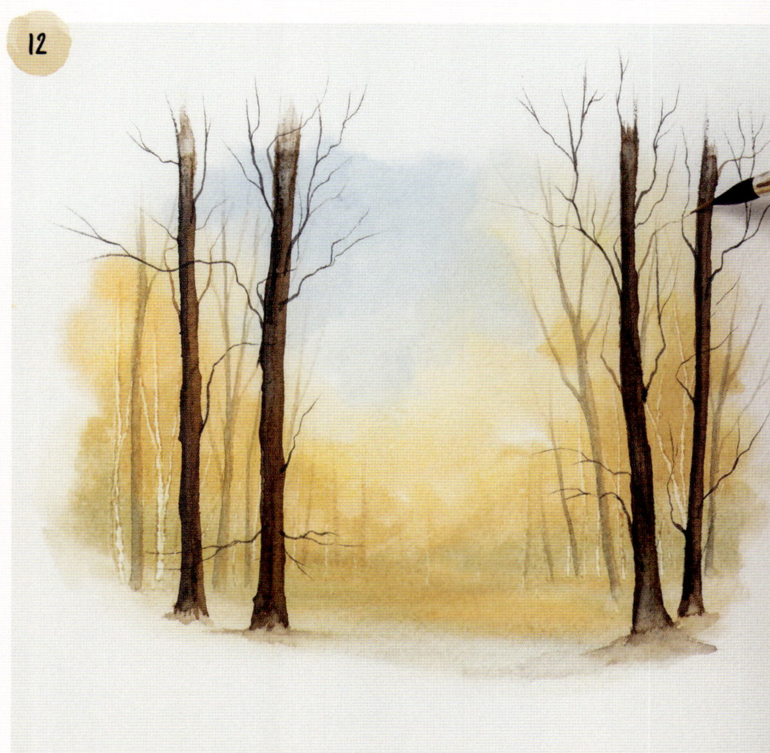

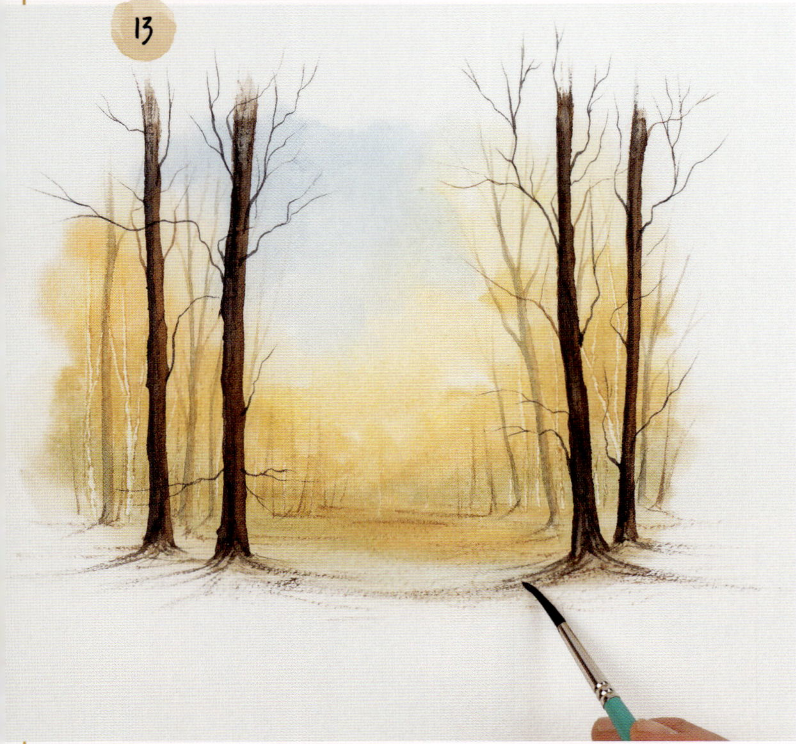

13. Time to add more detail. With a **dry brush**, use the a medium-strength G mix and the size 6 Round to add a few tiny vertical strokes around the centre of the painting, to suggest distant trees. Then, below some of the background and mid-ground trees, flick a few horizontal strokes to suggest subtle root textures. Change to a medium-strength F mix, then stroke in more defined root-like shapes at the bottom of the foreground tree trunks with a **dry brush**. These curve down and outwards until they line up with the horizon line. Leave the painting to dry.

14. Using the size 6 Round and a light-strength H mix, stroke in stronger cast shadows below all the trees, from the trees towards the bottom-left corner of the painting. Paint simple lines for the background and mid-ground trees; for the foreground trees, add a few branch-like shapes off the main stroke.

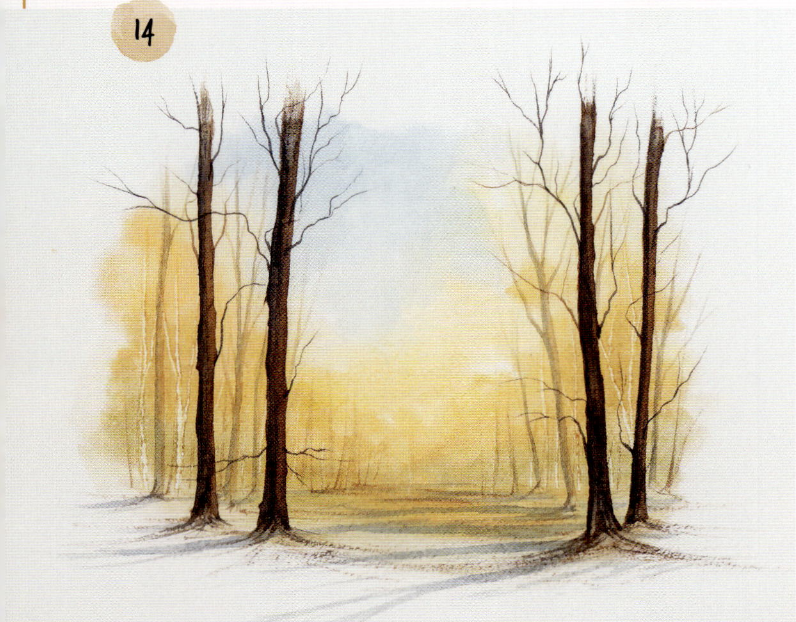

Adding more detail to the foreground trees' shadows helps suggest they're closer to the viewer

Cast shadows

These have come up a few times already, but if you're not familiar with the term: a cast shadow is the dark area created when an object blocks a light source, therefore projecting its shape onto the ground. Painting simple cast shadows is a great way to add depth to an artwork.

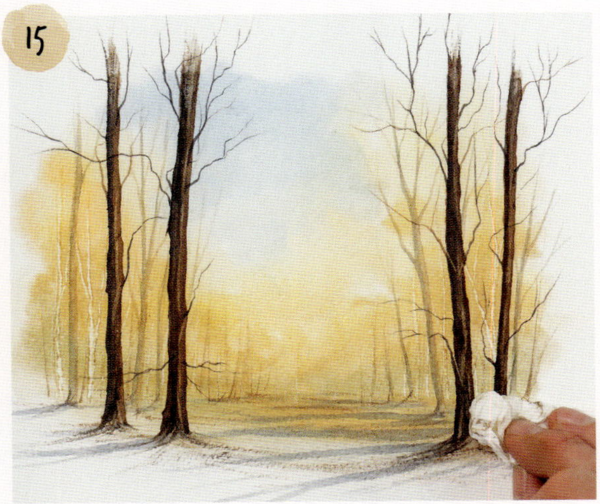

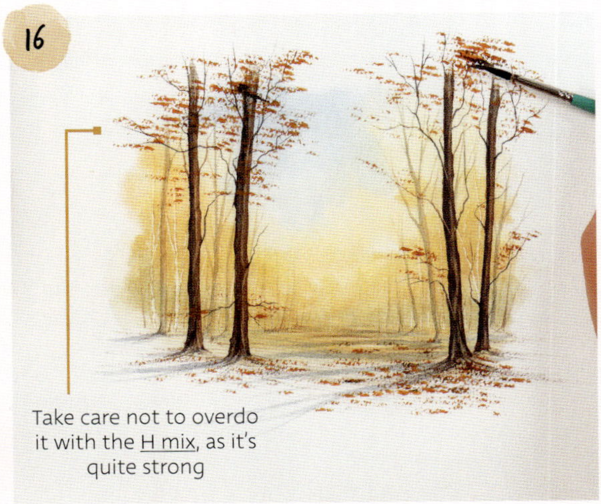

15. With a clean, slightly damp 6mm (¼in) Flat, 'scrub' away a few lines on the right-hand sides of the foreground tree trunks then dab with kitchen paper to **lift out** highlights. You can use this technique to add more shape to the tree too: shaping under branches where they connect to the trunk, and root shapes at the bottom of the trees.

16. With the size 6 Round and the K mix without blue in it, **stipple** in some leaves. Focus on the tops of the foreground and mid-ground trees, but colour can be tapped into some areas of the ground too, for fallen leaves. Repeat with the H mix, but take care not to overdo it with this shade.

17. To finish, using the size 6 Round and switching between the K mix and J mix when necessary, **dot and dab** a few individual leaves at the edges of the top leafy sections and around the branches at the bottom.

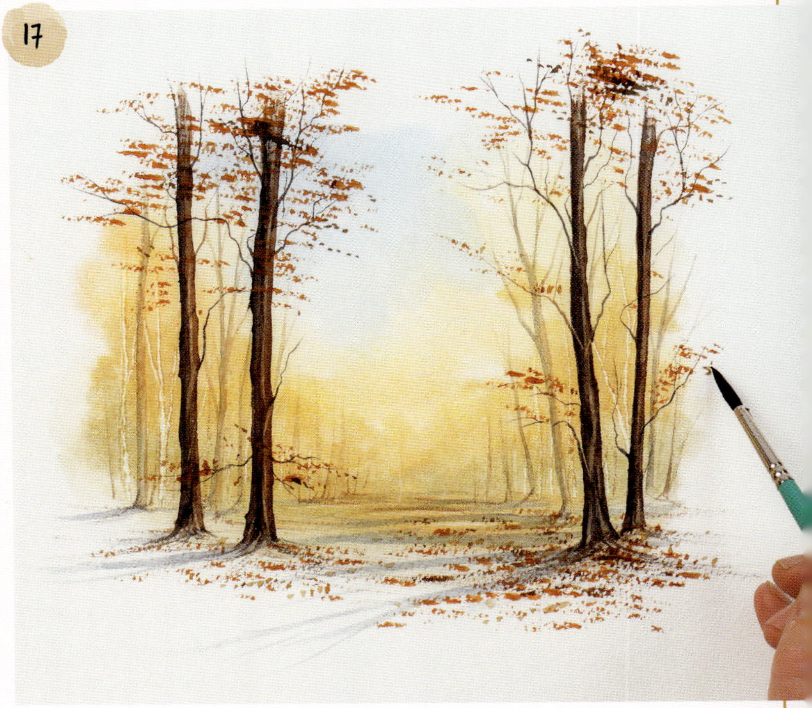

Lesson #11
WINTER WOODLAND

1. Tear off a long length of masking / painter's tape then narrow it by cutting it in half lengthwise with a craft knife. Slide the length between your fingers to remove some of the tape's stickiness. Loosely stick it horizontally onto the paper, about a quarter to a third of the way up from the bottom edge. Shape it with your fingers, pinching it in places and deliberately creating a wobbly hill shape. Then press down the tape firmly.

2. Wet the paper with a size 10 or 12 Round a few times to ensure there's an even layer of water all over. Then, immediately twist a medium-strength pure Yellow Ochre mix **wet in wet** in a triangle shape roughly in the centre, above the length of tape.

3. Clean the brush, then twist in the L mix around the yellow patch **wet in wet**. Work around the yellow patch at first as shown, then zigzag into it around the bottom, along the edge of the tape.

PURE COLOURS

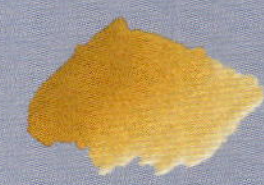

Yellow Ochre

MIXES

See page 14 or the cover flaps for details.

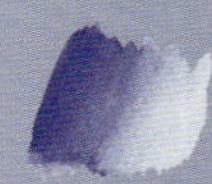

L

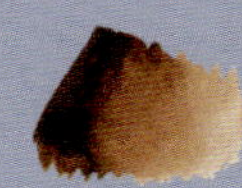

F

BRUSHES

- Size 10 or 12 Round
- Size 6 Round
- Size 2 Rigger or Detail

EXTRAS

- Masking / painter's tape
- Craft knife
- Titanium White gouache
- Optional: hairdryer

TECHNIQUES

- Wet in wet
- Fine branches
- Dry brushing
- Wet on dry
- Blending
- Feathering
- Dotting and dabbing
- Flicking

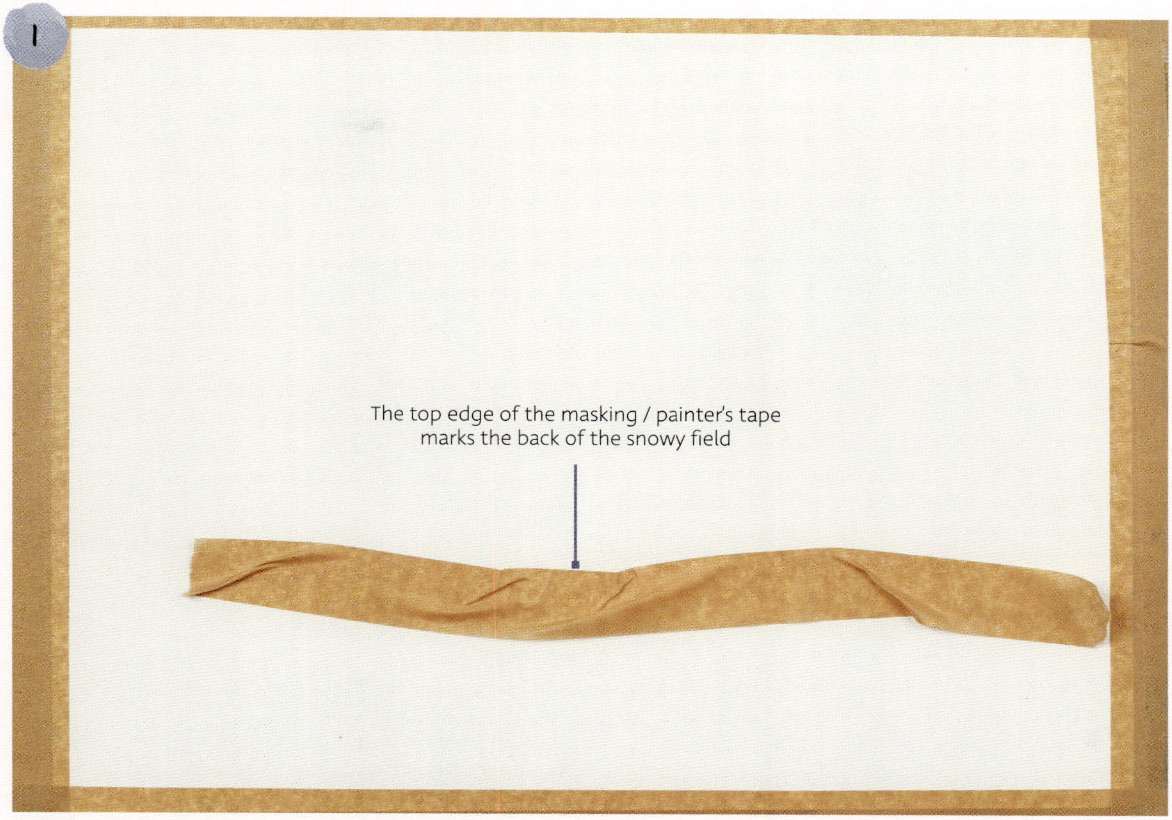
1
The top edge of the masking / painter's tape marks the back of the snowy field

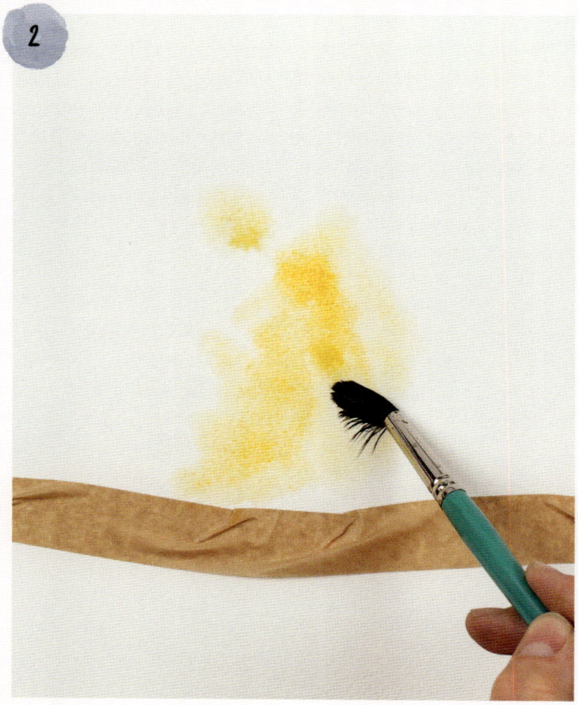
2

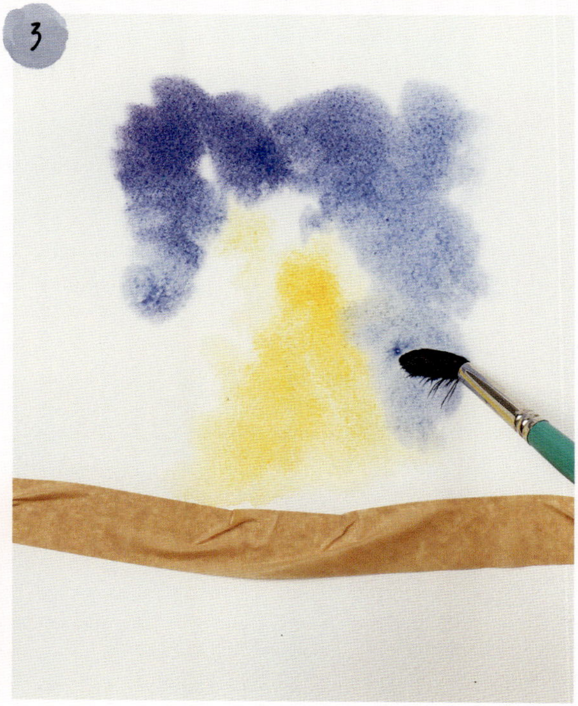
3

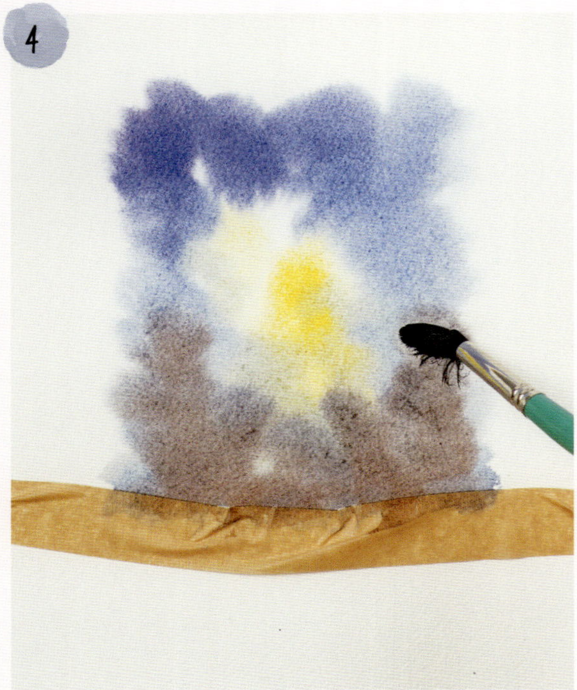

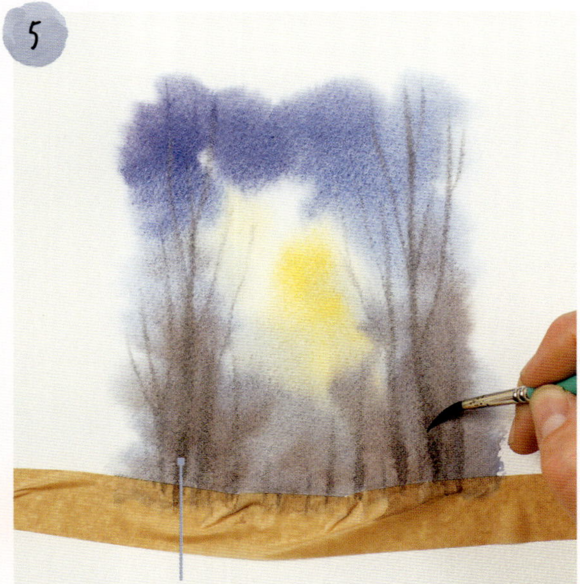

The damp paper will cause the paint to bleed a little; this creates a lovely 'misty' effect

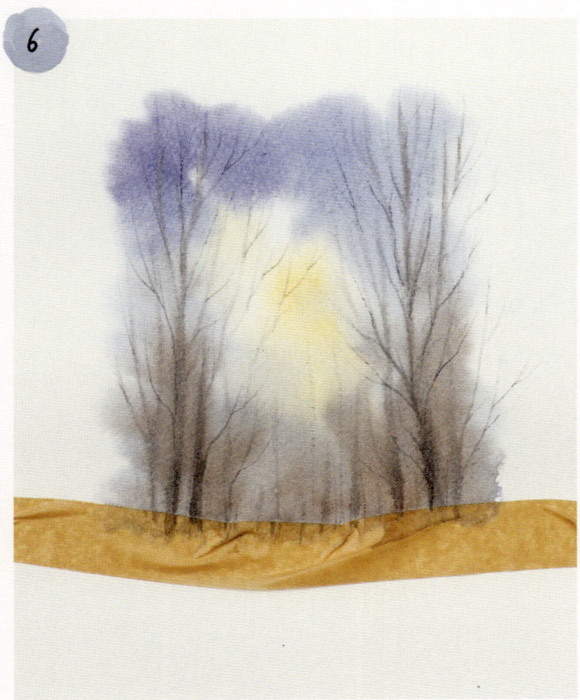

4. Clean the brush, then twist a medium-strength F mix **wet in wet** along the top of the tape, making a U-shape under the yellow centre to suggest distant tree shapes. The sky is complete.

5. While the painting is still damp, with the size 6 Round run lines of the F mix from the top edge of the tape up into the sky for tree trunks and branches. Make the lines taller at the outer edges of the scene (to suggest these trees are close to the viewer), then make them smaller towards the centre of the painting (to suggest trees in the background). Fine, vertical flicks can be used in the very centre for distant trees.

6. Switch to a size 2 Rigger or Detail, then add **fine branches** at the tops of the mid-ground and foreground trees using the F mix. Work on the mid-ground trees first, so that the lines are more defined on the foreground trees as the paper dries.

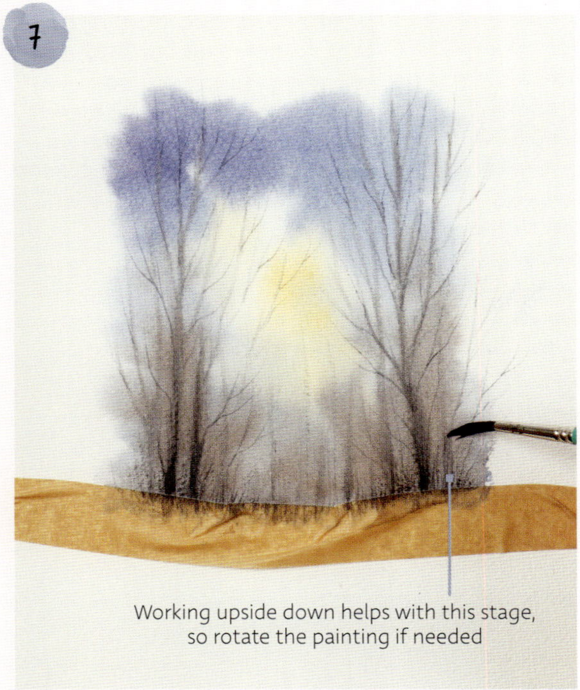

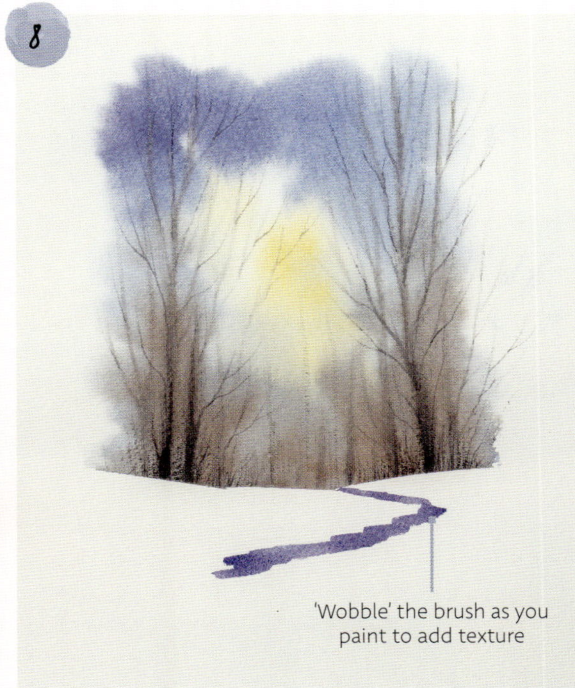

7. With a size 6 Round and strong F mix, flick up with a **dry brush** from the tape up into the foreground trunks; not only does this thicken the trunks, but it attaches the trees to the scene a little more too. Repeat for the smaller trees in the centre with tinier flicks. Leave the painting to dry completely.

8. Carefully remove the tape, using a hairdryer if necessary to melt the glue. With the size 10 or 12 Round and a medium-strength L mix, zigzag a path from the horizon (i.e. the top of the ground area) to the bottom of the painting, **wet on dry**.

9. Immediately, clean the brush, tap off the excess water onto kitchen paper then **blend** the edge of the pathway towards the right-hand side of the painting.

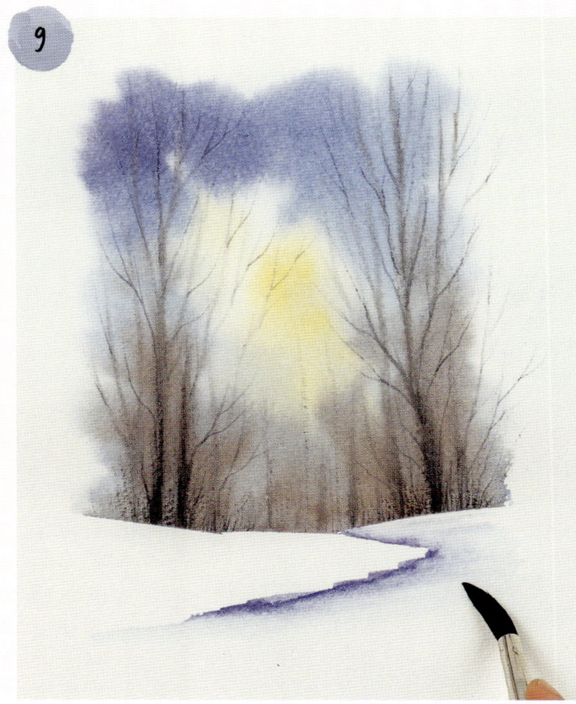

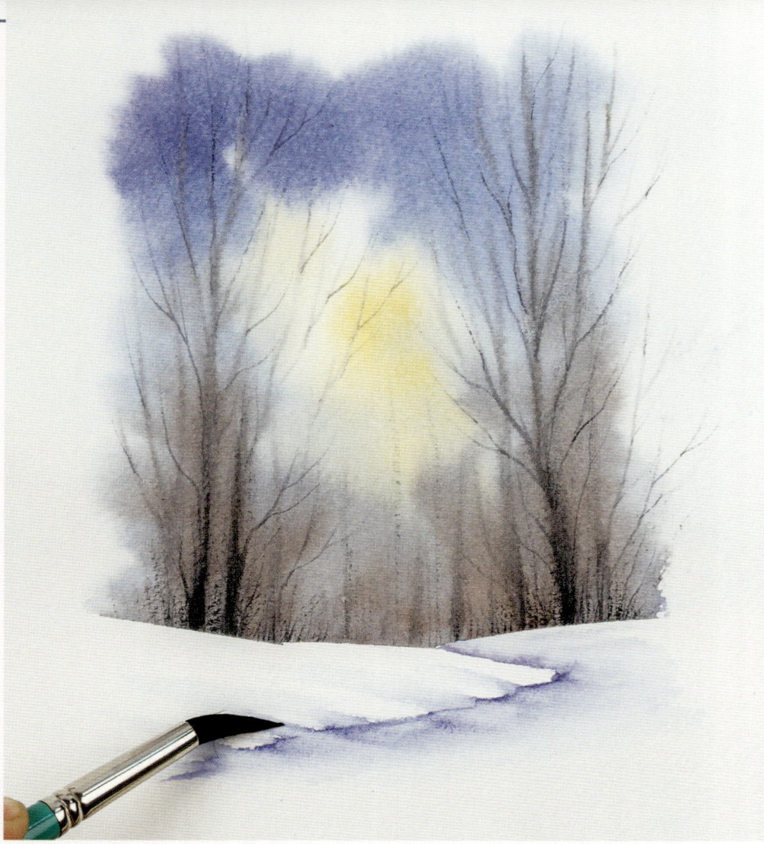

10. Repeat on the left-hand side of the path, this time adjusting the angle of the brushstrokes to suggest a snowy bank sloping up to the left. Leave the painting to dry completely. If you wish, you could finish the painting at this stage.

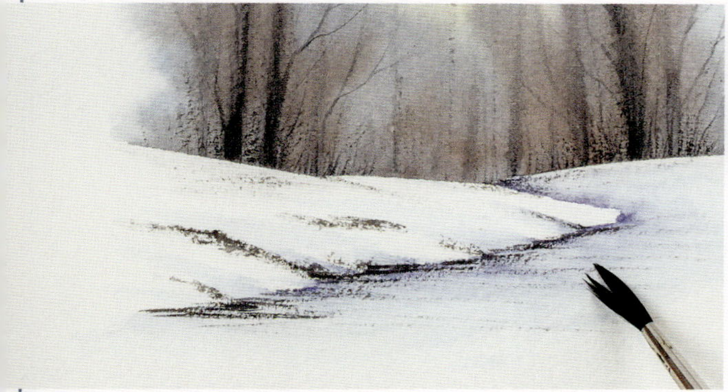

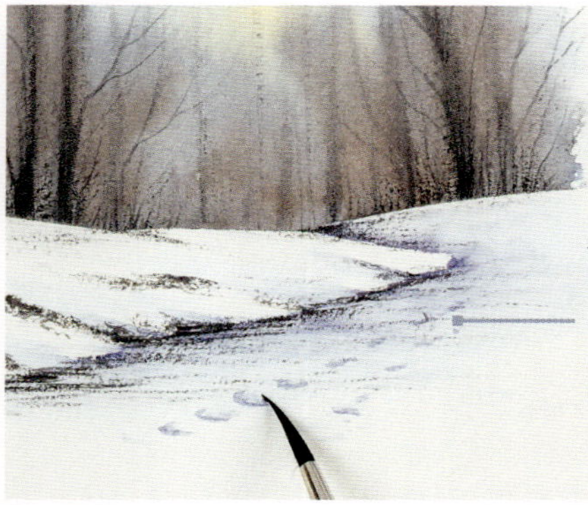

11. Using the size 6 Round, F mix and the **dry brush** technique, drag little horizontal strokes from the bottom edge of the bank into the pathway, from left to right, **wet on dry**. Here and there, pull a few strokes up into the snowbank itself, to outline a few mounds in the snowbank and give it shape.

12. With the tip of the size 6 Round and a medium-strength L mix, paint in little footprint shapes, from just below the horizon line to the foreground. Start out with little dots, then gradually paint stretched U-shapes as you near the immediate foreground. **Feather** the insides of the footprints to soften them, if needed.

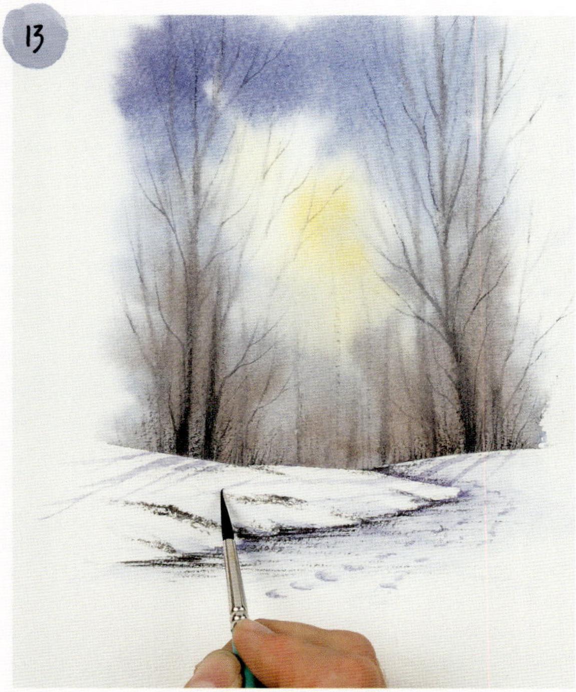

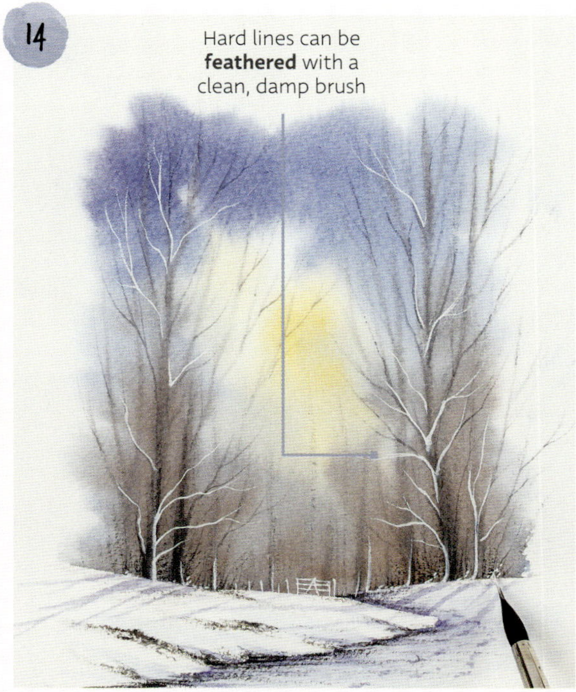

13. With a light-strength L mix, paint in the cast shadows of the foreground trees. Essentially these are reflections of the trees, but at an angle. Paint from the base of the trees into the foreground with single, smooth strokes, so the strength of the paint naturally reduces towards to the tip of the shadows.

14. With diluted Titanium White gouache and a size 2 Rigger or Detail, add lines of white in the foreground trees to suggest settled snow. Focus on the tops of branches and the trunks of the trees. If you wish, for more foreground interest, add a small gate for scale and **dot and dab** a few snowy shrubs at the base of some of the trees.

15. Pick up a little diluted Titanium White gouache, with the size 6 Round. Then, tap the ferrule of the brush (the metal casing) against your finger to **flick** the paint onto the painting, to suggest falling snow.

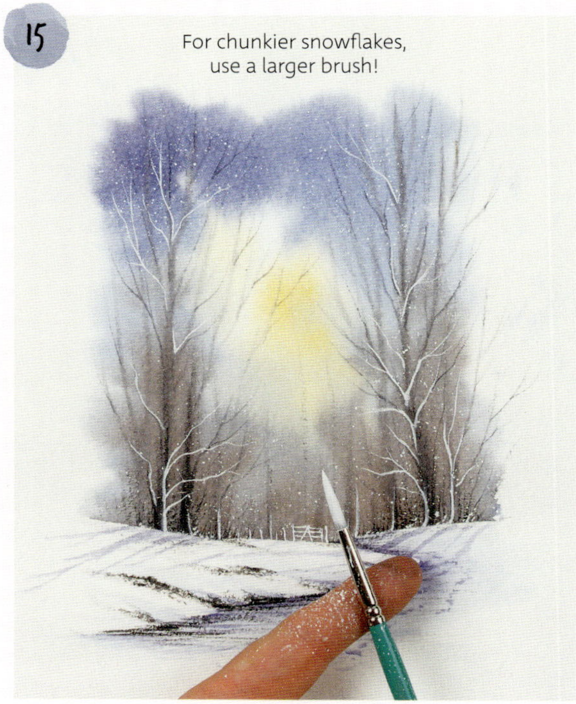

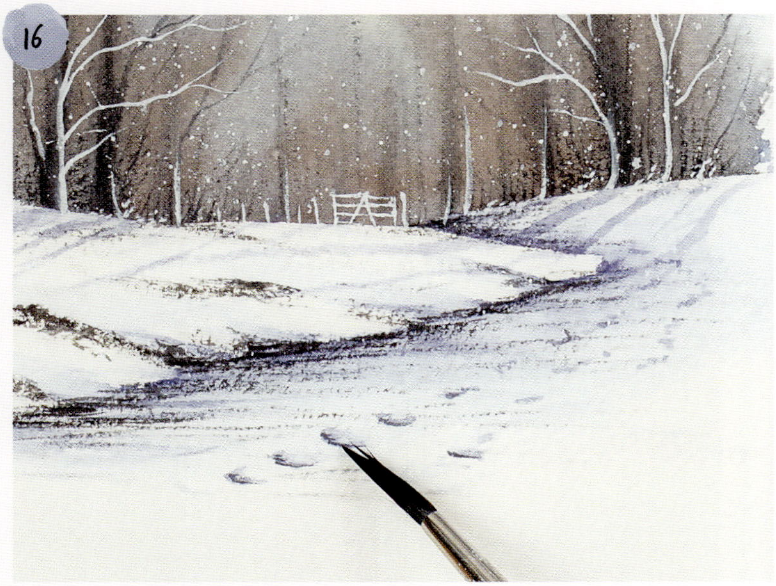

16. To finish, add more depth to the immediate foreground footprints by **dry brushing** a little amount of medium-strength L mix, along the curved edges with the size 6 Round.

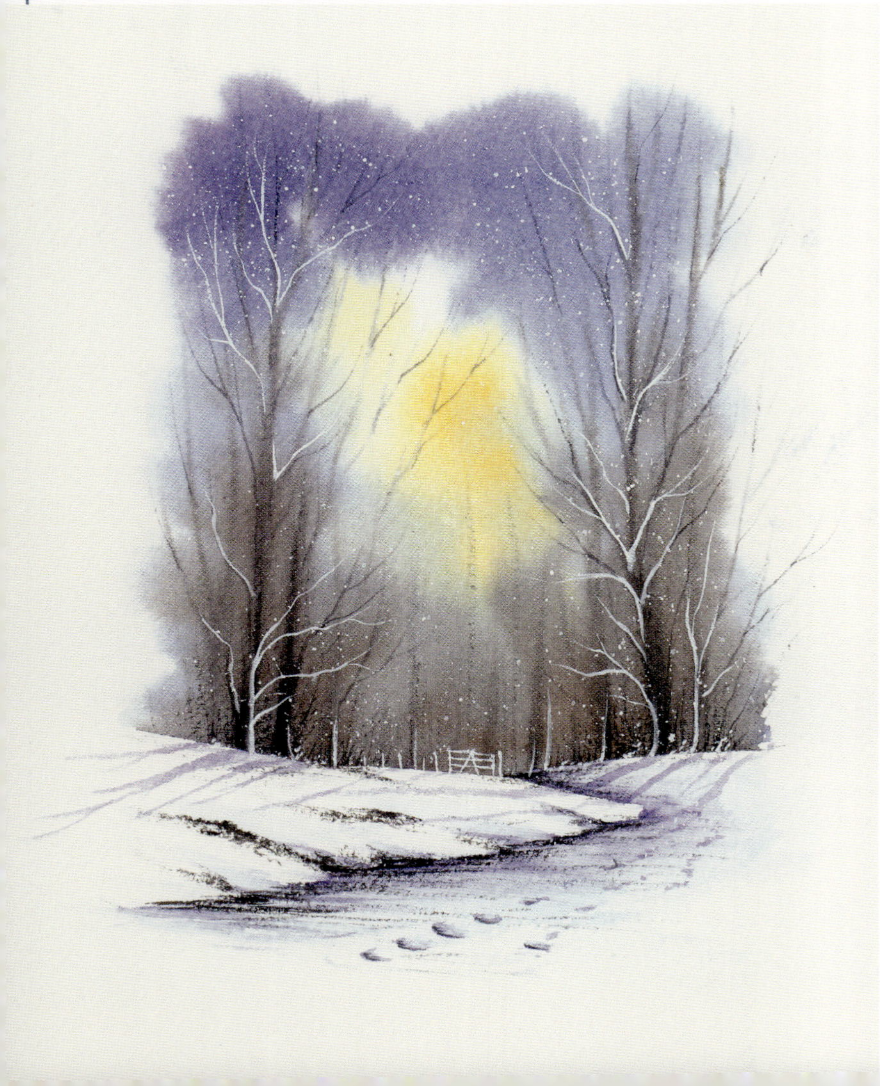

The finished painting.

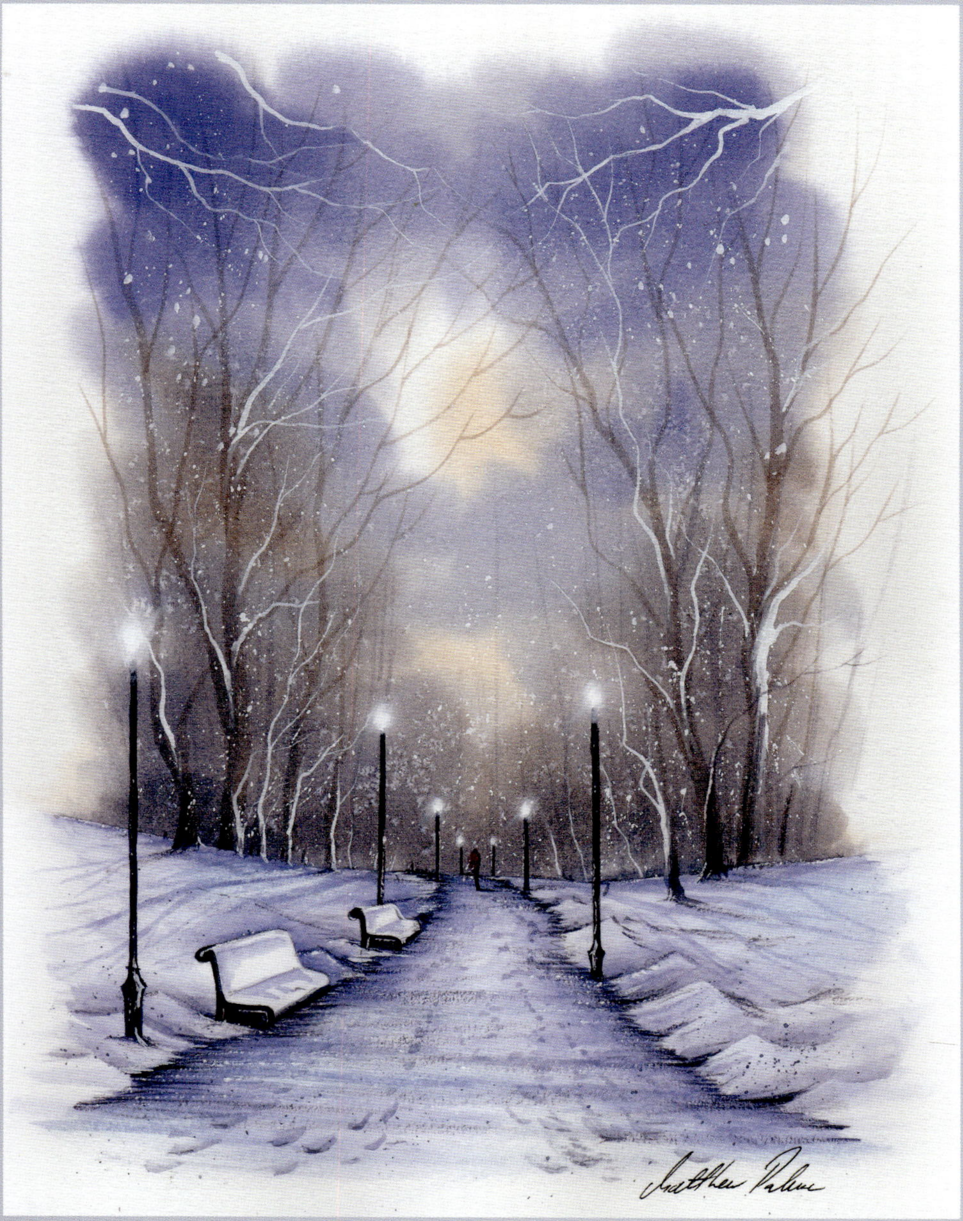

'WINTER IN THE PARK'

28 x 35.5cm (11 x 14in)

Several techniques applied in Lesson #11 were used to paint this detailed wintry scene. The streetlights and benches give a little extra atmosphere, along with the figure at the end of the pathway, and add a sense of scale too. The glow of the lamps was created by a combination of lifting out paint with a clean, damp brush, then intensifying the white using some Titanium White gouache.

Lesson #12
SPRING WOODLAND

1. Tear off a long length of masking / painter's tape then narrow it by cutting it in half lengthwise with a craft knife. Slide the length between your fingers to remove some of the tape's stickiness. Loosely stick it horizontally onto the paper, about a third of the way up from the bottom edge. Shape it with your fingers, pinching it in places and deliberately creating a wobbly line to mark the edge of the land, sloping slightly up to the left. When you're happy, press down the tape firmly.

2. Wet the paper with a size 10 or 12 Round a few times to ensure there's an even layer of water all over – but be careful not to overwet the area. Then, twist a medium-strength pure Cadmium Yellow or Aureolin mix **wet in wet** in a U-shape centrally above the length of tape.

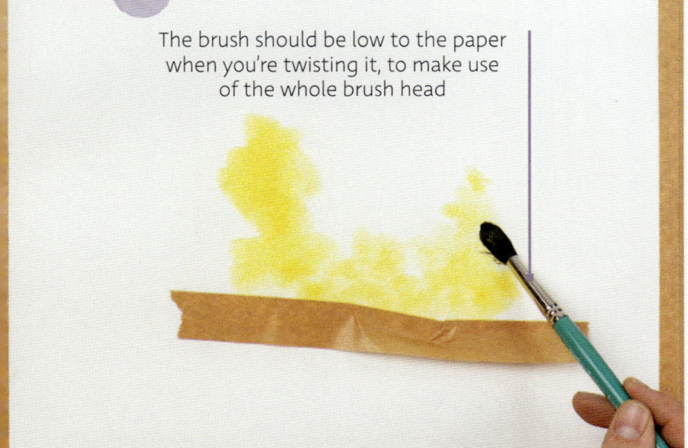

2

The brush should be low to the paper when you're twisting it, to make use of the whole brush head

PURE COLOURS

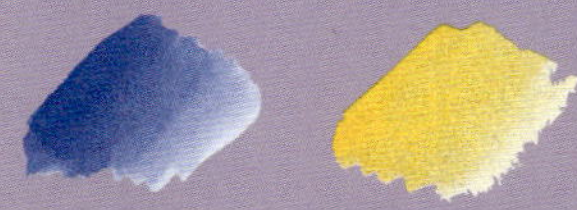

French Ultramarine | Cadmium Yellow or Aureolin

MIXES

See page 14 or the cover flaps for details.

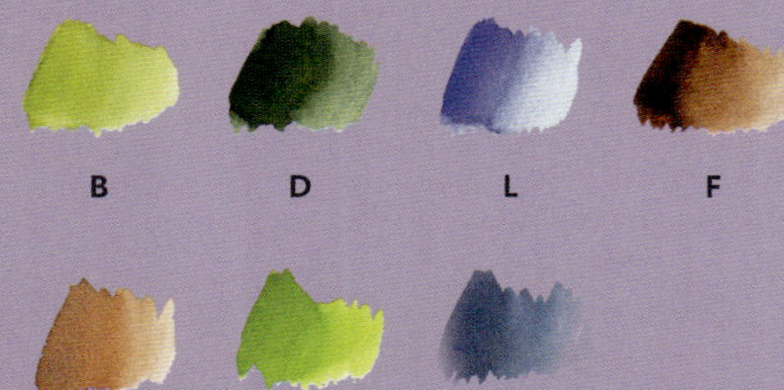

B D L F

G A H

BRUSHES

- Size 10 or 12 Round
- Size 6 Round
- Size 2 Rigger or Detail
- Medium Fan
- 6mm (¼in) Flat

EXTRAS

- Masking / painter's tape
- Craft knife
- Piece of hard card
- Titanium White gouache
- Kitchen paper
- Optional: hairdryer

TECHNIQUES

- Wet in wet
- Feathering
- Scratching out
- Dotting and dabbing
- Wet on dry
- Flicking
- Fine branches
- Dry brushing
- Stippling with a fan brush
- Lifting out

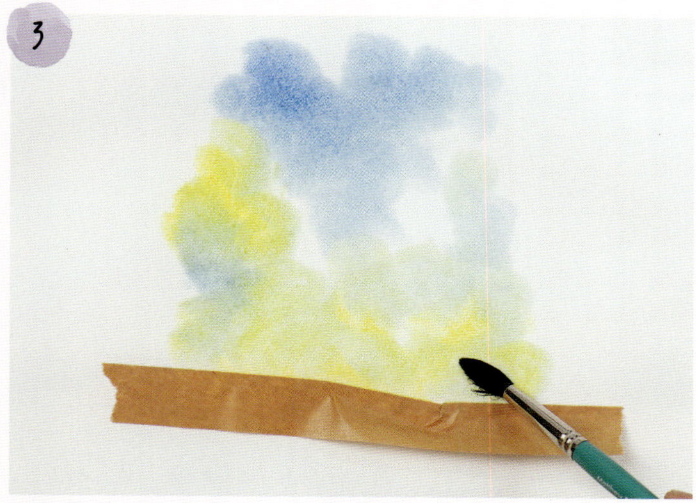

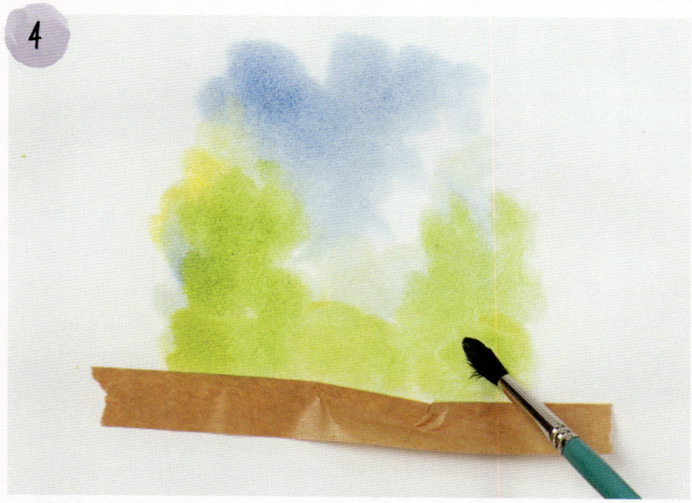

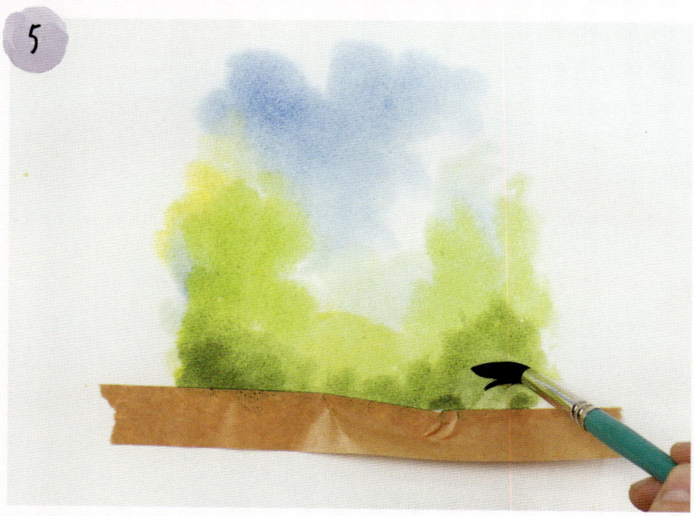

3. Still working **wet in wet** and with the same brush, twist in a medium-strength pure French Ultramarine mix above and into the yellow. Where the two colours meet, allow them to blend.

4. Working **wet in wet** still, twist in a smaller U-shape using a medium- strength B mix.

5. Into the bottom of the damp lighter green shape, twist in the D mix. If you find the paper has dried enough that the darker green isn't blending in, use a clean, damp brush to help **feather** the colour into the light green.

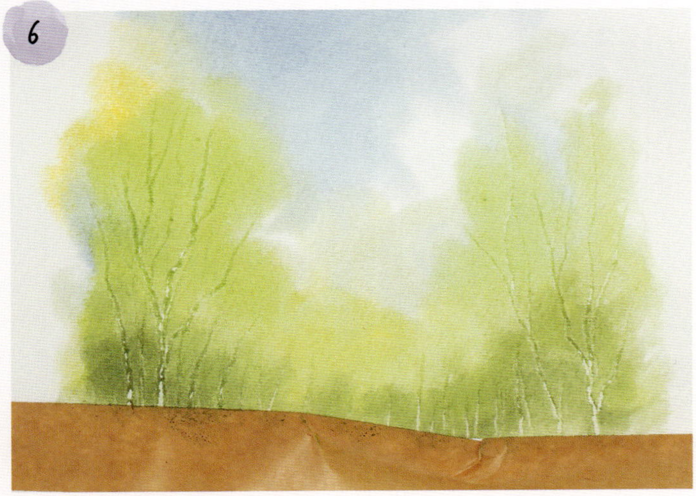

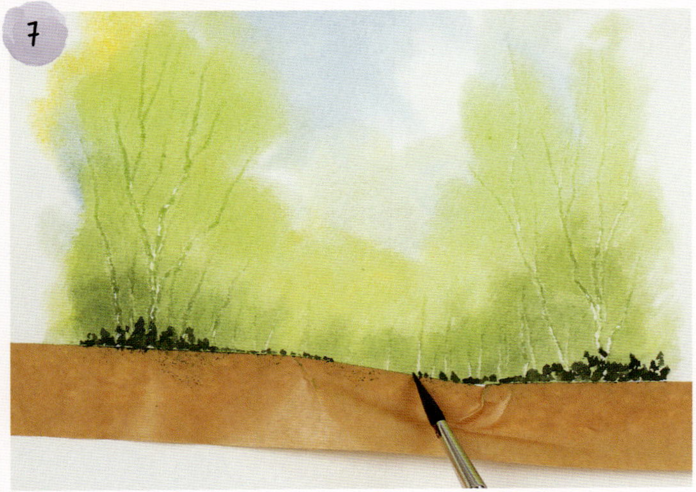

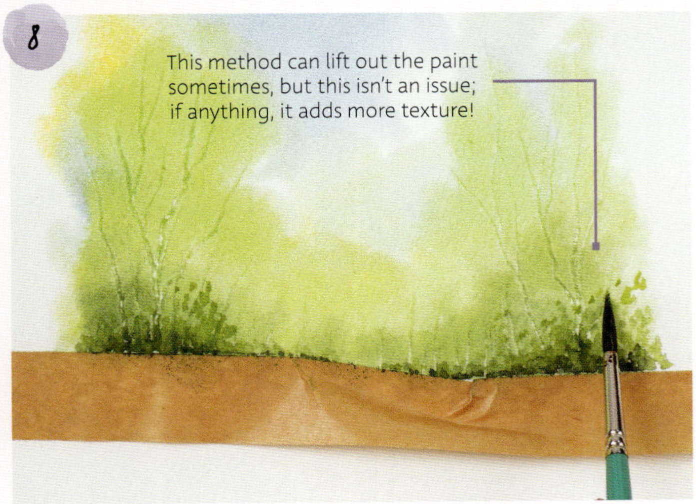

6. While the paint is slightly damp, **scratch out** distant tree shapes with the corner of a clean piece of hard card. Leave the painting to dry completely.

7. To suggest flora in the mid-ground and foreground, **dot and dab** along the top of the tape with the D mix **wet on dry** using a size 6 Round. Work from the edges of the painting inwards, making the clumps of flora smaller in size towards the centre, to add perspective.

8. Working **wet in wet**, pick up the B mix and **dot and dab** this into the top of the dark green flora, blending the two colours together. Steadily work upwards to extend the height of these shapes, gradually creating more distance between each dot as you move upwards to add perspective. You'll notice how blending the two greens softens the overall appearance of the flora.

9. Peel off the masking / painter's tape – use a hairdryer to help you remove the tape if it's proving difficult.

Using clean water, wet an area just below the tree line, about 2–3cm (1in) down, with a size 10 or 12 Round. **Wet in wet**, stroke in a light-strength L mix with same brush. Follow the contours of the land made by the tape, and create two mound shapes from the strokes – one below the left-hand background trees, and a larger one below the right-hand background trees.

10. Still working **wet in wet**, stroke the B mix into the gaps. This time, be careful these mixes DON'T blend.

11. Clean the brush, dab the excess water on to kitchen paper then very lightly skim the brush between the two colours. You can keep the brush low when you do this. Leave the painting to dry completely.

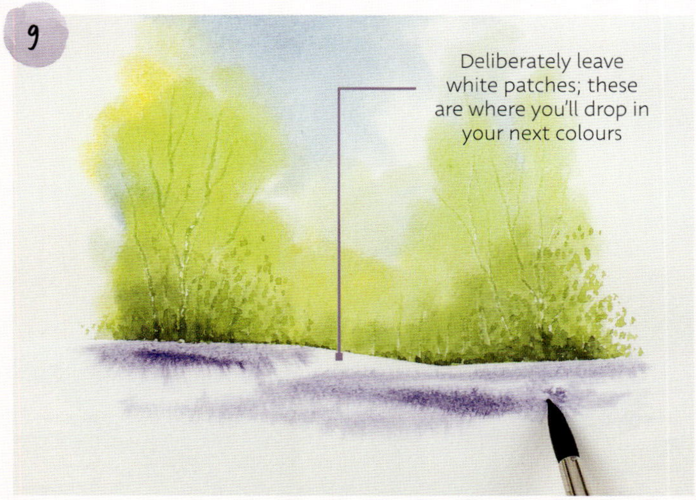

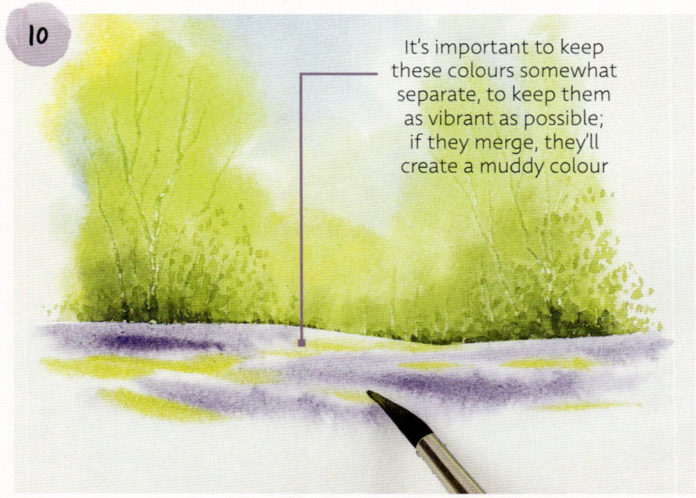

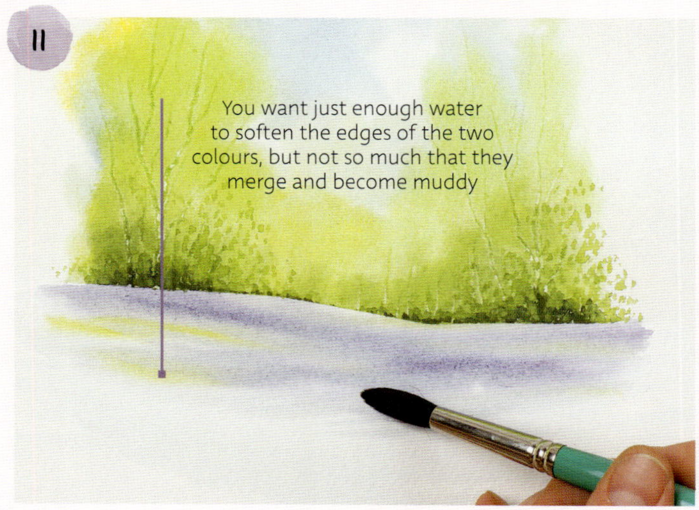

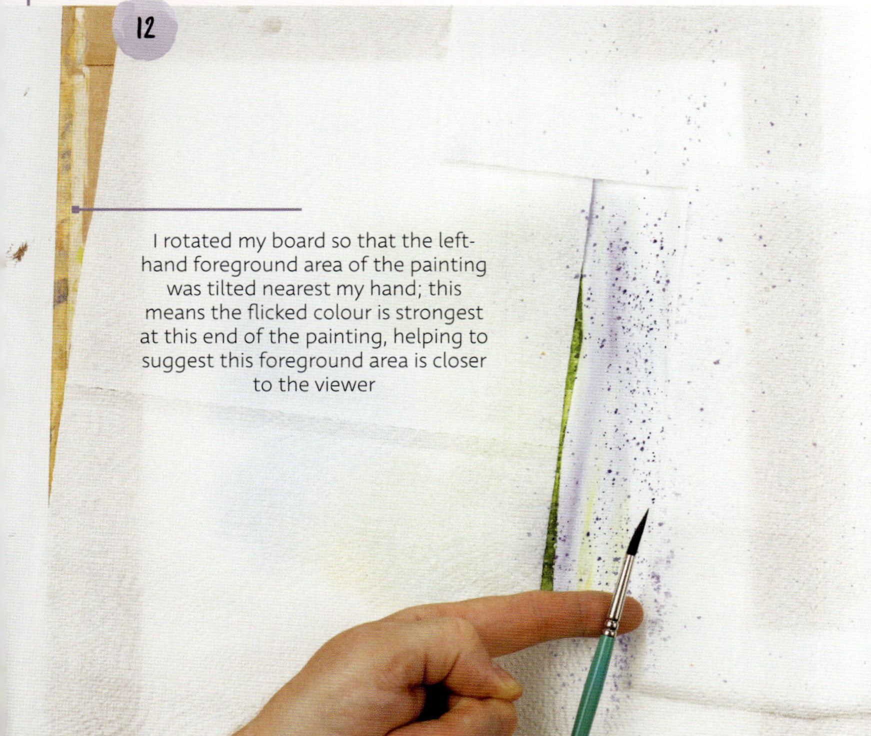

I rotated my board so that the left-hand foreground area of the painting was tilted nearest my hand; this means the flicked colour is strongest at this end of the painting, helping to suggest this foreground area is closer to the viewer

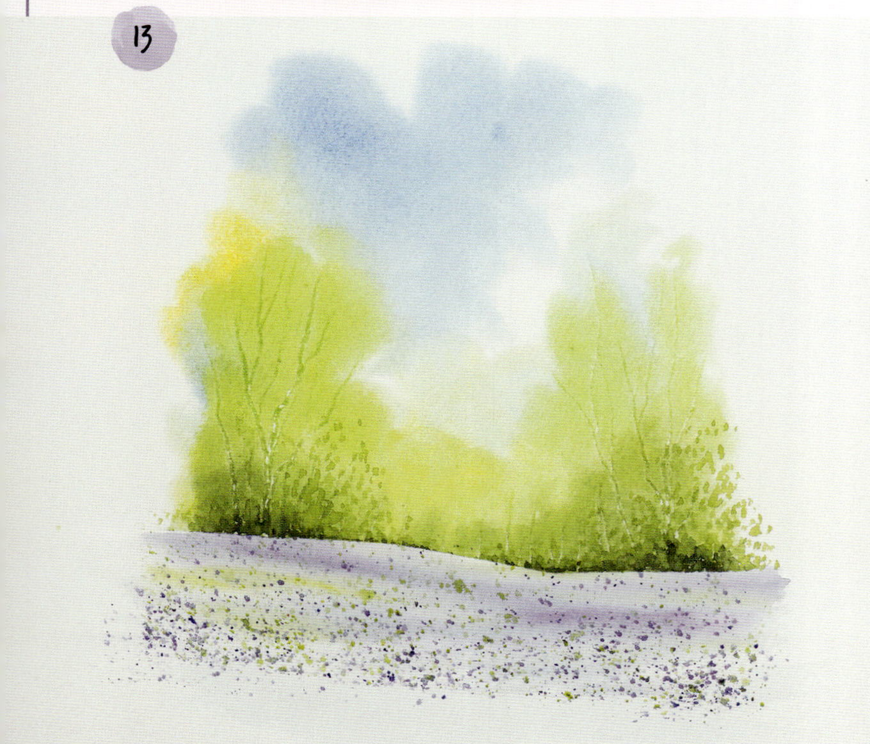

12. Cover the tree area and the sides of the painting with kitchen paper, so only the 'ground' area is revealed. With a size 6 Round and a medium-strength L mix, tap the ferrule of the brush against your finger to **flick** dots of colour towards the bottom of the painting, to suggest flowers in the immediate foreground.

13. Repeat the **flicking** process with the B mix to suggest tiny bits of greenery growing among the flowers. Leave the painting to dry.

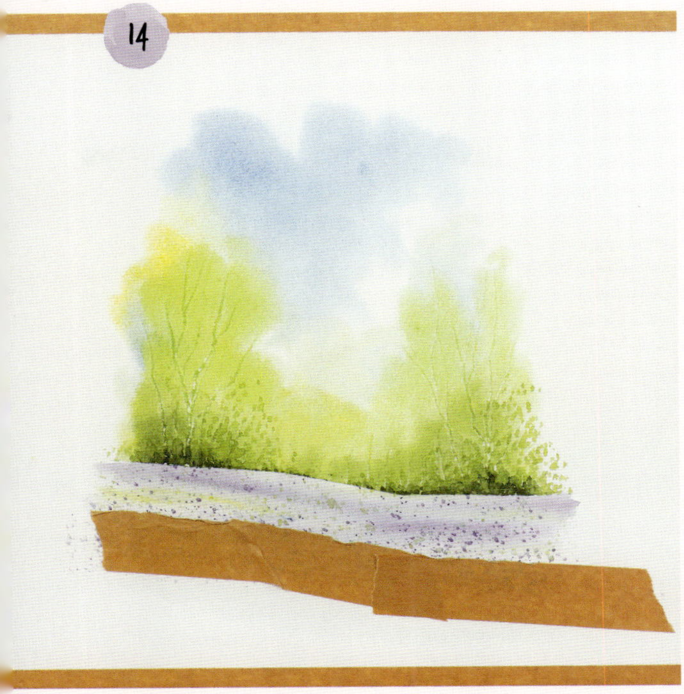

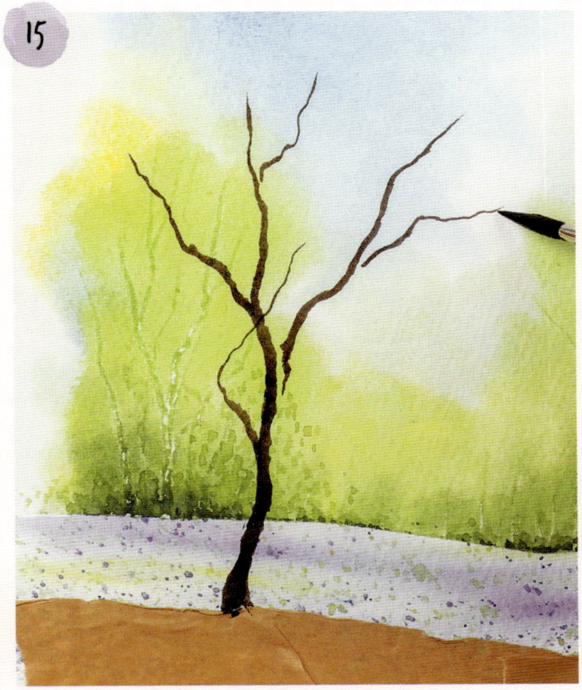

14. About halfway down the 'ground' area, tear off and lay two small lengths of masking / painter's tape across the paper, again creating a slight incline up to the left.

15. Working from bottom to top, and with the size 6 Round and a strong F mix, paint in the darker left-hand side of a tree in the immediate foreground **wet on dry** (see page 26 for help with this). Add a few thicker branches around the top.

16. With a strong G mix and the same brush, paint in the paler right-hand side of the tree. Incorporate some **fine branches** with the tip the brush. Alternating between the F mix and the G mix, and using a size 2 Rigger or Detail, add some very **fine branches** and twigs at the ends of the smaller branches.

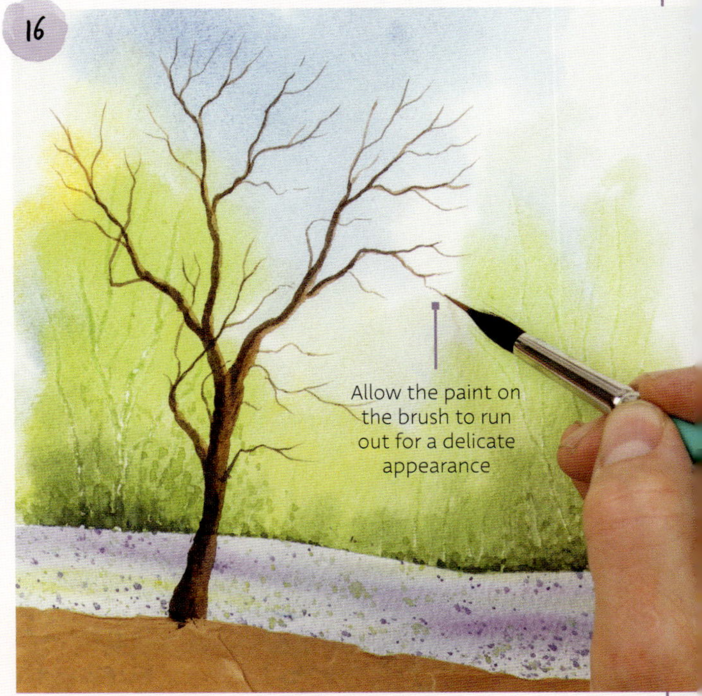

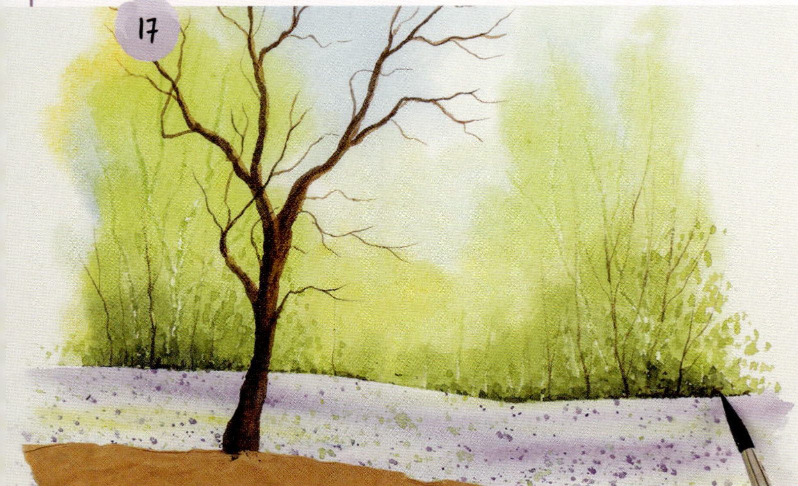

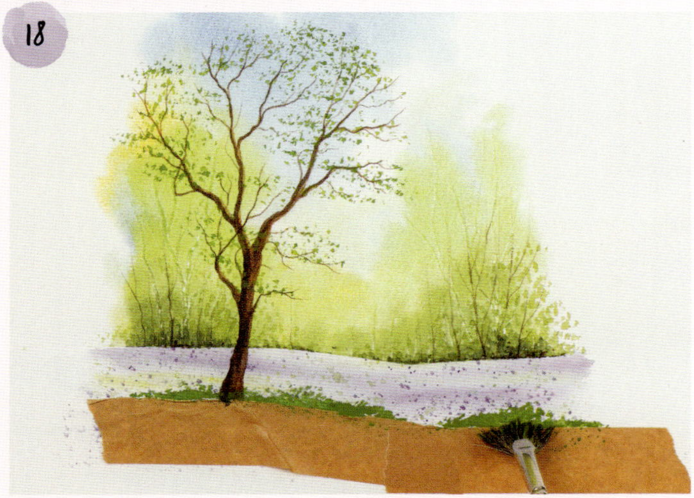

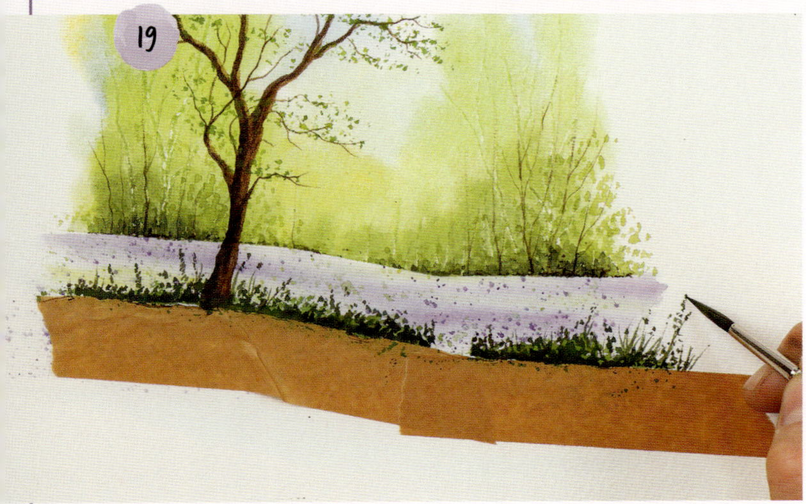

17. Use a medium-strength F mix, a size 2 Rigger or Detail and the **dry brush** technique to add in some simple mid-ground trees **wet on dry**, working from the first tape line towards the top of the scene. If you wish to add texture to the trunk of the tree, use the same brush, mix and the **dry brush** technique to scratch in some 'bark' with vertical strokes. To ground these trees, and connect them to the horizon line, **dot and dab** tiny amounts of the F mix at the base of the trees, along the initial tape line.

18. Squash the medium Fan into a strong A mix, spreading out the bristles and making the brush head quite spiky. **Stipple** in the foreground canopy. Don't add too many stipples, as spring trees don't have many leaves. Add a touch of French Ultramarine to the A mix and **stipple** in a few more leaves into the very top of the tree, using gentle taps to stop the colouring being too strong.

Along the top edge of the masking / painter's tape, and with the same mix, stipple in some immediate foreground foliage green. Leave a little gap where the 'ground' drops. Leave the painting to dry.

19. With a strong D mix and a size 6 Round, **dot and dab** over and around the light green ground area, along the tape. Then, using a mix of the greens you've got in your palette, flick in some grasses – **dot and dab** some details at the tops of some of the grasses with the same mix for extra texture. Leave the painting to dry.

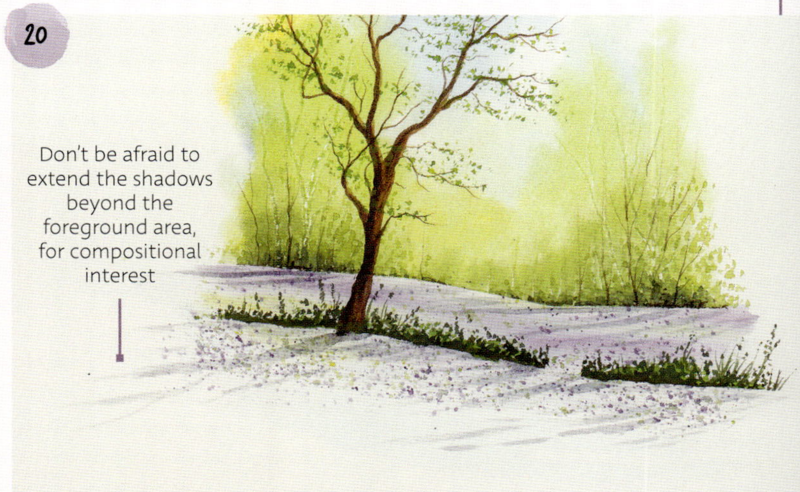

20. Carefully remove the tape in the foreground area. Using a light-strength H mix, paint in the cast shadows of the mid-ground trees, foreground tree and foreground flora **wet on dry** – these are long strokes of colour that start from the base of the tree or flora and taper off towards the bottom-left corner of the scene. With the cast shadow of the foreground tree, try to create a simple mirrored shape of the tree (including some of its branches) to give it more detail, and suggest its proximity to the viewer.

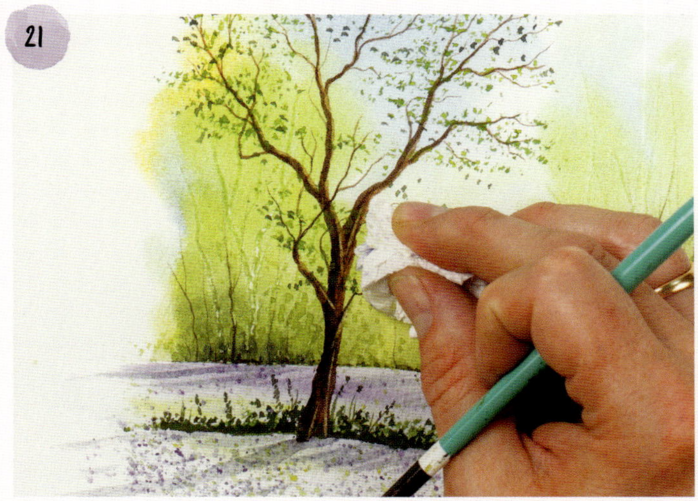

21. With a clean, damp 6mm (¼in) Flat, brush, **lift out** lines in the lighter right-hand parts of the tree trunk and branches to suggest highlights.

22. Using the size 6 Round, the last of the F mix and the **dry brush** technique, skim the base of the foreground foliage and tree to add texture, and help their bottom edges blend into the immediate foreground.

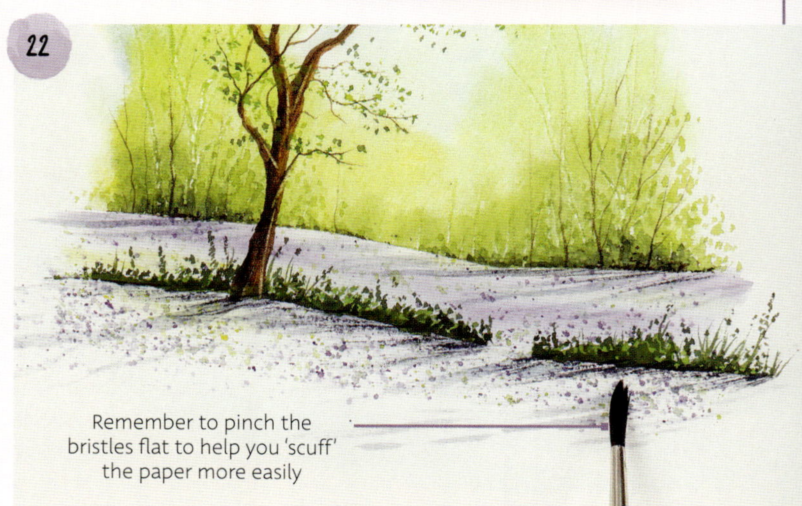

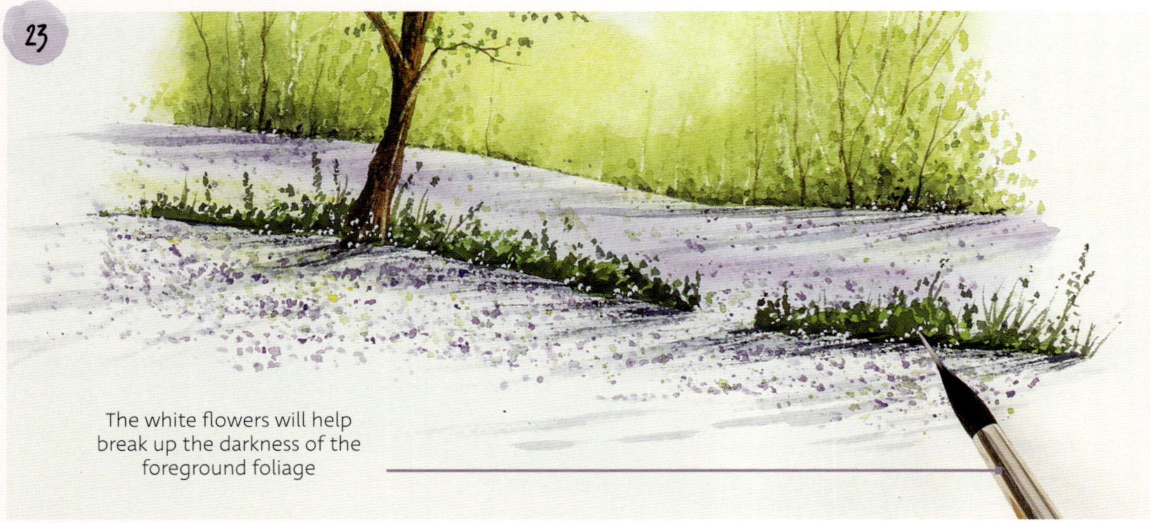

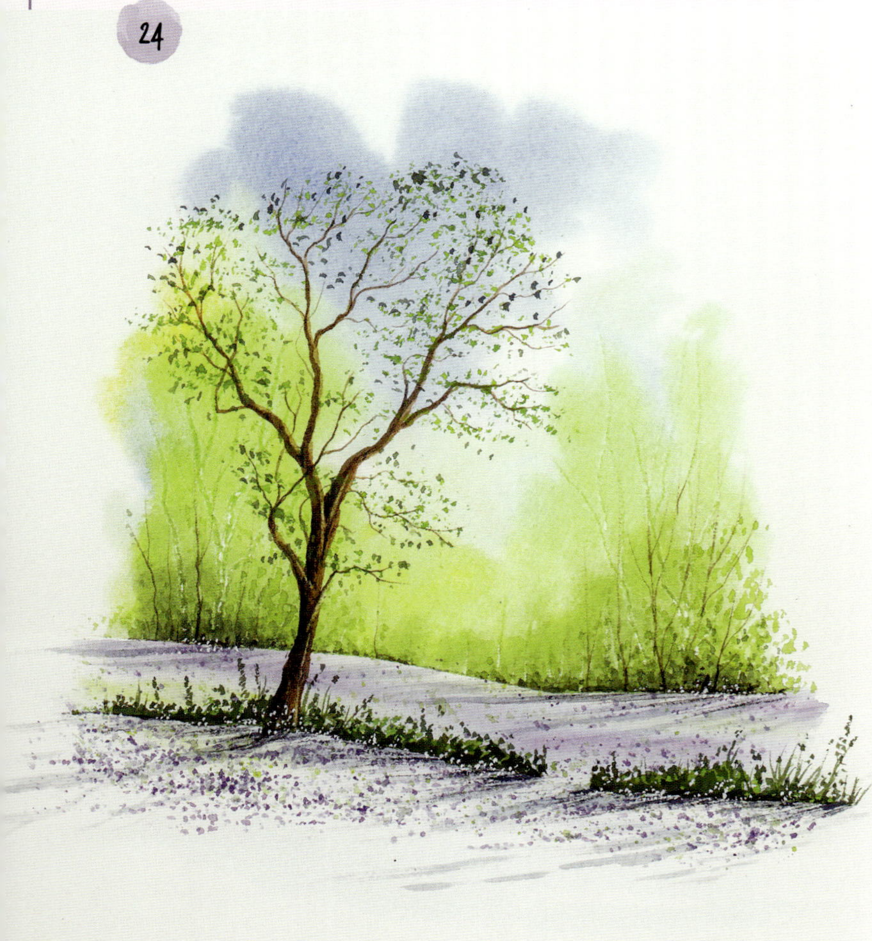

23. With a medium-strength L mix and the tip of the size 6 Round, **dot and dab** in a few foreground flowers to suggest they're close to the viewer. Work several flowers around the base of the tree for interest. Repeat with a little diluted Titanium White gouache using a size 2 Rigger or Detail.

24. With the left-over D mix on your palette, **dot and dab** a few final darker leaves into the top of the tree for some extra texture.

FINAL PROJECT

In this last section, we're bringing all the skills together that we've learnt through the previous lessons to paint a lovely riverside scene. This final project will not only flex your tree-painting muscles, but offer some small new challenges while capturing a landscape in paint.

PURE COLOURS

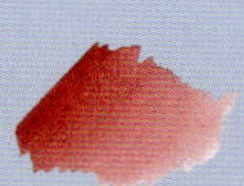

Alizarin Crimson

French Ultramarine

MIXES

See page 14 or the cover flaps for details.

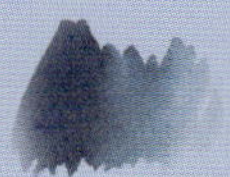

H

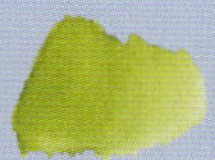

B

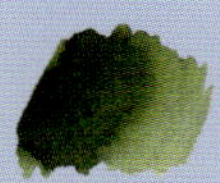

D

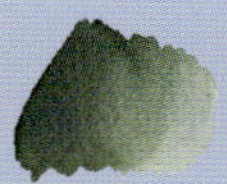

E

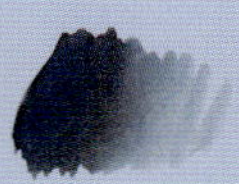

I

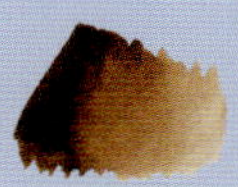

F

BRUSHES

- Size 10 or 12 Round
- Medium Fan
- Size 6 Round
- 6mm (¼in) Flat
- Size 2 Rigger or Detail

EXTRAS

- 2B pencil and 4B pencil
- Optional: tracing paper
- Masking / painter's tape
- Craft knife
- Piece of hard card
- Titanium White gouache
- Optional: hairdryer

TECHNIQUES

- Wet in wet
- Feathering
- Stippling with a fan brush
- Blending
- Dotting and dabbing
- Dry brushing
- Scratching out

1

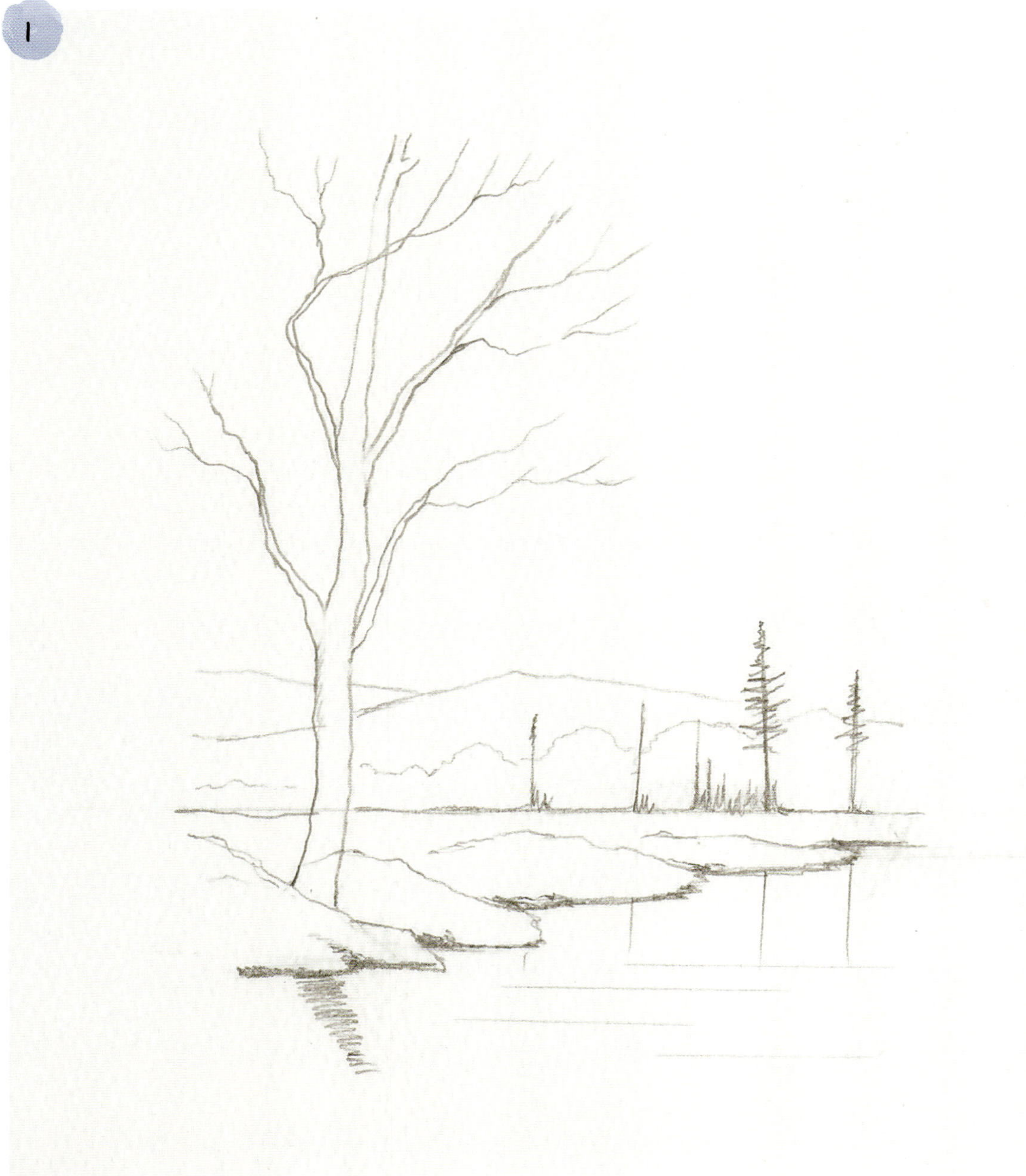

1. Trace or free-hand draw the scene above with a 2B pencil. To trace, first transfer the drawing onto tracing paper with a 2B pencil. Flip the tracing, then scribble over the lines on the back of the drawing with a soft 4B pencil. Flip the tracing back the right way up. Position the watercolour paper under the tracing, then carefully draw over the outlines again with a 2B pencil; the pressure of the pencil will transfer the graphite from the scribbling onto the paper.

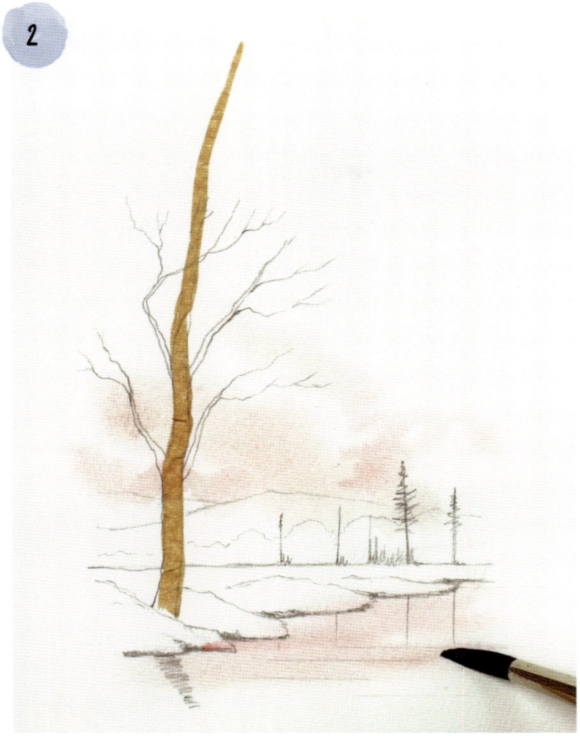

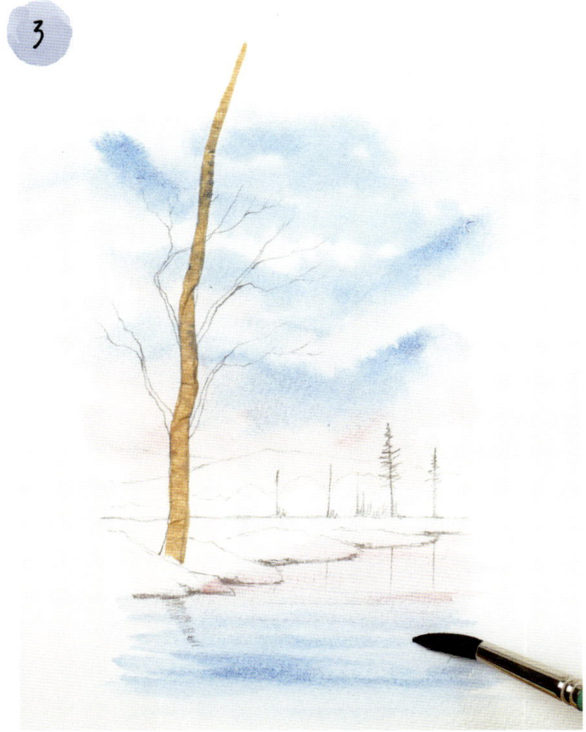

2. Mask off the tree trunk with a narrowed length of masking / painter's tape, shaping the tape where necessary with your fingernails.

Wet the paper a couple of times with size 10 or 12 Round. Twist a very light-strength pure Alizarin Crimson mix diagonally into the bottom half of the sky area **wet in wet**, working from the top-left corner down to the top of the tree line. Paint the top of the river with the same mix, using horizontal strokes this time, as shown.

3. Repeat Step 2 with a medium-strength pure French Ultramarine mix, this time painting above the red clouds and below the red section in the river.

4. With a size 6 Round, twist in a few darker, narrower clouds between the red and blue clouds using a medium-strength H mix. Work a few strokes from the left-hand edges of the bank in the water area, into the alizarin crimson. Leave the painting to dry.

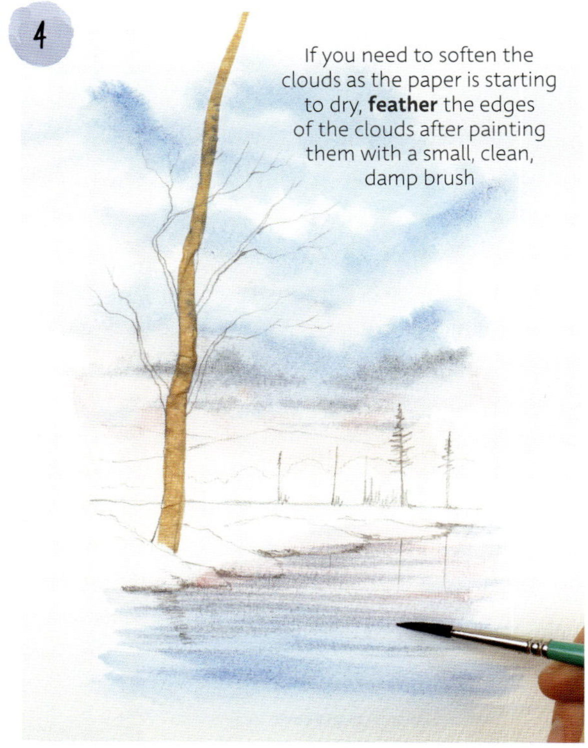

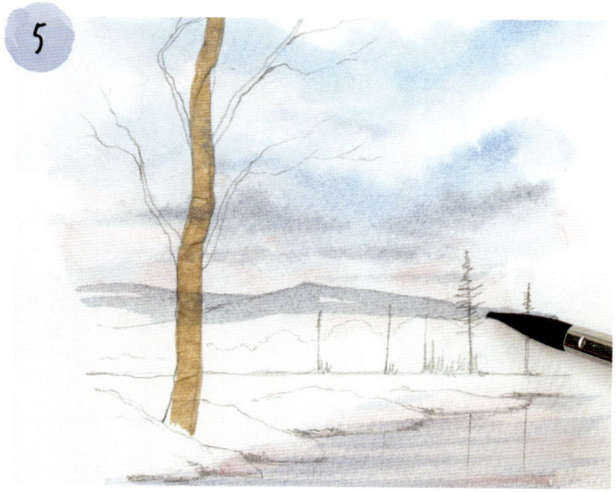

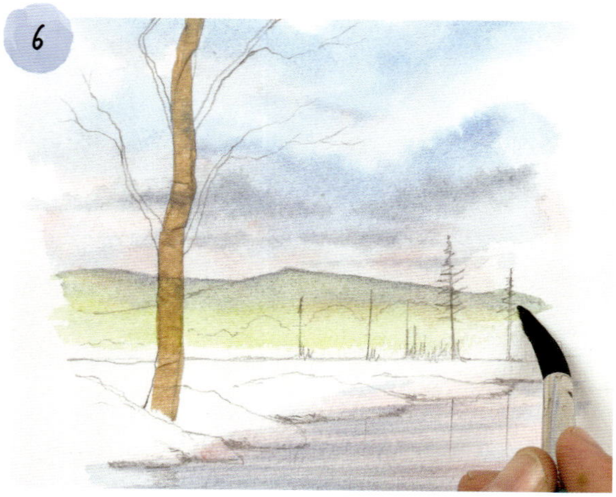

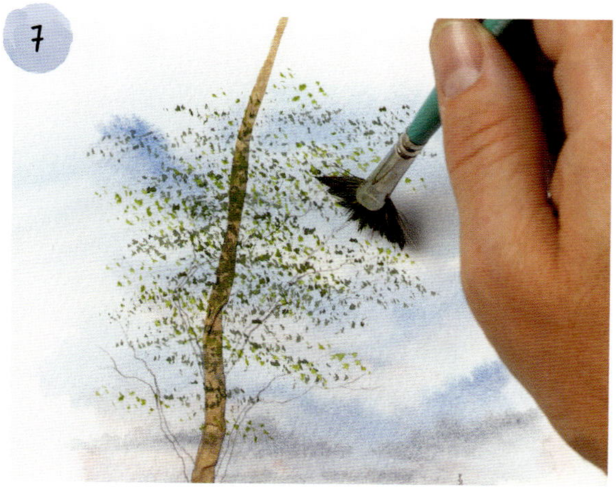

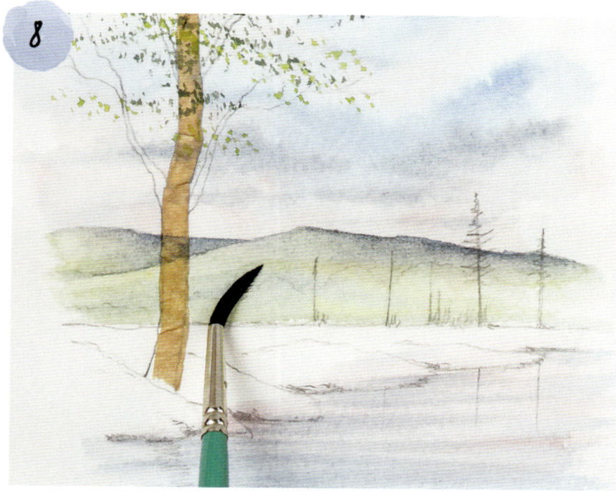

5. With the size 10 or 12 Round, run a line along the top of the distant mountains, from left to right, using a light-strength H mix.

6. A little way down from the top edges of the mountain, horizontally stroke in a medium-strength B mix, starting slightly in the grey then working down to the base of the mountains.

7. While the mountains are drying, **stipple** a medium-strength D mix at the top of the foreground birch tree with the medium Fan, working from the top down. To add more texture and variation, **stipple** in some medium-strength B mix too.

8. When the mountains have dried, stroke in a light-strength H mix along the top right-hand edge of mountain with a size 6 Round. Paint a sideways chevron shape (pointing to the right) on the far-right side of the left-hand mountain. **Blend** the colour diagonally down and towards the bottom-left corner of the mountains with a clean, damp brush.

9

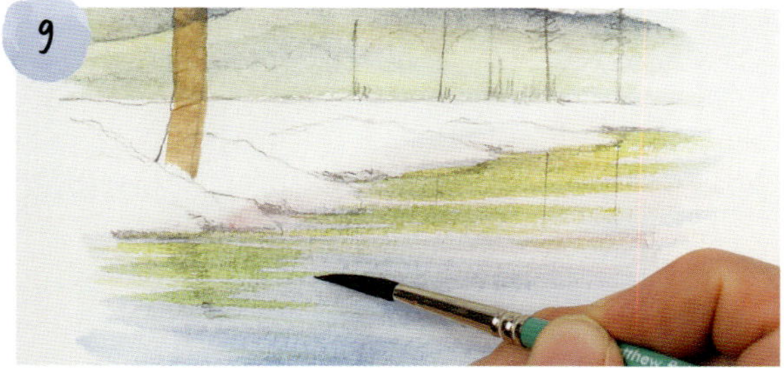

10

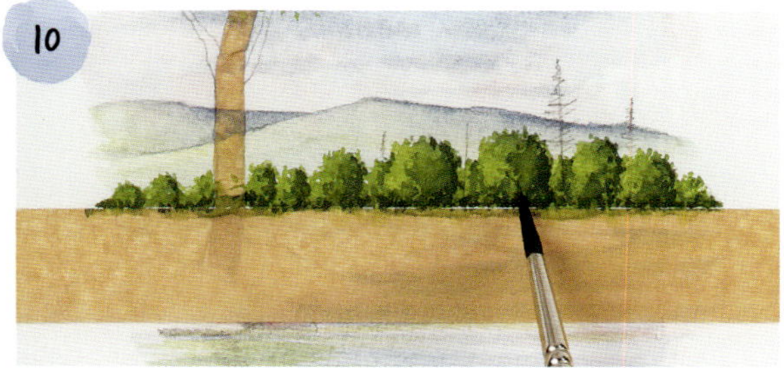

11

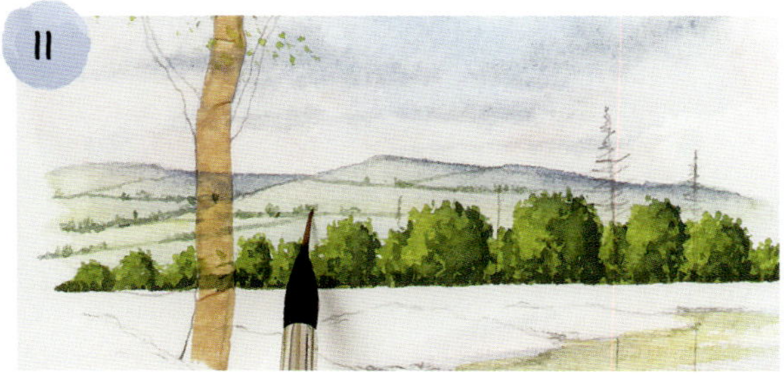

12

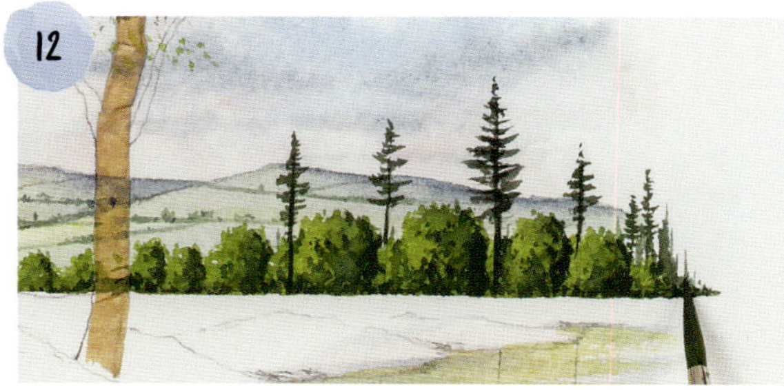

13

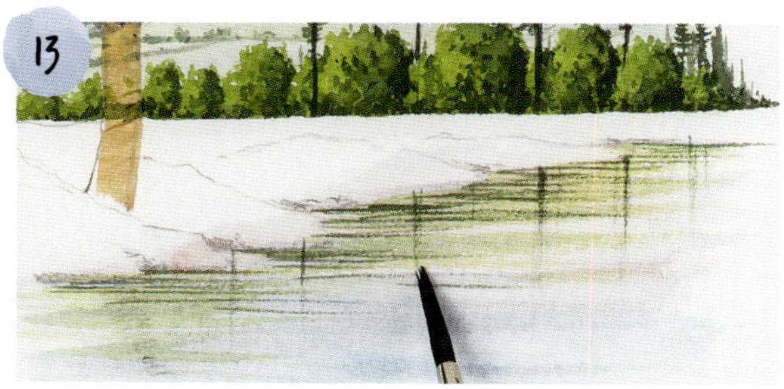

9. Add horizontal strokes of a light-strength B mix down the left-hand edge of the river, to create a reflection of the mountains. Leave the painting to dry.

10. Lay a strip of masking / painter's tape right under the line of trees. With a strong B mix, twist in a line of trees along the top edge of the tape, working from left to right and increasing the height of each tree towards the right-hand side of the painting, until they start to get smaller as they move into the distance again upriver, to add perspective. Pick up a strong D mix then **dot and dab** this into the bottom and right-hand edges of the trees **wet in wet**, allowing the two greens to merge. Leave the painting to dry, then remove the horizontal strip of tape.

11. With a light-strength D mix and a size 2 Rigger or Detail, **dot and dab** in tiny background trees along the mountainsides. Add a few tiny vertical lines here and there, along the mountainside, to suggest taller trees.

12. With a strong E mix, paint in some mid-ground pine trees on the right-hand side of the line of trees in the middle distance, working from top to bottom – see page 38 for a reminder on how to paint pine trees. To connect them to the ground, **dot and dab** little clumps of flora at the base of each tree, using the same mix.

13. With the size 6 Round, add both horizontal and vertical strokes of a light-strength E mix down the left-hand edge of the river, using the **dry brush** technique. This creates reflections of the pine trees in the river.

14
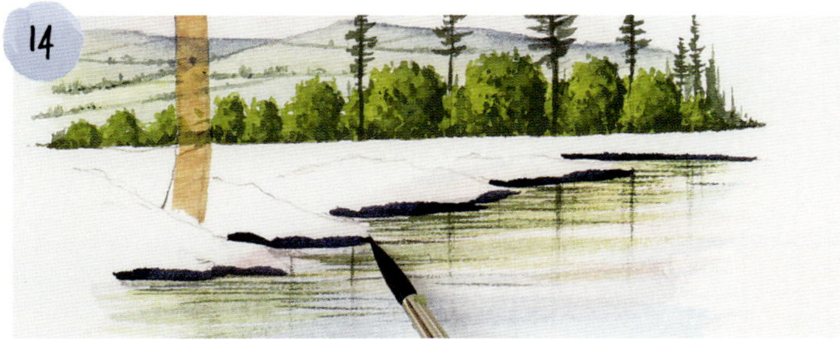

15
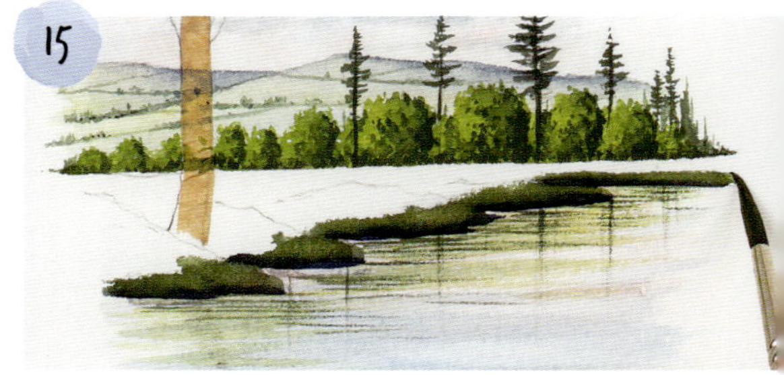

14. Run a strong H mix along the edge of the river bank with the size 6 Round. Note that I've only painted in the edges that are 'facing' the viewer.

15. Starting from the top of the grey river edge (so that the two colours merge slightly) and working upwards, paint in the bottom third of the river bank with a medium-strength D mix using horizontal strokes.

16. Repeat the process with a medium-strength B mix, starting from the dark green to merge the two colours and working up towards the top of the grassy area. Leave a narrow white edge along the top, so you can **feather** the top edge of the light green bank into it with a clean, damp brush.

17. Skim over the entire bank with a clean, damp brush, working from top to bottom, so this area is slightly damp. Using a piece of hard card, **scratch out** individual mounds in the bank, working from the water's edge up into the bank. It's worth practising the technique on a test painting first, to ensure you're happy with the results. Leave the painting to dry.

18. Remove the masking / painter's tape. Following Steps 7–10 on pages 53 and 54, using the I mix for the dark grey and F mix for the brown shade, and switching between the size 6 Round and the size 2 Rigger or Detail where necessary, paint in the foreground birch tree. Rotate the board when painting the branches, so you're always painting towards yourself, and have fun extending the branches beyond the boundaries of painting for interest. **Dry brush** some G mix from the bottom of the trunk a little way upwards, to help 'ground' it.

16
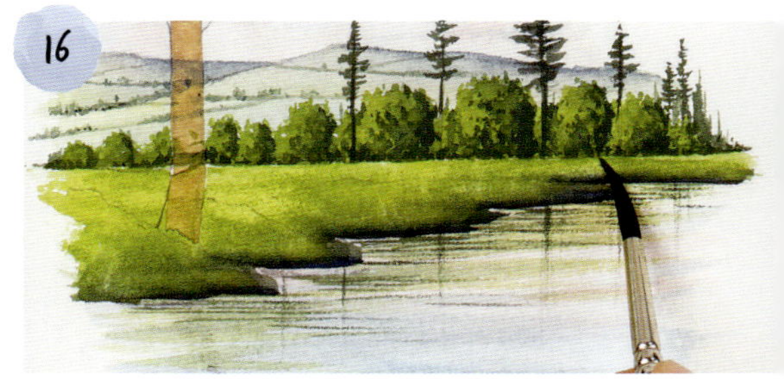

17
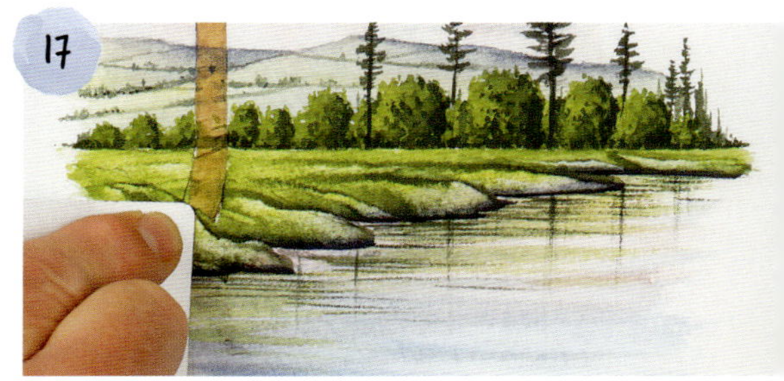

18
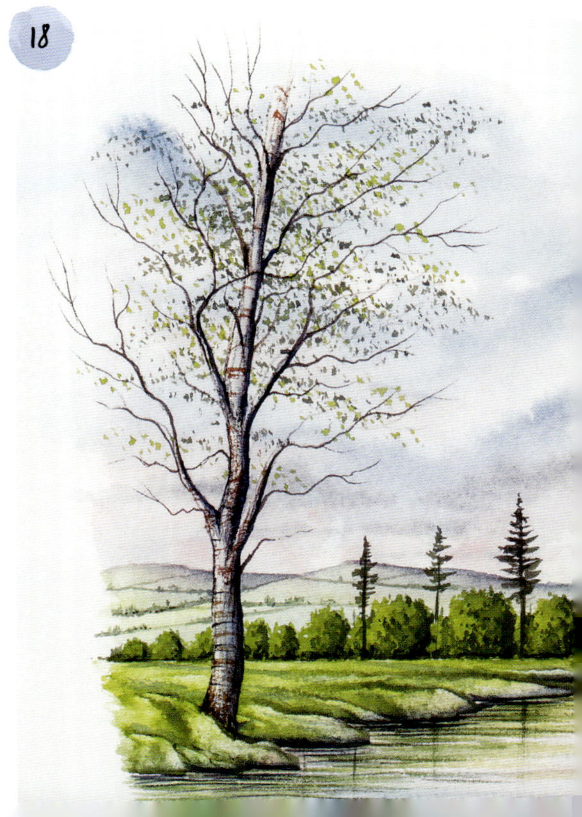

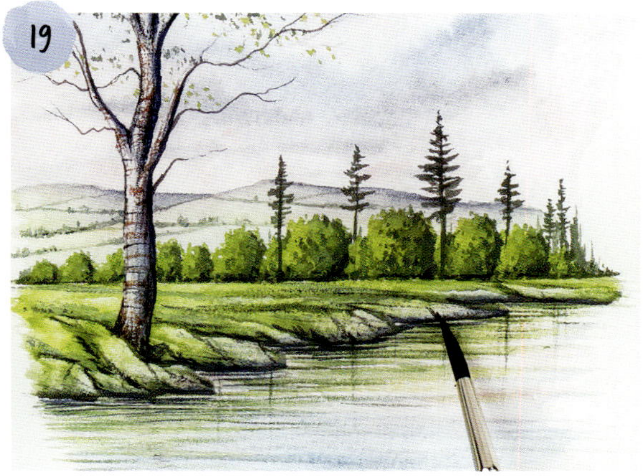

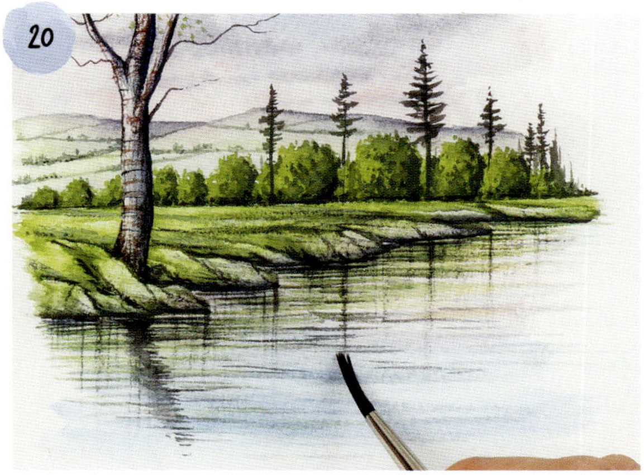

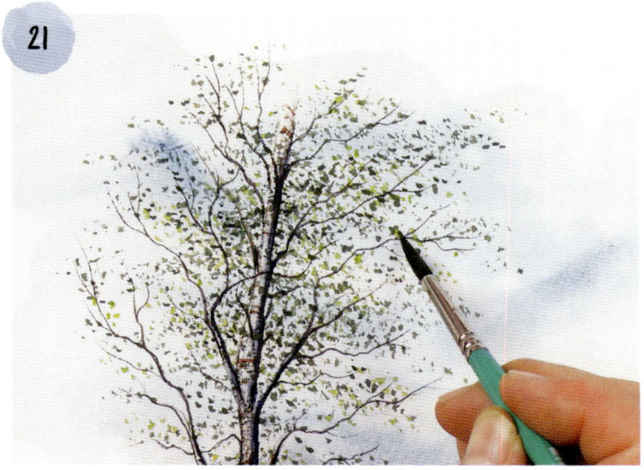

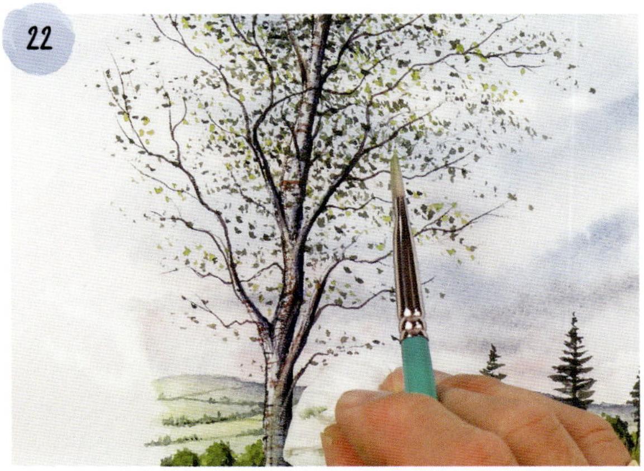

19. With the size 6 Round, skim over the bank with a medium-strength I mix using the **dry brush** technique, to add overall texture and connect the tree to the bank much more. Use a **dry brush** and the same mix to outline some rocky shapes in the water's edge, and adds in little textures too.

20. With the same mix and a damp brush, stroke little horizontal lines from the water's edge downwards to add the reflection of the birch tree. The strokes should start off the same width as the tree base, then get narrower as you work downwards. Remember the reflection mirrors the tree shape, so make sure it's 'pointing' in the right direction! Pull a few horizontal dark ripples here and there in the water with the **dry brush** technique, and strengthen some of the pine tree reflections with vertical strokes of the same mix. Leave the painting to dry.

21. With the birch tree trunk and branches in place, **stipple** in more leaves as in Step 7 on page 90. **Dot and dab** in a few individual leaves with the size 6 Round, as shown, to fill in any obvious gaps and add definition to main foliage.

22. To make the birch tree more 3D, **lift out** some highlights along the left-hand sides of the trunk and branches with the clean, damp 6mm (¼in) Flat. **Lift out** highlights on the left side of the taller mid-ground pine trees, too.

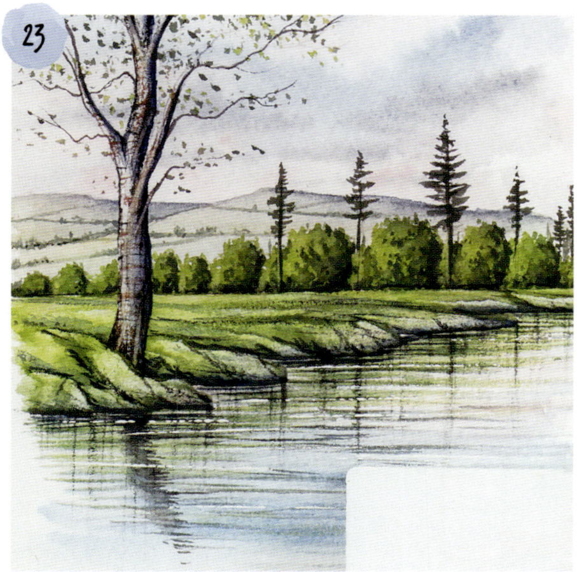

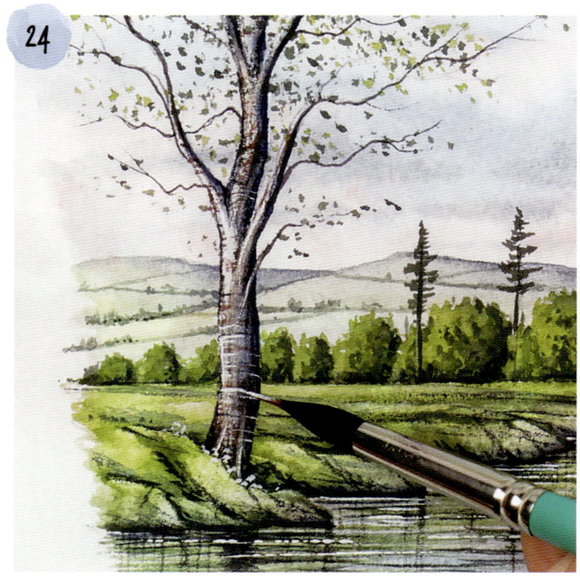

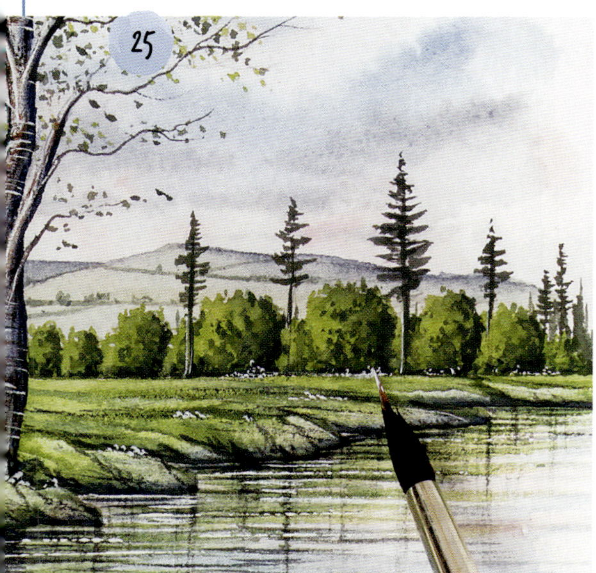

23. Mix up a little diluted pure Titanium White gouache on the palette, then paint this along the edge of your piece of hard card. 'Stamp' the card horizontally onto the river, mainly around the riverbank edge, to create sparkles in the water. For finer sparkles, add these by hand with the size 2 Rigger or Detail – these are just tiny horizontal strokes with the brush tip.

24. Add some highlights to the left-hand side of the birch tree trunk and branches with a size 2 Rigger or Detail and the diluted pure Titanium White gouache. Take the opportunity to paint some ring textures onto the tree trunk, too, as shown. **Dot and dab** a few white flowers around the bottom of the tree, and here and there on the river bank.

25. Run a thin line of dilute pure Titanium White gouache down the left-hand sides of the mid-ground pine trees. **Dot and dab** a few more white flowers around the base of the trees and into the bank as well, to balance the white flowers under the foreground birch tree.

26. With the tip of the size 6 Round and using whatever green is left in your palette, stroke in little patches of grass and foliage along the water's edge and base of the birch tree, flicking from the bank upwards. **Dot and dab** a few highlights on the right-hand edges of the immediate foreground riverbank mounds with the dilute pure Titanium White gouache to brighten and shape them further.

27. Finish by adding a few birds in the sky with a size 2 Rigger or Detail and whatever dark colour you have left in your palette. These are just simple little, slightly bent, V-shapes.

26

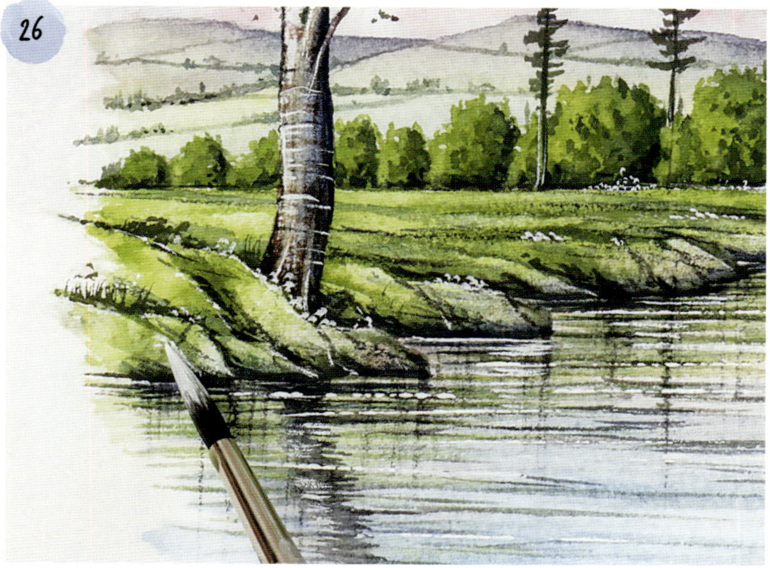

27

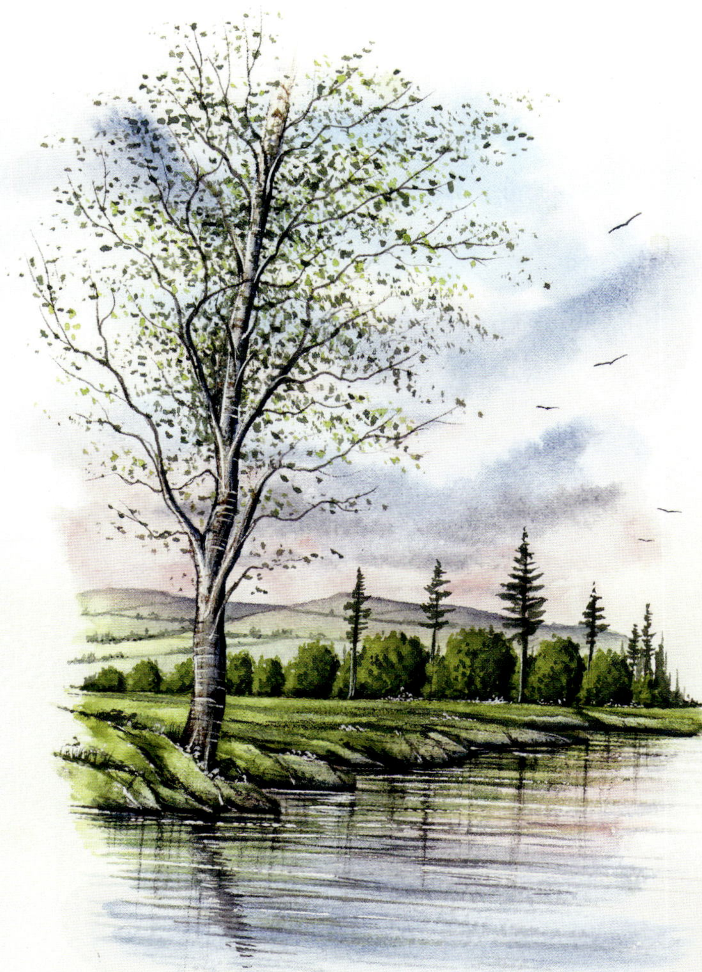

INDEX

ACKNOWLEDGEMENTS

I would like to thank all the staff at Search Press for making this book possible. A big thank you to Emily the editor and Mark the photographer. Thanks to all my friends and family for their continued support and keeping the paint flowing.